THE COMPLETE IDIOT'S GUIDE® TO

Solar Power for Your Home

Third Edition

by Dan Ramsey with David Hughes

ALPHA
A member of Penguin Group (USA) Inc.

This effort is dedicated to the Source of the sun and everything under it.

ALPHA BOOKS

Published by the Penguin Group

Penguin Group (USA) Inc., 375 Hudson Street, New York, New York 10014, USA

Penguin Group (Canada), 90 Eglinton Avenue East, Suite 700, Toronto, Ontario M4P 2Y3, Canada (a division of Pearson Penguin Canada Inc.)

Penguin Books Ltd., 80 Strand, London WC2R 0RL, England

Penguin Ireland, 25 St. Stephen's Green, Dublin 2, Ireland (a division of Penguin Books Ltd.)

Penguin Group (Australia), 250 Camberwell Road, Camberwell, Victoria 3124, Australia (a division of Pearson Australia Group Pty. Ltd.)

Penguin Books India Pvt. Ltd., 11 Community Centre, Panchsheel Park, New Delhi—110 017, India

Penguin Group (NZ), 67 Apollo Drive, Rosedale, North Shore, Auckland 1311, New Zealand (a division of Pearson New Zealand Ltd.)

Penguin Books (South Africa) (Pty.) Ltd., 24 Sturdee Avenue, Rosebank, Johannesburg 2196, South Africa

Penguin Books Ltd., Registered Offices: 80 Strand, London WC2R 0RL, England

Copyright © 2010 by Dan Ramsey

International Standard Book Number: 978-1-61564-001-0
Library of Congress Catalog Card Number: 2009937015

12   11   10   8   7   6   5   4   3   2   1

Interpretation of the printing code: The rightmost number of the first series of numbers is the year of the book's printing; the rightmost number of the second series of numbers is the number of the book's printing. For example, a printing code of 10-1 shows that the first printing occurred in 2010.

Printed in the United States of America

Note: This publication contains the opinions and ideas of its author. It is intended to provide helpful and informative material on the subject matter covered. It is sold with the understanding that the author and publisher are not engaged in rendering professional services in the book. If the reader requires personal assistance or advice, a competent professional should be consulted.

The author and publisher specifically disclaim any responsibility for any liability, loss, or risk, personal or otherwise, which is incurred as a consequence, directly or indirectly, of the use and application of any of the contents of this book.

Most Alpha books are available at special quantity discounts for bulk purchases for sales promotions, premiums, fundraising, or educational use. Special books, or book excerpts, can also be created to fit specific needs.

For details, write: Special Markets, Alpha Books, 375 Hudson Street, New York, NY 10014.

Publisher: *Marie Butler-Knight*
Editorial Director/Acquiring Editor: *Mike Sanders*
Senior Managing Editor: *Billy Fields*
Senior Development Editor: *Phil Kitchel*
Senior Production Editor: *Janette Lynn*
Copy Editor: *Andy Saff*

Cartoonist: *Shannon Wheeler*
Cover Designer: *Bill Thomas*
Book Designer: *Trina Wurst*
Indexer: *Angie Bess Martin*
Layout: *Ayanna Lacey*
Proofreader: *John Etchison*

Contents at a Glance

Appendixes

Contents

Appendixes

Introduction

Houston, we *still* have a problem!

We're running out of oil! The petroleum that fuels our daily lives is getting harder to find. Turning fossils into electricity is hazardous to our health. And the numerous costs of burning fuel are skyrocketing!

Fortunately, we're not running out of options. We can cut back on the energy we use. And we can turn to the energy sources that have been there all along: the sun, wind, and water.

So why didn't we make this decision years ago? Economics! Fossils fueled the industrial age. We became dependent on cheap, available oil to keep things moving toward a brighter future. Well, the future is here—and the *easy* fuels are nearly depleted. Maybe soon, maybe *very* soon. Prices are up and down like a runaway roller coaster. Fortunately, technology is moving faster to offer some options.

So what can you, a homeowner or renter, do *right now* to reduce the world's dependency on petroleum fuels? You can read this book!

No, I'm not a "tree hugger." I don't believe that the ecology equation excludes mankind's needs. I also don't believe ecology has been given a fair shake in our greed for more stuff. Moderation is the key to life. Give and take. Unfortunately, we've been blindly taking, and it's time to *at least* cut back.

That's what *The Complete Idiot's Guide to Solar Power for Your Home, Third Edition,* is about: considering solar and other renewable energy resources to power our lives efficiently. It's also about becoming aware of the energy problem and finding some easy-to-implement solutions *right now.* Most important, it helps you discover whether the solar option is *your* best option and shows you how to implement it.

If you're like most folks, you don't know much about the sun except that you're not supposed to stare directly at it. Well, it's Earth's primary energy source and we're using it to grow food and do other things, but we're not giving it a fair chance to power our homes and lives. So this book is written to give you first an overview, then more and more specifics on how to put the sun to work for you.

You may have heard that solar power is expensive. Well, compared to here-today-gone-tomorrow fossil fuel, it is—in the short term. However, advances in renewable energy technology have really brought prices down over the past few years. And governments have stepped up to offer impressive rebates and incentives that make solar power much more economical. In fact, today's systems can pay back costs in just a few years—then furnish nearly free power for many more. Think of the investment as prepaid utility bills. There's even some great financing available for solar power systems.

These are the things you'll learn about as you read this book. It's your first investment in the solution. Even if you choose not to install a complete solar electric generation system in your home, this book will still be an excellent investment in knowing how to reduce oil dependency by cutting your energy costs. It shows you how you can save many hundreds of dollars each year in energy bills.

This book *isn't* for solar experts. They already understand the problem and the solutions. It's for *you!* You've read the news stories, heard the dire warnings, and want to know more about your options. You want to be part of the *solution* rather than the problem. You're certainly not a "complete idiot," but you do want to have solar and other renewable power options explained in clear and usable terms. This book answers the question: Does solar power make sense for *you?* It includes what you need to know about buying, installing, and maintaining solar and other renewable power systems for your home. This latest edition includes more detailed information about installing your new power system.

One more note: Prices offered in this book are estimates and guidelines to help you determine the relative value of solar power. Your power system suppliers and contractors can offer costs more specific to your needs and region. This book can help you become a smarter power consumer and save many dollars.

How to Use This Book

The Complete Idiot's Guide to Solar Power for Your Home, Third Edition, contains 19 clear chapters and 4 practical appendixes. Here's how it's laid out:

Part 1, "Solar Basics," tells you about the technology, rebates, and financing available to those who go solar. You'll also get an overview of solar power installation in your existing home or a new one. You'll learn about design issues that can dramatically cut heating and cooling costs without a solar power system. You'll learn the basics.

Part 2, "Solar Energy Solutions," takes curious minds into the proven world of solar and other power resources. You'll learn how solar power is generated with photovoltaic cells and modules. And you'll find out how to store and distribute power. You'll also discover the most efficient application of solar energy: making hot water. You'll also learn about heating your home with passive solar energy. You'll see the solutions.

Part 3, "Solar Power Systems," is for plug-and-play folks. It covers the various types of solar power systems available today. These systems include all the components you need to go solar within days. You'll find systems to power your entire house, smaller systems to handle part but not all of the load, emergency systems for backup power, and even portable systems for travelers. You'll learn about grid-tied and off-grid power systems, supplemental power, and other ingenious ways to produce home energy. You'll understand how the systems work.

Part 4, "Solar Power Projects," guides you through buying, installing, and maintaining a solar power system—whether you'll build and install it yourself or hire a contractor to do some or all of it. Lots of specific information is included here, provided by designers and installers. You'll find clear step-by-step instructions for solar power installations.

You'll also find four comprehensive appendixes. The first guides you in estimating your home's energy needs and the second offers 50 ways to cut your home energy bill right now! Remember: every dollar you save in energy efficiency reduces the cost of your solar power system by $3 to $5! The expanded Solar Glossary clearly defines all those words and terms you may come across as you consider and shop for solar power. The updated Solar Resources appendix is your one stop for all the resources you'll need, including federal, state, and local government resources; solar equipment dealers and suppliers; energy-efficiency contractors; catalogs and magazines; and more. You can find the latest Solar Resources online at SolarHomeGuides.com.

Yes, there is a structure to this book. However, don't let it get in the way of enjoying the discovery process. If you're curious about how PV cells work, turn to Chapter 7 right now. If you're interested in how you can use net metering to earn extra money from your system, flip over to Chapter 12. If you think wind and water technology may be a good option, check out Chapter 8 first. This book is written for both front-to-back readers and browsers. Enjoy!

Extras

Throughout this book, additional guides clarify new terms, offer additional information, or caution you about potential problems. They look like this:

Bright Idea

Check these boxes for hot tips that will save you time, money, and effort.

Sun Spots

These boxes give you some background on getting the most from your solar power system and some ideas for going solar.

Solar Eclipse

These cautions keep you from spending too much money or spending time in the hospital. Follow their advice so you can enjoy solar power.

def•i•ni•tion

These boxes offer clear definitions of words or terms used in selecting, installing, and using solar power equipment as well as in making your home more energy efficient.

Acknowledgments

It's amazing how many solar experts there are under the sun. I tapped into many of them while researching and writing this book for you. Here are the names of those who contributed their time and knowledge toward making this book informative and accurate. Thank you, one and all!

This updated and expanded third edition greatly benefits from the knowledge and experience of David Hughes, president of Affordable Solar Group (affordable-solar.com). David's credentials are extensive and his skills invaluable. Thanks for your hard work, keen eye, and voluminous solar knowledge.

Also, a special thanks to my insider at the U.S. Department of Energy whose knowledge and patience I frequently tested: Paul Hesse. Paul is an excellent resource for all things solar. He's also a credit to the Department of Energy and the government's attempt to inform us about energy options. Great job, Paul!

Thanks also to Doug Pratt, a.k.a. Dr. Doug. He knows the solar industry, what's available, and where to get it. He's a great resource. He served as one of the first edition's technical advisors, reading to make sure that the info I give you is accurate. Thanks, Dr. Doug!

My other insider is Greg Dunbar. Greg is a licensed general contractor with lots of construction experience. Greg lives off-grid, away from utility lines, generating his own electricity. Happy *new* birthday, Greg! (Greg was also my technical reviewer for two editions of *The Complete Idiot's Guide to Building Your Own Home*; Alpha Books, 2002 and 2004.)

Many others contributed to this book as well. They are included in Appendix D. They contributed time and information toward making this book both informative and friendly. Thank you, one and all.

Editorially, thanks to Mike Sanders at Alpha Books, whose vision started the process. My appreciation also goes to Phil Kitchel, Andy Saff, and Janette Lynn, whose sharpened pencils and pointed questions enhanced the value of this book. Thanks, too, to my agents, Sheree Bykofsky and Janet Rosen. And thanks to Judy, who, for 40 years, has been my editor and friend.

Special Thanks to the Technical Reviewer

The Complete Idiot's Guide to Solar Power for Your Home, Third Edition, was reviewed by an expert who double-checked the accuracy of what you'll learn here, to help us ensure that this book gives you everything you need to know about solar power. Special thanks are extended to David Hughes.

Trademarks

All terms mentioned in this book that are known to be or are suspected of being trademarks or service marks have been appropriately capitalized. Alpha Books and Penguin Group (USA) Inc. cannot attest to the accuracy of this information. Use of a term in this book should not be regarded as affecting the validity of any trademark or service mark.

Solar Basics

Puff, puff … we're running out of energy!

Maybe not today or tomorrow, but soon the headlines will again read "Energy Crisis!" And maybe this will be the Big One. Maybe it will *really* happen and we'll need a cosigner to pay home utility bills. Or maybe we'll just float along for a while, enjoying relatively cheap power. It could happen.

What do we really mean by a "nonrenewable" energy source? We know it means that one of these days we're going to run out of cheap energy.

The solution is the sun. By figuring out what's really happening in the energy world—and energy technology—you can make some informed choices that will make everyone's life a little better. As we get older, we learn that energy is nonrenewable and doesn't last forever. It's time to take a closer look at our energy diet!

Looking into the Sun

In This Chapter

- What's all the fuss about energy
- How to investigate our renewable energy sources
- How and why solar energy works
- How technology and attitudes are changing in favor of solar power

Life is good. Electricity keeps our food cold or warms it up, washes the dishes, and entertains us while we eat. It also runs our computer, washer, lights, and garage-door opener.

Then the electric bill comes. We pay it because it's a bargain! All this neat stuff works for us for just a few bucks a day. We wouldn't consider totally doing without the comforts, helpers, and gadgets that electricity powers in our lives. Nobody's ready to pull the plug.

But we all know in the back of our minds that the monthly electric bill isn't all we're paying. There's another bill—an energy-use bill—that we pay every day in the form of spent resources that we can't get back, smog and health problems, taxes for energy regulations, wars, and other concerns. These costs total into the billions of dollars. We get the other bill in increased health costs, higher consumer costs, and higher taxes.

Unfortunately, some of our long-term bills will be delivered to our children and their children. We don't know exactly what the total bill will be.

So what can we do? We can look to alternative energy sources, especially those such as the sun, that minimize those long-term bills. Maybe we can't change the whole world, but we can change our little piece of it. We can consider solar and other renewable energy sources to power our homes.

Photovoltaic panels can "catch" the sun's energy and convert it into electricity.

Finding the Energy

We've always needed energy to live. Energy has grown our food, baked our bread, and powered our bodies for thousands of years. It's always been that way, and it will probably always be so.

Even satellites use solar power.

Lately, however, technology (applied science) has put increased demands on us to find additional sources of energy that can be put to work for us. We need power to light our homes, run our computers, move aircraft, turn wheels, and put satellites in orbit. We depend on power every day as we monitor hospital patients, watch television, refrigerate food, send e-mail, fight wars, and build structures. Technology can be good.

Solar panels can add functionality to any style of home.

Unfortunately, technology requires lots of power. For the past century or so, we've been getting this power from fossil fuel, a limited resource. Even the experts don't know if we'll discover enough fossil fuels to keep us going at this pace for another 10 or 100 years. We *do* know that eventually we will run out of this finite source of energy. And even if we had an unlimited supply of fossil fuels, using solar and other renewable energies is easier on our environment.

The good news is that within 20 years we can get as much as half our power from the sun—if we make smart decisions today.

Where does all our energy get used? About 25 percent is burned up in getting from here to there—transportation. Industry uses more than 20 percent. Homes and businesses use nearly 12 percent. The biggest chunk, nearly 40 percent of all energy used in the United States, goes to produce electric power!

> ### Sun Spots
> Energy is the ability to *do* work. Power is energy *at* work.

So should we cut back on technology and all its benefits? Certainly we can trim down on our energy requirements (see Appendix A). We can weigh the costs and benefits to strike a balance. We can also use our noggins to find and use energy sources that don't have hidden costs or steal from our children's future. We can use renewable energy sources.

Using Renewable Energy Sources

Renewable energy sources are continually replenished by nature: the sun, wind, water, thermal heat, and plants (or "bio"). These sources have been here since the world began—long before us.

Renewable energy technologies turn these fuels into usable forms of energy—electricity, heat, mechanical power, and chemicals. Let's take a closer look at our options.

Renewable energy power system options for your home include solar, hydro, wind, biofuel, and public utilities. Later in this book, you'll learn how to sell some of your excess renewable energy back to the power company!

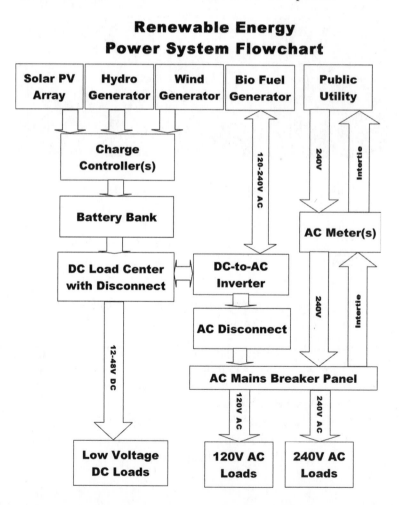

Renewable Energy Power System Flowchart

Solar PV Array · Hydro Generator · Wind Generator · Bio Fuel Generator · Public Utility

Charge Controller(s) → Battery Bank → DC Load Center with Disconnect → DC-to-AC Inverter → AC Disconnect → AC Mains Breaker Panel

AC Meter(s)

12-48V DC → Low Voltage DC Loads

120V AC → 120V AC Loads

240V AC → 240V AC Loads

120-240V AC · 240V · Intertie

Solar Energy

The sun, our star, has been around a long time, and chances are it will be around a lot longer. We're counting on it. Daily, we count on the sun to provide energy to us in the forms of light and heat. We've been doing so since mankind first breathed life. In fact, many civilizations through the ages have believed that the sun is the source of all life on Earth.

Homes that aren't serviced by public utilities are excellent candidates for solar power.

In the past 100 years, technology has been seeking a way to turn the sun's energy into electric power. We'll cover solar energy in the next section and throughout this book, so let's take a quick look at other renewable energy sources.

Sun Spots

Nevada Solar One is the second largest concentrated solar power plant in the world. It uses concentrated solar power (CSP) to collect thermal energy—at 750° Fahrenheit (F)—to produce steam that powers electric generators. Located near Boulder City, it produces *134 million kilowatt hours* of electricity a year—enough to energize 40,000 homes. The Department of Energy says that if CSP plants were built on just 9 percent of Nevada's land, they could generate enough electricity to power *the entire United States!*

New building-integrated photovoltaic (BIPV) systems also can serve as roofing so your home doesn't look "solar."

Wind Energy

The wind has been around forever as well, harnessed to move sailing ships and to pump water with windmills for hundreds of years. Today, wind turbines produce electricity in California, Texas, and many Great Plains states. Hawaii has them, too. Canada and Europe also use wind turbines.

Smaller turbines can produce 50 *kilowatts* of power; larger turbines can turn the wind energy into 1 to 2 *megawatts* of power. Large utility-scale projects with hundreds of turbines spread across acres are called wind farms. Though technology continually improves the efficiency of wind turbines, only about ¼ of 1 percent of all electricity generated in the United States comes from the wind—although this percentage has more than doubled in the past few years. (We'll explore this in detail in Chapter 8.)

def•i•ni•tion

A **kilowatt** (kW) is 1,000 watts of electrical power. A **megawatt** (mW) is 1,000kW of electrical power.

Solar Eclipse _____

Wind power has been on the increase in the past few years, peaking at 8,500mW in 2008. Large wind-turbine farms are in the planning stage, but some larger installations are on hold until economic conditions improve.

Hydro Energy

Less than 10 percent of U.S. energy needs are filled by hydro energy, mostly in western states. Large hydroelectric dams on the Columbia and Snake rivers of the Pacific Northwest and the Colorado River in the Southwest use the power of moving water. Water motion rotates turbines that generate the electricity.

Because energy is released without using up the water, hydro energy is a renewable resource. As long as clouds pick up water and deposit it at higher elevations to flow downhill, hydro energy will be an important source of electric power.

Bio Energy

Bio means "life," so bio energy is energy released from recently living things. It can be methane gas from decaying biomass at landfills, or biofuels such as ethanol alcohol made from corn and other plants. Biodiesel, for example, is made from used vegetable oil. Home fireplaces burn wood (although not very efficiently), another renewable source of bio energy. Wood by-products are used to meet some industrial energy needs.

Bio energy is primarily used to replace or supplement other fuels, because power from fossil fuel is cheaper. For example, ethanol (grain alcohol) is added to gasoline to reduce total emissions. Biomass is used with coal to lower emissions at coal power plants. These renewable energy sources will not soon replace coal and gasoline; biomass and biofuels produce less than 2 percent of U.S. electrical energy.

Geothermal Energy

The center of Earth is cooking at 9,000°F. That's a lot of energy! Fortunately for us, some of that energy escapes to the surface in the form of steam and hot water that can be harnessed to produce electric power. Geothermal power plants need water of only 225 to 360°F to produce electrical power.

You either live near a source of geothermal energy or you don't. All geothermal power plants in the United States are located in the western states of California, Nevada, Utah, and Hawaii. Together they produce *less than* ½ of 1 percent of the electricity generated in the United States. Not much, but it all helps.

Other Energy Sources

Add it all up and you'll discover that the energy produced in the United States using renewable resources is just 12 percent of the total—less than one eighth of what we use! But what about other energy sources? Nuclear power, becoming less popular because of long-term environmental concerns, produces 20 percent of our electricity. Petroleum and natural gas make another 18 percent. The subtotal is still less than half.

> **Sun Spots**
>
> The United States consumes about 20 million barrels of petroleum *per day,* importing 58 percent of it from other countries. A barrel of oil is 42 gallons. The United States also consumes 22 billion cubic feet (cu. ft.) of natural gas per year, importing about 20 percent of it, mostly from Canada.

The majority of U.S. electric generation uses coal. In the process, fossil-fueled electric power plants released nearly 3 billion tons of carbon dioxide, 15 million tons of sulfur dioxide, 9 million tons of nitrous oxides, and a bunch of other stuff that isn't good for us.

We should also talk about the other uses we have for nonrenewable energy. Cars and trucks burn up a lot of gasoline and diesel fuels. In fact, we use about twice as much fossil fuels to run our cars as we do to power our homes. The result is that our energy resources can't keep up with demand and the U.S. market now imports more than half of its fossil fuel needs. Thirty years ago, we relied on importing a third of fossil fuels. Within 20 years, we'll need to import nearly two thirds. As a comparison, 100 years ago the United States relied almost entirely on home-grown renewable energy resources.

So why should we consider renewable energy sources such as the sun? There are several compelling reasons:

◆ Fossil fuels are finite; the sun's energy is infinite.

◆ The sun offers many times more energy than we can ever use. At noon on a clear day at sea level, the sun delivers an average of 1,000 watts (1 kW) of energy per square yard!

◆ Costs of renewable energy will go down as more people use it.

- Solar energy doesn't pollute our environment (although the manufacturing of solar power equipment does slightly).

- Solar thermal energy can take care of our water and heating needs.

- Using solar energy will eliminate fuel imports and the associated economic and political problems.

Here Comes the Sun!

Think of the sun as the ultimate energy source. It's a nuclear reactor, but at a nice, safe 93 million miles away. Plants and animals that eventually became fossil fuels were once nourished by the sun. The sun's heat powers the Earth's winds and the clouds that transport water.

The first users of residential solar heating on this continent were the ancient Native Americans who built homes in rock cliffs that faced south to collect and store solar thermal energy. Solar energy works. Open the door of a car that's been sitting in the hot sun, and you will feel solar thermal energy. Or take a drink from a hose that's been lying in the sun.

The good news is that the lucky old sun, with nothing to do but roll 'round heaven all day, can satisfy Earth's energy needs many times over without depleting itself. The bad news is that solar energy today is used to produce less than 1 percent of our electricity. That's not very much!

> ### Sun Spots
>
> The American Recovery and Reinvestment Act (ARRA) of 2009 dramatically increased government spending in clean energy beginning in 2010. The act includes $39 billion in energy investments and $20 billion in tax incentives. Additional funding is budgeted for the next decade. The American Clean Energy and Security Act (ACESA) will require 25 percent of U.S. energy to come from renewable resources by 2025. Canada has similar goals and incentives, described online at ecoaction.gc.ca. Additional solar resources are available online at SolarHomeGuides.com.

The problem is not the availability of the sun, obviously. It's always there, even when it's behind the clouds. The problem is that solar electricity is, in the short term, more expensive to generate than other electricity. It seems easier and cheaper simply to pay for the electricity conveniently delivered to you. Where does it come from? How did it get here? What are the longer-term costs to our world? These are questions worth considering.

The sun radiates energy. If it were any closer than about 93 million miles, we would be cooked. If it were farther, we would freeze to death. About 10 percent of that radiated energy arrives to Earth in the form of sunlight. Fortunately, that's the form we need most here on Earth.

How much sunlight a given point on Earth receives depends on when it is, where it is, and what's in between. Any point on Earth is tilted farther away from the sun during winter months and closer during summer months. Places closer to the equator get more sun than those farther north or farther south. Finally, clouds, smoke, and pollutants diffuse or reduce the solar radiation hitting different points on Earth.

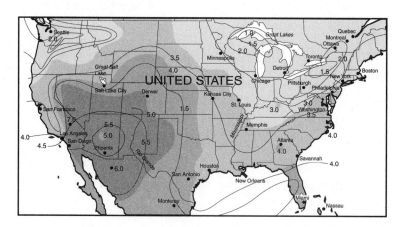

Map of the average number of hours each day the sun shines in the United States.

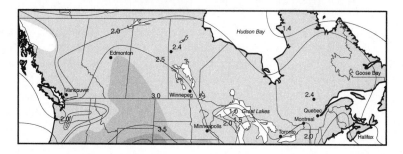

Map of the average number of hours each day the sun shines in Canada.

In addition to producing electricity, solar energy can reduce our need for electricity by heating water and air in our homes. Solar thermal energy—heat—can generate power when sunshine is concentrated at places such as California's Mojave Desert. So the sun can offer our homes both heat and electricity.

Here are some ways the sun's energy can work in our homes:

- Lighting rooms with sunlight
- Preheating water for showers, baths, and laundry
- Preheating air to maintain comfortable room temperatures
- Providing electricity to power appliances and tools

How can sunshine become electricity? I'll cover the "how" in detail in Chapter 7. But in a nutshell, modules or groups of silicon solar called *photovoltaic* (PV) cells collect sunlight and convert it into electricity. The PV modules can be mounted on or near your home. In addition, solar energy can be used to warm air and water without the middleman, electricity. Fortunately, solar power systems are becoming increasingly efficient and cost effective, so that even renters and campers can afford portable systems. The PV modules also last a long time. Many early units are still working after 30 years. A life span in excess of 20 years of constant use is expected and most modules are warranted for 10 to 25 years.

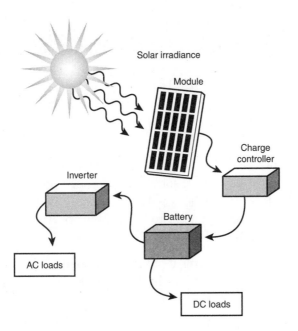

How sunlight can be used to make electricity.

In addition, solar radiation can be collected and used to heat water using flat-plate panels mounted facing south on your home's roof. I'll give you the specifics in Chapter 9.

You can also design or redesign your home to have sunrooms and other air spaces that collect and distribute **passive** solar energy, thus cutting your power bill.

def•i•ni•tion

Solar energy is **passive,** delivered to your doorstep without a truck or power line. If it needs machinery, such as PV modules or pumps, to work in your home, it is *active* solar power.

Changing Technologies and Attitudes

Prices for PV systems have come down about 25 percent in the past few years. At the same time, those who have been pleading with us to consider solar energy are being heard. The federal government and many state governments both use and encourage solar energy. Many push industry to share solar technology and lower equipment costs. Others offer impressive tax incentives for investment in solar electric systems (see Chapter 2). And some have even required utility companies to buy electricity from users who have excess! Attitudes and opportunities are changing.

Sun Spots
What do you need to turn solar power into electricity? Clear, unshaded access to the sun at least five hours each day, adequate roof or ground space for the solar collectors, and some solar power generation equipment. There's more, of course, but those are the basic requirements. It's easier than you may think.

For example, the U.S. Department of Energy's Solar Energy Technologies Program is focusing more attention on the benefits of solar power through policies and research. Working with the marketplace, its goal is to make the United States competitive in the photovoltaics marketplace and produce 5 to 10 gigawatts of PV power—enough for 1 to 2 million homes—by 2015.

The purpose of this book is to inform you about the solar solution, the economics, the importance of solar power, and your options. In the following chapters, you'll learn how to select, buy, finance, and install solar power for your home.

In the meantime, don't stare at the sun!

The Least You Need to Know

- ◆ The sun provides free energy to Earth that can be used to power our lives.

- ◆ Nonrenewable fuels currently provide most of our electric and engine power—and nearly all of our pollutants.

- ◆ Homeowners and even renters can reduce energy costs with solar power.

- ◆ Solar power is becoming a cost-effective investment through applied technology.

Solar Power Incentives and Paybacks

In This Chapter

- Discovering federal tax credits for energy efficiency
- Getting information about solar rebates
- Taking advantage of state tax incentives for solar power
- Selling power to the utility company
- Earning valuable renewable energy credits
- Learning your solar light rights

Solar energy is a readily available power source. So why aren't all homes and power companies using it? Cost! The fact is, it's currently more expensive to produce electricity using a solar power system than it is with a nonrenewable source such as fossil fuel. The problem certainly isn't availability, as there's more sunlight than there is coal, oil, and gas in the world. The problem is mass production. Until more people and utility companies decide to use solar energy, the cost of producing solar electric and thermal power systems will remain higher than for entrenched energy sources. When fossil fuel became less expensive than whale oil, the use of fossil fuel expanded and whale hunters found new jobs. It's an economic thing.

So when will the economics of solar energy make it cost less than fossil fuel? Soon.

This chapter tells you how you can cut the costs of solar power for your home with clout and incentives from various governments. By being aware of and using these opportunities, you can reduce solar power costs for yourself as well as for others.

Federal Tax Credits for Energy Efficiency

Here's good news: recent changes in federal law, including those of the Internal Revenue Service (IRS), encourage consumers and businesses to invest in both new and retrofit equipment and services that increase energy efficiency. Here's a summary:

◆ Federal tax credits are available for 30 percent of the cost of retrofitting homes with energy-saving products, including windows, doors, insulation, roofs, heating and air conditioning (HVAC), nonsolar water heaters, and biomass stoves. The current limit for tax credits is $1,500 and they are set to expire in 2010 (although Congress may extend them).

◆ Federal tax credits are available for 30 percent of the cost of installing energy systems in new and existing homes. There is no upper limit on the credit, though it is set to expire in 2016. These energy systems include solar panels, solar water heaters, small wind energy systems, geothermal heat pumps, and fuel cells.

As you can imagine, there's lots of fine print. In addition, specifics and definitions can help you determine whether your energy investment qualifies. To qualify for the tax credit, you must have Manufacturer Certification Statement for each of your purchases. These are available from the manufacturer, online, or from the retailer.

For more specifics, visit energystar.gov/taxcredits. Note that not all ENERGY STAR homes and products qualify for this federal tax credit. Make sure you get a Manufacturer Certification Statement and contact the IRS (irs.gov) for specific filing requirements.

Sun Spots
Be a smart consumer when purchasing products that say they are qualified for the Federal Tax Credit for Energy Efficiency. Only those with a Manufacturer Certification Statement are allowed by the IRS. In addition, some manufacturers are charging premium prices for products that do qualify for the tax credit—in some cases, a premium that exceeds the potential credit. Shop and compare.

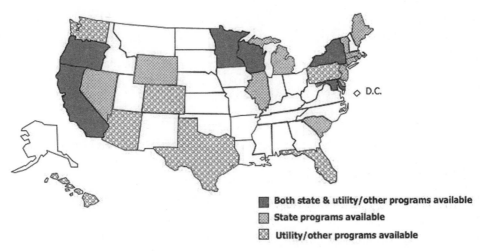

■ **Both state & utility/other programs available**
■ **State programs available**
▨ **Utility/other programs available**

Rebate programs are available in many states for renewable energy technology investments.

American Recovery and Reinvestment Act (ARRA)

For decades, the U.S. Department of Energy (DOE) has been trying to encourage the use of solar energy by power companies, industry, and home builders. Most of that support has been in the form of technical assistance. The DOE funds programs that teach how to apply solar energy to meet power needs.

In 1997, the DOE announced the Million Solar Roofs Initiative (MSRI), a program intended to encourage the installation of solar energy systems in 1 million federal buildings by coordinating the efforts of various federal, state, local, utility, financial, and industry groups toward that goal. The MSRI was intended to be a facilitator with clout. The federal government can coordinate such an extensive project more easily than any other single entity. The American Recovery and Reinvestment Act (ARRA) of 2009 has taken over this responsibility, focusing on federal buildings and public housing.

Of course, the DOE gets its funding and some of its direction from Congress, so it must satisfy the political side of the equation. People must use the program and keep pressure on Congress to keep it focused and funded. So far, so good.

The MSRI and ARRA have a number of noble goals. They are trying to reduce *greenhouse gases* and other emissions by replacing fossil power with solar power and other renewable energy resources. It estimates that a million solar power systems will reduce carbon emissions into our atmosphere equivalent to the annual emissions from 850,000 cars.

def•i•ni•tion

Greenhouse gases trap the heat of the sun in Earth's atmosphere, producing the greenhouse effect, which increases temperatures around the world. The two major greenhouse gases are water vapor and carbon dioxide. Other greenhouse gases include methane, ozone, chlorofluorocarbons, and nitrogen oxides.

The ARRA also wants to create thousands of new high-tech jobs resulting from increased demand for photovoltaic (solar electricity), solar hot water, and related solar energy systems. And it is trying to encourage the growth of an industry—solar power—that can compete in the world market. Of course, all this means that if more folks buy solar energy systems, prices will come down. It's a matter of supply and demand.

You can follow the progress of the ARRA online at recovery.gov. It's your tax dollars at work.

Rebates

A rebate is money given back. Many manufacturers use rebates to get folks to try their products. Federal, state, and local governments try to get people to buy and install solar power by using rebates. About half of all the United States and utilities have some type of solar incentive program. The money may be paid to the consumer, the installer, the retailer, or the manufacturer. Ultimately, the consumer benefits through lower initial costs—as long as the consumer knows about the rebate.

One form of rebate is known as a *buy-down*. Someone, typically a government program, pays part of the initial cost of a solar power system. Usually, the buy-down amount is established by the state legislature for a specified period. The buy-down amounts are based on the system's generating capacity, measured in watts or kilowatts. In some programs, rebates are given on a first-come, first-served basis. Those who apply earliest get the higher rebate.

Can you qualify for a state buy-down? How? Good questions! The best place to start answering these questions is your state's energy department. In addition, you can contact the National Association of State Energy Officials at (703) 299-8800 or online at naseo.org. Its website includes a map on which you can click to find out about your state's energy office. From there you can find out what solar energy rebates and resources are available. Additional solar resources are available online at SolarHomeGuides.com.

Here's another great resource: the North Carolina Solar Center and the Interstate Renewable Energy Council developed and maintain the Database of State Incentives for Renewable Energy (DSIRE). You can see it online at dsireusa.org. It tells you, state by state, what resources and opportunities are available to those considering renewable resources.

For example, California has its Emerging Renewables Program, which offers incentives and rebates for homes that take advantage of solar power. A comprehensive guidebook is available from the California Energy Commission (energy.ca.gov). Other states also have renewable energy incentive programs (see SolarHomeGuides.com).

Local governments, too, try to encourage renewable energy resources. The city of Chicago offers a Green Building Incentive to advise and encourage solar and other renewable energy buildings. Information is available at cityofchicago.org.

State Tax Incentives

Do states offer tax credits and other incentives? Some do and some don't. Again, check online at dsireusa.org for the latest information for specific states, counties, municipalities, and communities. An interactive map on the main page will help you select your state and learn more about tax incentives. Included are green building incentives, local loan and rebate programs, product incentives, property tax exemptions, utility grants, and other opportunities. As always, you must follow the regulations exactly to benefit from these programs.

How can you learn what rebates and tax incentives are available to you? The resources listed in this chapter and online at SolarHomeGuides.com are the best place to start. In addition, talk with local solar equipment suppliers and contractors; their job is to know about rebates and incentives that help them sell more systems.

Selling Your Excess Power

The federal Energy Policy Act of 2005 (Sec. 1251) says that all public electric utilities are now required to allow *net metering* programs. If individuals and businesses generate excess renewable-generated power and want to sell it, the local utility must buy it at "avoided" or wholesale cost. Some states have net metering programs with major public utilities in the state. For example, California's Self-Generation Incentive Program (SGIP) is a joint venture of the state's primary utilities for a standardized structure for handling customer-generated power options and incentives. The latest

def•i•ni•tion

Net metering allows your electricity meter to spin forward when electricity flows from the utility into your home and backward when your power system delivers unused power to the utility. However, you must make sure your system is a qualified facility (see Chapter 12) and your local utility allows net metering.

SGIP handbook is available from primary California utility companies. In addition, some Canadian provinces have net metering programs.

Fortunately, many states have passed laws to force utilities to make net metering easier for consumers. Some states even allow you to sell electricity to the utility at the peak-usage rate and buy from it at the low-usage rate. Chapter 12 offers more specifics on the program. This can dramatically decrease the long-term costs of your solar power system, so find out now whether net metering is available to you. Besides state energy offices, a solar power system retailer (see Chapter 16) or solar power contractor (see Chapter 17) can offer localized advice.

Yes, some utilities offer incentives to customers to generate their own renewable energy. To learn more, contact your electric company and ask:

◆ Do you net meter (run the meter backward) if I sell power to you? If not, how much do you credit me compared to how much I pay you? Some utilities will pay the "avoided cost"—the cost of the fuel they do not have to use. This may be about one quarter of what you pay them.

◆ Can I have a time-of-use (TOU) meter? The advantage to you is that peak cost usually coincides with peak production from your solar electric system. The utility may pay you more for your peak kilowatts.

◆ How much do you charge to set up a buy-back agreement? This charge should include an additional meter, the contract, and an inspection by the utility before the power can be accepted.

Utilities that credit at retail rates for PV electricity will not pay retail for your excess electricity. They may carry over your credit for a month, a year, or the life of the system, but they will settle up at the lower avoided cost rate if they pay you at all.

Renewable Energy Certificates

Here's something new under the sun. Because utility companies are mandated to sell more power from renewable energy sources, a system of credits has been developed to keep track of power developed from renewable energy. These Renewable Energy

Certificates or RECs (pronounced "rex") are the documented proof that grid-tied electricity was produced from a renewable source. They have some value and may be bought by either a utility or agency that's subject to a Renewable Portfolio Standard (RPS) or by an aggregator or broker who sells to these public or governmental utilities.

For example, New York State recently mandated that investor-owned utilities in the state must get at least 24 percent of their electricity from renewable sources by the year 2013. The utilities will rely on some of their grid-tied customers to provide a portion of the renewable energy power. How do they keep track? With RECs—credits earned by the customers for delivering renewable energy (RE) to the grid via net meters. Nifty!

Bright Idea

When you install grid-tied electric systems, make sure you get to keep the RECs so that you can resell them yourself, or at least get additional value for them. RECs are similar to money in the bank. Just make sure you know how much they are worth, as some RECs are earned per kilowatt-hour (kWh) and others per megawatt-hour (mWh). (One REC is approximately equal to 1 mWh of electricity produced from a renewable, carbon dioxide–free resource.)

Your Right to Light

You have rights! As a property owner, you may have the right to unobstructed, direct sunlight. No one can build or block your property's solar access. I say "may" because not all communities give you that right. It comes under zoning laws. Several communities in the United States have specific solar access planning guidelines and ordinances. The ordinances are specific; their intent is to encourage the use of solar energy systems.

For example, San Jose, California, defines solar access by the amount of shade a dwelling has at solar noon on December 21, the shortest day of the year. It says that solar shading from a structure or vegetation can't be more than 20 percent of a south-facing wall or 10 percent of a south-facing window. That's specific!

Many states have enacted laws to protect landowners' rights to sunlight. For example, California Civil Code Section 801.5 follows:

> a) The right of receiving sunlight as specified in subdivision 18 of Section 801 shall be referred to as a solar easement. "Solar easement" means the right of receiving sunlight across real property of another for any solar energy system.

As used in this section, "solar energy system" means either of the following:

(1) Any solar collector or other solar energy device whose primary purpose is to provide for the collection, storage, and distribution of solar energy for space heating, space cooling, electric generation, or water heating.

(2) Any structural design feature of a building, whose primary purpose is to provide for the collection, storage, and distribution of solar energy for electricity generation, space heating or cooling, or water heating.

b) Any instrument creating a solar easement shall include, at a minimum, all of the following:

(1) A description of the dimensions of the easement expressed in measurable terms, such as vertical or horizontal angles measured in degrees, or the hours of the day on specified dates during which direct sunlight to a specified surface of a solar collector, device, or structural design feature may not be obstructed, or a combination of these descriptions.

(2) The restrictions placed upon vegetation, structures, and other objects that would impair or obstruct the passage of sunlight through the easement.

(3) The terms or conditions, if any, under which the easement may be revised or terminated.

Check with local governments to learn what your solar access rights—and obligations—are. They may give you the right to have trees removed that block your home's solar access. In addition, it may mean that you can't build a two-storey house that will block someone else's solar access. You'll learn more about this topic in Chapter 6.

In the meantime, let's move on to Chapter 3, which offers dozens of ideas and resources for financing your solar home.

The Least You Need to Know

- The American Recovery and Reinvestment Act is a federal program aimed at bringing solar resources together to bring down costs and create jobs.

- You can earn Energy Policy Act Renewable Energy Certificates to reduce your taxes.

- State and local rebates and buy-downs reduce the out-of-pocket costs of solar energy systems (see dsireusa.org).

◆ Federal and state tax incentives can further reduce solar power costs.

◆ You may be able to generate extra solar electricity and sell it back to the utility company.

◆ Your property may be subject to solar access zoning laws that can impact the cost of your system.

Financing Your Solar Home

In This Chapter

- ◆ Finding the money to pay for your solar home
- ◆ Understanding why your home needs an energy rating
- ◆ Learning all about federal solar financing programs
- ◆ Obtaining state financing resources
- ◆ Getting your utility or solar power vendor to finance your system

Solar power can be expensive. Depending on whether you're seeking solar electricity, hot water, hot air, or all of the above, a solar power system for your home can cost $51,000 for a large 6 kW system. Add a swimming pool heater and the price goes up.

Fortunately, the previous chapters have introduced you to solar power systems and started you thinking about what you want. You then learned about programs, rebates, buy-downs, tax credits, and other incentives that can cut the cost of solar power by more than half.

Sun Spots

Want to get a quick estimate of the solar power system your home will need? Use the online estimator at http://www.affordable-solar.com/gt-estimator.htm. Input your monthly electrical use (in kilowatts), the average bill (in dollars), the percentage of power you want from your solar system, and the average peak sun hours for your location (four to six in most locations). The calculator then will recommend a system size and tell you what your savings will be. Batteries not included.

Even before you decide exactly what kind of solar power system you will install in your home and start getting bids, you need to know what funds are available. So the next step is to find out what money is available to stretch your investment over a longer period. That's what this chapter is all about. There is a surprising amount of money out there waiting for smart solar investors!

About Financing

Maybe you don't need to finance your solar power system. Maybe you have the cash on hand from winning the lottery or something. Even so, consider financing solar equipment and installation. The interest rates are typically very low, so you often can invest that money somewhere else for a greater return.

You have options. You can finance purchases with a consumer loan, a supplier loan, or a *first* or *second mortgage*. Which makes the most sense? Consumer loans don't require collateral, except your promise to pay them back, so their interest is usually the highest. Examples include credit cards and finance company loans. Interest on the loan will range from about 12 to 24 percent. In most cases, it does not make sense to put your solar system on a credit card and make payments for years.

Alternatively, whoever sells you the solar equipment or system may offer financing, using the equipment as collateral. Interest is typically lower, ranging from 6 to 10 percent. In some cases, suppliers offer manufacturer rebates or buy-downs that will lower the interest rate, similar to car manufacturers that sometimes offer below-cost financing. Their "loss" is rolled up in the final purchase price.

The lowest rates are available to homeowners who are building a new home or retrofitting an old one with solar equipment. The reason is that if you default, the lender can collect against the value of the house and not just against the solar equipment. Without rebates, first and second mortgage rates currently run between 6 and 9 percent for fixed-rate mortgages and lower for adjustable-rate mortgages.

def•i•ni•tion

A **mortgage** is a document in which the borrower (mortgagor) gives the lender (mortgagee) rights to property as security for the repayment of the loan. A **first mortgage** offers lenders first rights to take money from the proceeds of selling a defaulted property. A **second mortgage** offers second rights after the first rights have been satisfied. The mortgage lien is removed after the debt is repaid. A **home equity line of credit** (HELOC) is similar to a second mortgage except that it gives you a maximum loan amount that you can draw on as needed.

Another advantage to financing solar power systems with a mortgage is that mortgage interest currently is deductible against federal and most state income taxes. For example, if you're in a 30 percent tax bracket, $1,000 in interest paid earns a tax credit of $300. It's similar to actually paying just $72 in interest. For more information, contact the Internal Revenue Service at 1-800-829-1040 or online at irs.gov.

Where can you apply for a consumer loan or a first or second mortgage? If you currently have a mortgage or consumer loan, contact that lender first. It can help start your education. If you are buying a new home, your lender can include the costs of solar planning and solar equipment in the first mortgage. If you already have a first mortgage on an existing home, you can either refinance the mortgage for an amount large enough to cover the system or apply for a second mortgage. A second mortgage makes sense if the interest rates on your first mortgage are lower than you could get by refinancing (including new loan costs). Or your first mortgage may be held by a private party (contract) not willing to invest in improvements. Of course, you also need to make sure the loan fees are calculated into the cost of a new loan.

If you decide to get a new first or second mortgage, you can get a conventional loan or a special loan through conventional lenders (such as banks or savings and loans). Special loans include those that offer rebates, buy-downs, and lower rates for energy-efficient projects. Many mortgage lenders can help you get one of these special loans, but you should make yourself an informed consumer so you know you're getting the best deal. The forthcoming section on energy-efficient financing will guide you through the maze.

Financial resources for solar power system loans are available online at SolarHomeGuides.com. Be sure to check with local banks and credit unions if you live in the solar rebate states with the most incentives: California, Colorado, New Jersey, New Mexico, and New York.

Home Energy Rating

Before getting knee-deep in mortgages and acronyms, consider that you will probably need a home energy rating. Most financing programs for energy-efficiency projects we discuss in this chapter encourage you to have your current home (or building plans) reviewed and rated by a certified professional energy rater.

The energy rater's job is to inspect the energy-related features of a home, such as insulation levels, window efficiency, heating and cooling systems, and air leakage. The resulting report will include the home's energy rating and an estimate of annual energy use and costs. The report may also recommend energy-efficient improvements, their costs, potential savings, and expected payback time for improvements. The rating will be a score between 100 for the typical home and 0 for a home that needs no outside energy sources. Obviously, you want improvements that will lower your home energy rating score.

To get the best financing package possible, you need to assure the lender that the improvements are cost effective and will save you more money than you're borrowing to install them. This works to your advantage because it typically helps you qualify for a higher loan amount—or lower interest rate—than a lender can give you without the potential savings.

Who pays for the home energy inspection and rating? Ultimately, the homeowner, though it may be rolled into the lender's loan costs. Check solarHomeGuides.com to find out more about the Home Energy Rating System (HERS) and certified inspectors in your area. Also, your lender may have a favorite inspector.

> ### Sun Spots
>
> A typical HERS report will include estimated annual energy uses and cost by system (space heating, space cooling, water heating, and other energy uses) for the current home both with and without energy-efficient improvements. It then uses a one- to five-star rating system that compares uses and costs before and after improvements. For example, a two-star rating means that energy costs in the current home are 200 to 300 percent higher than in an ideal or reference home.

Energy-Efficient Financing

There are two primary types of energy-efficient mortgages (EEMs): new and existing home. Which one you choose obviously depends on whether you're building a new energy-efficient home or investing in a house that's already built to which you'll add solar. Most lenders described here will be happy to help you with either type, though you may find that some are easier to work with on new-home mortgages and others are more experienced with mortgages for retrofits.

As you look at these resources, keep in mind that nothing is safe from change while Congress is in session. That is, today's program may become tomorrow's history. New programs may get announced but not funded. Limits change. Even so, many of these programs have been around for a few years with minor changes, so we're safe discussing them. Talk with your lender(s) about the latest wrinkles in these programs.

Fannie Mae

Fannie Mae is the newer name for the Federal National Mortgage Association (FNMA). Everyone has referred to FNMA as Fannie Mae for so long that it's now the official name. Fannie Mae is a private, shareholder-owned corporation set up by Congress to keep money flowing into the mortgage market. It doesn't actually lend money directly to home buyers. Instead, it purchases mortgages from lenders to ensure that funds are available. In 2008, Fannie Mae was placed under the power of the Federal House Finance Agency to work out some problems it was having. However, this doesn't change what Fannie Mae does.

Fannie Mae encourages lenders to offer EEMs by providing guidelines and incentives. Fannie Mae buys conventional mortgages as well, up to $417,000 on new homes (as of 2009)—higher in some areas. They also buy residential energy efficiency improvement loans (REEIL, for you acronym fans) up to 100 percent of the cost of retrofitting older homes with a maximum of 15 percent of the home's new value. The REEIL mortgages are at interest rates *below* current market rates, making them very attractive to homeowners. The mortgage must fund energy-efficient upgrades such as solar electricity (PV), solar water, and solar space heating systems. Even conventional mortgages for new home construction are at market rates and often very attractive. Adjustable and fixed interest rates are available as well as balloon or large payments at the end of a specified period.

Solar Eclipse

Can you get a Fannie Mae mortgage for constructing or retrofitting an off-grid house? Theoretically, yes. However, some lenders may not want to write a loan for a house that isn't connected to an electric utility. Before you start spending money, make sure area lenders are willing to finance your solar home.

Who offers Fannie Mae EEMs? Conventional mortgage lenders do. Work through your bank, savings and loan, mortgage company, or mortgage broker. For the latest information on Fannie Mae mortgages and loans, call 1-800-732-6643 or visit online at fanniemae.com.

Freddie Mac

Not to be outdone, the Federal Home Mortgage Loan Corporation (FHMLC) likes to be called Freddie Mac. Freddie Mac also buys conforming mortgages from lenders, packages them as securities, and sells them as guaranteed investments to insurance companies and pension funds. It's in what's called the secondary mortgage market. In 2008, Freddie Mac was placed under the power of the Federal House Finance Agency to work out some financial difficulties it was having. However, this doesn't change how Freddie Mac works.

Freddie Mac's programs are similar to Fannie Mae's except that it is more interested in long-term EEMs than in short-term loans. The current mortgage terms and limits on energy-efficient mortgages are similar to those of Fannie Mae. Interest rates are very attractive with fixed mortgages at market rates and variable mortgages at the prime rate plus 2 percent. First mortgages can be written for up to 95 percent of the property's value.

Freddie Mac mortgages, too, are available through traditional mortgage lenders. For additional information call 1-800-FREDDIE (373-3343) or visit the website at freddiemac.com.

Farmer Mac

Building or retrofitting a country home? The U.S. Department of Agriculture (USDA) has money to lend both rural homeowners and rural utility services. It is especially interested in helping new and existing rural utilities use solar electricity and solar thermal energy. Why? Because Congress told them to.

The USDA's division called the Farmers Home Administration (FmHA) is referred to as Farmer Mac. (Isn't it cute?) It guarantees and insures rural housing mortgage loans, encouraging those that use solar energy. Farmer Mac, a stock-owned, publicly traded corporation that answers to the U.S. Department of Agriculture, has not faced the problems or restructuring that Fannie and Freddie have. For additional information and specific loan requirements, contact the USDA at 202-720-4323 or visit online at usda.gov.

Department of Energy (DOE)

The Department of Energy doesn't actually lend money to develop solar energy systems. However, it does fund programs such as the State Weatherization Assistance Program (SWAP), which helps states fund weatherization projects for low-income Americans. The program can also install solar hot-water systems. Since 1976, SWAP has provided weatherization funds to 6.2 million low-income families. It recently received additional funding from the American Recovery and Reinvestment Act. The funds go to the states for distribution. Contact your state energy and weatherization office (see SolarHomeGuides.com) for details.

As you've learned in other chapters, the DOE funds various solar research and information projects that benefit consumers. One of the most popular is the National Database of State Incentives for Renewable Energy (DSIRE), which was covered in Chapter 2. Its website (dsireusa.org) offers state-specific charts and data. For example, financial incentives for renewable energy in Massachusetts include personal, corporate, sales, and property tax breaks; rebates (state and utility); grants; and loans. The site offers up-to-date financial opportunities for all states, the District of Columbia, and Puerto Rico.

Department of Housing and Urban Development (HUD)

HUD's function is to develop communities of opportunity, funding affordable housing for low- and moderate-income families. Within that charter, it encourages the purchase and retrofitting of energy-efficient homes. Specifically, HUD loans can include solar power (PV), thermal space, and water heating projects. Depending on the loan type, the loan value can actually exceed the property's value.

HUD has a variety of ongoing programs to encourage energy-efficient home owner-ship. They include the Community Development Block Grant Program (CDBG); the HOME Investment Partnership Program; HOPE VI, which replaces old housing with new; and, the most famous, the *Federal Housing Administration (FHA)* program.

def•i•ni•tion

The **Federal Housing Administration (FHA)** is a HUD division that insures home loans to make them more attractive investments and thus keep interest rates down. Many Americans have purchased their first (and subsequent) homes using FHA-insured mortgages. There are a variety of programs, including the popular Energy Efficient Mortgage (EEM) program that recognizes solar and other renewable energy sources. FHA has insured more than 34 million properties since 1934.

FHA EEMs can be written for new and existing one- to four-unit properties that have a home energy rating, provided by local energy rating inspectors. The borrower must make a 3.5 percent down payment based on the sales price or appraised value. The maximum loan depends on the property's location. The EEM can be used with other FHA loans such as the 203(b). Visit hud.gov and search for "FHA EEM" for additional information.

Another resource is Title I Property Improvement Mortgage Insurance, which helps homeowners get a second mortgage of up to $25,000 for solar and other home improvements. Visit hud.gov and search for "Title I" for additional information.

There are other FHA-insured financing opportunities as well. Your lender may or may not be up on the latest programs and requirements, so check area telephone books for your local HUD office or visit it online at hud.gov.

Department of Veterans Affairs (VA)

Like the FHA, the Department of Veterans Affairs (VA) doesn't actually lend money on homes. It guarantees that the purchaser will pay off the loan. The purchasers have to be qualified veterans of the U.S. armed services.

VA loans are guaranteed first mortgages of up to 100 percent of the home's value plus loan costs. Interest rates are fixed and are very attractive because the VA is guaranteeing the loan. The loan is actually made by a conventional lender that follows VA lending guidelines.

VA loans can fund to build a new home, buy an existing house, or retrofit a house with solar or other energy systems. VA-guaranteed loans can also fund the purchase of a lot and manufactured home.

For additional information on VA loans for energy-efficient and solar homes, visit the website at homeloans.va.gov or contact your regional office of the Department of Veteran Affairs.

Environmental Protection Agency (EPA)

Even the Environmental Protection Agency is getting into the solar home mortgage business. Its stated mission is to protect human health and safeguard the natural environment, so encouraging solar homes fits right in.

Here's how the EPA does it. It manages the ENERGY STAR Financing Program, working with lenders to finance new homes that are ENERGY STAR–rated. To qualify as an ENERGY STAR home, the structure must be 15 percent more energy efficient than the typical home, called a model. Some of these homes utilize solar electric and solar thermal systems to qualify.

The benefits to buyers go beyond the home's higher efficiency. The ENERGY STAR lender can give you a larger mortgage than one you could otherwise qualify for. Interest rates are attractively low. And the EPA helps pay some of the lender's closing costs for you.

Unfortunately, not all lenders can offer ENERGY STAR financing. Currently, only a few national and regional lenders are authorized to package these loans. In addition, not all builders are qualified to construct ENERGY STAR homes. Fortunately, interest in these homes is growing and more builders and lenders are getting certified.

For additional information on EPA ENERGY STAR housing and financing, call toll-free at 1-888-STAR-YES (782-7937) or visit the website at energystar.gov. Information on ENERGY STAR new home ratings is offered in Chapter 4.

State Energy Financing

Many states are pioneers in helping residents finance solar homes. Others are followers. Fortunately, most states now offer some form of financial assistance to those who are buying or retrofitting solar-powered homes.

What does your state or territory do to help finance solar homes? The first place to check is with the National Association of State Energy Officials at 703-299-8800 or online at naseo.org. It's a central clearinghouse for information on requirements and financing for solar and other energy resources by state governments.

In addition, the Residential Energy Services Network (RESNET) is a national network of mortgage companies, real estate brokerages, builders, appraisers, utilities, and other energy and housing professionals. Its aim is to improve the energy efficiency of

Bright Idea

For more information about solar financing, visit the DOE Energy Efficiency and Renewable Energy website at eere.energy.gov. The site includes extensive articles and resources on solar energy technologies, weatherization, wind, hydropower, and other efficient topics.

the nation's housing. It offers state-by-state directories of conventional EEM lenders and energy raters. RESNET is online at natresnet.org. The website can direct you to certified inspectors in your area; also, your lender may have a favorite.

Utility Financing

Here's another important financial resource: your local utility. Most public utilities and many private ones are encouraging energy efficiency by coordinating all the resources. Most offer information and advice, develop lender packages, certify and recommend builders, identify and certify energy system inspectors, and perform related tasks.

The first place to look for utility information is on your monthly utility bill. There will be a customer service telephone number or website address for general information. That's a start. You can ask about energy efficiency programs, resources, and funding. Some (those mandated by legislature to do so) will be cooperative and helpful. Other utilities (private and commercial) may not. The best ones will direct you to an on-staff energy counselor who can talk you through the process and help you find the right financial package.

Solar Vendors

The more you can afford, the more solar power system vendors can sell. So it is in their best interest to know about the best financial packages available to energy projects. In some cases, the manufacturer or distributor of solar equipment will finance packages at attractive interest rates. This may be your best resource if you're buying a solar water heating system that doesn't require a mortgage on your home.

Which vendors offer or know of financing? Most of them. Again, a good place to start is online at SolarHomeGuides.com. Also check your telephone book yellow pages under "Solar Products—Dealers and Services" as well as "Building General Contractors." Ads and a few telephone calls will help you identify solar power system vendors that offer financial packages.

Will you be building a new solar home or retrofitting one? Chapter 4 offers valuable information and tips for those considering a new home, and Chapter 5 is for retrofitters. In these and subsequent chapters, you'll also learn exactly how much your project will cost.

The Least You Need to Know

- ◆ The federal government sponsors numerous cost-effective financial packages to encourage solar homes.

- ◆ State governments and local utilities, too, can help you find the money to invest in energy efficiency.

- ◆ Various home energy rating systems are in use to help measure savings from solar and other renewable energy sources.

- ◆ The best source of funding smaller solar power systems is often the contractor or vendor that sells you the equipment.

Chapter 4

Building Your New Solar Home

In This Chapter

- Finding out about local building codes
- Having an overview of the construction process
- Discovering the basics of solar design
- Orienting your solar home for peak energy efficiency
- Finding the right architect, contractor, and suppliers

Congratulations! The lender has okayed your new construction loan and you're ready to build or retrofit an energy-efficient solar home. Now what?

Not so fast. We haven't gotten into the specifics of designing and selecting solar power and heat components. That will come in Parts 2 and 3. Meantime, you're probably eager to see how it's all going to be built.

This chapter offers an overview of the solar home construction process, including an introduction to passive and active designs. For more specifics on construction, read my book *The Complete Idiot's Guide to Building Your Own Home, Third Edition* (Alpha Books, 2007), which covers all aspects of the process in greater detail.

Building Codes

Not every community is ready for those who want to build solar homes. It's not that the communities are unfriendly, it's that they may say "no" to something they've never seen. Fortunately, more communities are learning about solar options and are actually encouraging solar homes, doing their best to help builders and owners.

So what can you do to make sure that your community will allow your solar home?

◆ Contact your local building department early to discuss your plans for a solar home and ask for relevant ordinances and codes.

◆ Study local building codes and construction guidelines.

◆ Ask about local contractors who have experience constructing solar homes.

◆ Check with your homeowner or neighborhood association to see if there are any restrictions or support for solar homes.

Note that, to construct a new home anywhere, you will need someone's permission. Typically, that's the building department for your city or county. It will want to make sure that the home you build is safe for you and for future owners. In addition, the building department wants its building permit fee, which pays for the building inspector(s) who visit your construction site. Don't even try to start building a home without the proper building permits.

Bright Idea

Some cities and counties are attempting to encourage more solar and energy-efficient—called green—construction. They are doing so by waiving some or all building permit fees. Check with your local building permit department to find out whether it has such programs.

Beginning the Construction Process

Building a home can take from 3 to 12 months, depending on how complex the design is and who is building it. However, the work starts even earlier as the building site is selected and the home's plans are developed.

Designing your home can be frustrating fun. It's frustrating because you probably have a budget limited by what the lender says you can afford. It's fun because this is *your* home and *your* design ideas.

Besides the solar elements, which we'll get to later in this chapter, there are livability questions:

- How many bedrooms will your home have?

- How many baths will it have?

- Will there be any special-use rooms (office, family room, entertainment room)?

- Are there storage and recreation requirements (RV parking, swimming pool)?

- Will it have a single, double, or triple garage?

- In what town and neighborhood will it be located?

- On which lot or parcel will it sit?

- Which services are available (electric, water, sewer, cable) to the building site?

- What is your preferred architectural style?

- What is your solar orientation (which way is the sun)?

- What are the typical lot costs, including utility hookup fees?

Bright Idea

Buy a blank notebook and start your own Solar Home Book with ideas, resources, costs, and designs so you can begin the building process. You also can use it to collect literature on solar products and services.

As you will see, passive solar laws are simple to understand but more complex to implement. You'll need a qualified solar architect to help you design the most efficient passive solar home for your climate and building site. Chapter 10 offers a valuable overview of designing a passive solar home, one where the home itself is the collector of solar energy.

Home construction has become an efficient process over the past 100 years. Even so, there is room within the process for variations, such as including passive and active solar components. Unfortunately, not all building contractors are familiar with these variations, so you will need to find one who understands solar power. If a solar building contractor isn't readily available where you're building, make sure that you hire an architect who will draw up specific plans that can't be misinterpreted. Additional solar resources for finding qualified contractors are available online at SolarHomeGuides.com.

Sun Spots

An ENERGY STAR new home must meet guidelines for energy efficiency set by the U.S. Environmental Protection Agency. By design, they are at least 15 percent more efficient than homes built to the 2004 International Residential Code (IRC). Many are up to 30 percent more energy efficient. The gain comes from using approved insulation, windows, heating and cooling equipment, and construction techniques. For more specifics, visit energystar.gov and search for "new homes." ENERGY STAR home plans and builders are also available from that website.

It's also best if the building inspector on your project is knowledgeable about solar power systems. The best way to hire the right team is to contact your local building authority (from the county or city) and discuss your plans with a senior inspector or other official. She or he may recommend a local contractor who has solar experience. A specific inspector may also be recommended, at least for the solar components of the job.

The conventional residential construction process includes the following 20 steps, in roughly the order they'd be accomplished:

- Preconstruction preparation
- Excavation
- Pest control
- Concrete
- Waterproofing
- Framing
- Roofing
- Plumbing
- Electrical
- HVAC (heating, ventilation, and air conditioning)
- Siding and/or masonry
- Barriers (doors and windows)
- Insulation

- Drywall

- Trim

- Painting

- Cabinetry

- Flooring and tile

- Gutters and downspouts

- Landscaping and driveways

Solar construction is incorporated into these steps, primarily in the preconstruction preparation, plumbing, electrical, HVAC, and landscaping stages. Depending on your solar design, your solar construction may also impact excavation, framing, roofing, insulation, and other steps. Otherwise, your solar home is constructed in the same manner as conventional homes.

Solar panels can be less obtrusive if installed on a garage roof.

Solar Design

In Chapter 1, I introduced the terms "active" and "passive" in regard to solar design. An *active solar home* is a house that collects thermal heat in water or air, then
distributes that heat using pumps or fans. A *passive solar home* is a house that uses a
room, floor, or another part of the building as a solar collector. The room's air or
walls (or both) collect thermal heat from the sun and store it for use in other parts of
the home *without* pumps or fans.

How can a passive solar power system distribute thermal energy without pumps or
fans? You've probably noticed that heat moves from warmer materials to cooler ones
until there is no longer a temperature difference between the two. In fact, the wind
is the movement of air warmed by the sun. A passive solar building distributes heat
throughout the living space by way of *conduction, convection,* and *radiant heat.* These are
the natural laws. You can't break any of these laws, but you can take advantage of them
as you design and build your own home.

def•i•ni•tion

Conduction is the movement of heat through materials. An electric stove burner heats up
a skillet. Convection is the circulation of heat through liquids and gases. Warm air rises
to the ceiling. Radiant heat moves through the air from warmer objects to cooler ones.
A sun-heated floor warms the air around it.

Another law is that opaque objects absorb solar radiation. Darker objects absorb more
than lighter colors. This was clarified for me at an outdoor auto show a few years ago
where two classic cars of the same model, one black and one white, sat in the sun. The
light car was cool to the touch while the black car was very hot to the touch. That's
why solar collectors are dark, to capture the greatest amount of solar radiation. And
that's why it seems that everyone in the southern United States drives a white car.

The difference between a passive solar home and a conventional home is design.
A passive solar home incorporates a collector, absorber, thermal mass (storage),
distribution, and control that best takes advantage of the local climate.

There are three types of design techniques:

  ♦ **Direct gain** is the simplest passive design technique. Sunlight enters the house
    through south-facing windows with special glazing or glass. The sunlight then
    strikes dark masonry floors and/or walls that absorb and store solar heat. At

night, as the room cools, the heat stored in thermal mass radiates into the room. Because water stores twice as much heat as masonry, specially designed walls can be filled with water for greater solar heating efficiency.

♦ **Indirect gain** stores its solar thermal energy between the south-facing windows and the living space in a special solar heat-absorbing wall called a Trombe wall (named after Felix Trombe, one of its inventors). The wall then radiates thermal energy into the living space. The main difference between direct-gain and indirect-gain designs is the distance between the glass and the thermal mass. Indirect-gain components are closer to each other.

Bright Idea

Want a solar home but not sure you want to build one? Consider a new or preowned solar home that's already built. Your local real estate agent can help you find one. In addition, visit websites such as greenhomesforsale. com, listedgreen.com, and greenhomefinder.com.

♦ **Isolated gain** is another popular passive solar design. A sunspace, also known as a solar room or solarium, uses solar energy to warm the air in a room. It works in much the same way as a greenhouse, except that a sunroom requires more ventilation control so people inside don't get too hot or cold.

Orienting Your Solar Home

As you can see, designing your home to take advantage of the sun's energy can save you thousands of dollars in energy costs over the years. That's why it's vital that you make sure your home is not only designed but *oriented*, or placed on the building lot to take full advantage of solar radiation.

The most productive hours of sunlight are from about 9:00 A.M to 3:00 P.M., called solar noon. For much of the year, your site will probably receive solar radiation before and after these times, but it will contain less energy. The least sunlight will be at solar noon on the shortest day of the year, December 21. The most will be six months later, or approximately June 21.

Orientation is important in designing a solar passive home, but it is most critical for one that will use PV to develop solar electricity. And it's especially important if the PV modules are installed in a fixed position without a tracking system. In Chapter 7, I'll cover the specifics of selecting, orienting, and mounting PVs. Generally, a house that is slightly longer in the east-west dimension will be warmer in the winter and cooler in the summer.

The best solar orientation is facing the widest part of the house to the south.

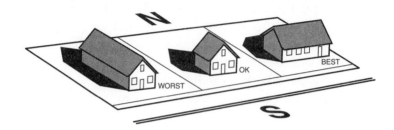

For now, know that there are resources and tools to help you orient your house for optimum solar reception. The Solar Pathfinder (solarpathfinder.com), for example, is a small plastic dome and tripod that helps track solar travel over a specific site. In addition, Chapter 7 and SolarHomeGuides.com include numerous products and free Internet sites to help you orient your new home.

Solar panels don't have to be mounted on the home's roof. They are rack-mounted at ground level.

Energy-Efficient Design

You can save on the cost of solar equipment and design by first making your home design as energy efficient as possible (Appendix B). What does that mean? Here's what most energy-efficient home designs have in common:

♦ A well-constructed and tightly sealed thermal envelope

♦ Energy-efficient doors, windows, and appliances

♦ Properly sized, high-efficiency heating and cooling systems

♦ Controlled ventilation

Let's take a closer look at each of these components of building an energy-efficient home.

Thermal Envelope

A thermal envelope is everything about the house that shields the living space from the outdoors. It includes the wall and roof assemblies, insulation, vapor retarders, windows, and weatherstripping.

Today's wall and roof assemblies are designed to keep interior air in and exterior air out. For example, structural insulated panels (SIPs) of plywood or oriented-strand board (OSB) are glued to foam board that serves as an insulation barrier.

An energy-efficient house has much higher insulation R-values than required by most local building codes. An *R-value* is the ability of a material to resist heat transfer. ("R" is the scientific code for "resistance.") The lower the value, the faster the heat loss. For example, a typical house might have insulation of R-11 in the exterior walls, R-19 in the ceiling, and no insulation in the floors and foundation walls. An energy-efficient home will have wall insulation of R-20 to R-30 and ceiling and floor insulation of R-50 to R-70.

Bright Idea

It makes little sense to save money on winter heating just to spend it on summer cooling. A passive solar home design must provide summer comfort as well, primarily by using intelligent window placement—which can be supplemented by awnings, shutters, and trellises.

In addition, an energy-efficient home will have vapor retarders that minimize the condensation of water vapor on exterior walls. In colder climates, warm indoor air condenses inside exterior walls. In humid climates, warm outdoor air condenses on the outside surfaces of exterior walls. Condensation leads to heat loss as well as mildew and other problems. An efficient thermal envelope minimizes heat loss and mildew with vapor barriers.

Doors, Windows, and Appliances

Many homes lose more than 25 percent of their heat through windows and surrounding window framing. That's a lot of expensive heat lost to inefficiency. South-facing windows should have a high solar heat gain coefficient (SHGC) to allow winter sun and heat into the house. North-, east-, and west-facing windows should have low SHGC to reduce loss. Your home's designer, contractor, and materials supplier can help you select the most energy-efficient windows and doors for long-term value.

Modern appliances are much more energy efficient than those of a decade ago. Those with the ENERGY STAR label exceed the federal government's minimum efficiency by a large percentage. Energy-efficient appliances may cost more to purchase. However, they then cost less to operate, meaning they eventually cost less than inefficient appliances.

> ### Sun Spots
>
> Heat pumps, a combined heater and air conditioner, are much more efficient to operate than separate furnaces and air conditioning systems. However, heat pumps work too hard in very hot and very cold climates, so they aren't as efficient as in moderate climates.

The highest gains in energy efficiency are found in buying efficient models of those appliances that commonly use the most energy. That means getting energy-efficient water heaters, clothes washers and dryers, dishwashers, and refrigerators.

A newer product for energy efficiency is solar tubes. They are vertical tubes of reflective material installed vertically between the home's exterior roof and interior ceiling. The special diffusers on each end collect the light and deliver it to the home interior without the sun's heat. Ask your contractor or window supplier for additional information.

Heating and Cooling

With energy-efficient insulation and a well-designed thermal envelope, your home will need much less heating and cooling. In fact, smart designing can save you thousands of dollars by requiring a system only half the size needed by a nonefficient home.

To keep from buying a system that costs more to purchase and operate than you really need, make sure your home designer gets the latest information on energy-efficient HVAC systems. If you'd like to do your own research, visit energystar.gov and search for "HVAC."

Controlled Ventilation

An energy-efficient house must be tightly sealed, but it also needs some controlled air flow or ventilation for the health of the house and the people inside. There will always be ways for air to escape. Unfortunately, with the outgoing air goes expensive heat and cooling.

Airtight homes use energy recovery ventilators (ERV) that salvage as much as 70 percent of the energy from the stale exhaust air. A heat exchanger inside the ERV pulls the heat or cold from the air for recycling. Other systems are also used to make sure that stale air is removed from the house, but many systems don't recycle the energy.

Is a controlled ventilation system right for your new home? Much depends on the local climate and how much it costs to keep the home comfortable. If the loss is of minimal value, it may not be worth the expense of engineering and equipment to try to capture and reuse the energy. Your utility supplier and architect can give you more specifics.

In addition, you can gain ventilation by installing ridge vents in the roof. Ridge vents are components on the highest points of a roof, called the ridge, that allow hot air trapped in the attic to exit without allowing rain to enter. Your contractor can help you determine whether roof ridge vents are a good option for your new energy-efficient home. For additional information, visit energystar.gov and search for "ridge vent."

Contractors and Suppliers

Hiring the right contractor and supplier is always important when building a house. It's especially important when you're building a nonstandard home such as a solar home.

A building contractor usually doesn't pound nails or rough in plumbing. He or she is the construction manager and makes sure that everyone is doing the job according to the approved building plans. In most cases, your building contractor will …

- Supervise all aspects of the work done at the building site.

- Hire, supervise, pay, and fire subcontractors as needed to get the job done.

- Buy all materials and supplies needed in construction.

- Make sure that the site is inspected and approved by the local building department.

- Get building permits and any variances.

- Make sure that all subcontractors are legal and have the needed insurance (such as worker's compensation).

For this effort, the general contractor (GC) typically gets 15 to 20 percent of the total cost of the project. Alternatively, the GC could be hired to manage the project for a specified hourly rate, or a lump sum may be agreed upon.

What does it take to be a licensed general contractor? Contractors are licensed based on knowledge, experience, and other assets. For example, in California, a licensed general contractor must …

- Be 18 years of age or older.

- Prove at least four full years of experience as a journeyman, foreman, supervisor, or contractor in the appropriate classification.

- Pass a written test.

- Have a specific amount of operating capital.

- Register a contractor's bond or cash deposit ($10,000).

- Pay the examination fee ($250) and licensing fee ($150) plus a biannual renewal fee ($300).

Most states have more than one type of general contractor. There's a general engineering contractor, who must have specialized engineering knowledge and skills. And there's a general building contractor for constructing houses and other shelters.

In addition, there are various specialty contractors or subcontractors for specific trades (electrical contractor, carpentry contractor, and so on). The one you're most interested in is the solar contractor. Most states license solar contractors, which means they have to pass a special test and show that they have solar construction experience.

How do you hire the *best* contractor? It's similar to buying anything else. You first find out what's available, then get the cost, and finally compare your options to get the best value. Of course, you're not buying toothpaste here. You're buying a building partner, and there is a lot more money involved.

Start the process early by asking building inspectors, solar equipment suppliers, and solar home owners about local contractors. Keep notes in your Solar Home Book, that notebook you set aside for writing down ideas, resources, costs, and designs as you begin the construction process. You want to know who's qualified, who's available, and who's recommended by people with more building experience than you.

After you've developed or selected a specific home design and plans, ask qualified contractors to bid on construction. You'll probably have to supply a set of detailed plans to any contractor from whom you want a detailed bid.

> **Solar Eclipse**
>
> Keep in mind that the lowest cost isn't necessarily the best value. The lowest bidder may not have solar experience. Or the bidder may not be fully licensed and insured. There are often reasons besides efficiency that allow a contractor to bid low. Some reasons are legitimate, while others aren't. It can save you thousands of dollars and days of frustration if you can pick the best *value* in a building contractor.

Again, check out my book *The Complete Idiot's Guide to Building Your Own Home, Third Edition*, for lots more information and guidelines on selecting a qualified contractor—and for being your own building contractor.

What if you've decided to retrofit your current or next home with solar power rather than build a new home? That's the topic of the next chapter.

The Least You Need to Know

- Find out early how cooperative your local building department will be toward building or retrofitting a solar home.
- The standard construction process can easily be modified to fit the requirements of solar home construction.

◆ Your solar home can take advantage of passive and active solar designing to save money.

◆ Make sure that your home's design and orientation fit the solar opportunities and limitations of your building lot.

◆ Make sure that your solar home is as energy efficient as possible to keep your investment in solar power equipment as low as possible.

◆ Find an architect and a building contractor with solar construction experience to ensure that the home is planned and built for efficiency.

Chapter 5

Retrofitting Your Home for Solar Power

In This Chapter

- Understanding your home's solar climate
- Determining how your home's orientation enhances or limits sunlight
- Planning your solar power system
- Learning what it will cost
- Trading in energy-guzzling appliances and upgrading insulation

Solar power is the future. But what do you do if your home was built in the past? How can you retrofit your current home to take advantage of solar energy?

This chapter offers dozens of ideas on replacing home energy components (retrofitting) with solar power, heating, cooling, appliances, and more. It shows you how to make the most of what you have as well as the best that's available today.

Solar Climate

You already have a home, cabin, RV, or other structure, and you want to put solar power to work. Good for you! Let's see what you have to work with. First, let's take a closer look at the local climate. We'll then figure out how solar power can be applied to your current home.

Weather is what happens today. Climate is what happens over many, many days. For example, a home near Phoenix, Arizona, may be getting cold and rain today, but the local climate is hot and dry. A home atop a nearby mountain may get more snow in winter and sunshine in the summer than a similar home in town. The hilltop home has a microclimate—that is, the climate immediately surrounding the home.

Sunlight, weather patterns, and microclimates affect the performance of solar power and thermal energy systems. The more direct sunlight a system receives, for example, the more electricity or heat it produces. In contrast, clouds, fog, frost, rain, and falling snow reduce the amount of solar energy that can be captured. Water and trees can make a solar energy system work more effectively or less effectively, depending on where they are located.

So the first step in retrofitting your home is to figure out how much solar energy is available to it. The amount of sunlight (solar radiation) reaching a specific site depends on the latitude, time of day, and time of year.

Think about this: locations nearer the equator get more sunlight through the year than places at higher latitudes. In the United States, for example, the southern states receive more solar radiation than the northern states. But two cities at the same latitude can get differing amounts of sunlight through the year. Seattle, Washington, for example, doesn't get the same amount of sunlight as Minot, North Dakota, even though they are at about the same latitude. And Minot gets much colder weather.

There are many factors besides proximity to the equator. Clouds scatter and absorb solar radiation, creating diffuse sunlight with less energy than direct sunlight. Smog can have the same effect. The flat land around Minot doesn't stop cold weather from Canada from crossing the border without permission. Seattle, however, is protected on the west by the Olympic Mountain Range and tempered by the nearby waters of Puget Sound.

A solar radiation map, shown in Chapter 1, offers an approximation of the amount of sunlight your location gets. Of course, microclimates and local obstructions will impact this.

Sun Spots

Earth's equator isn't directly under the sun. Earth is actually tilted 23.5° relative to the sun. This tilting results in *longer* days in the Northern Hemisphere (north of the equator) from the spring or vernal equinox to the fall or autumnal equinox. At the same time, the Southern Hemisphere has *shorter* days. An equinox is the time when both the day and night are 12 hours long. Spring equinox occurs each year about March 23 and fall equinox about September 22.

Because Earth is round, the sun strikes its surface at different angles ranging from 0° (just above the horizon) to 90° (directly overhead). When the sun's rays are vertical, Earth's surface gets all the energy possible. The more slanted the sun's rays are, the longer they travel through the atmosphere, becoming more scattered and diffuse. That's why mornings and evenings are cooler than midday.

The polar regions of Earth never get a high sun, and because Earth is tilted slightly, the poles get no sun at all during part of the year.

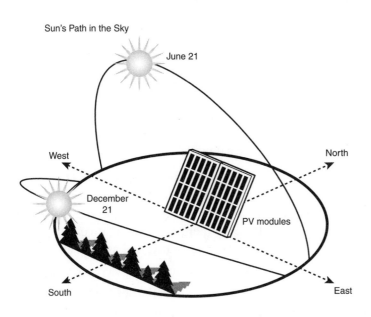

The sun's noontime height above the horizon changes seasonally, an important factor when you're orienting PV modules.

The continental United States is in the middle latitudes (between the North Pole and the equator); thus it receives more solar energy in the summer because the days are longer *and* because the sun is nearly overhead.

That's a review of solar energy for those who slept through science class in high school. Of course, there's a lot more to the topic. But it does remind you of the basics so you can better understand how the location, orientation, and climate at your home site impact the job of retrofitting for solar energy.

Your Current Home

So let's take a look at where you live. Hey, nice place!

Chances are, you're not going to be able to turn your house to take more advantage of the sun—unless you're living in an RV. Where it is, it is. Fortunately, the solar power and thermal energy systems you're going to install can be oriented or turned to take advantage of the greatest amount of solar radiation. In fact, PV modules can be installed on motorized frames that actually follow or track the sun's relative movement through the sky to gather the greatest solar energy. Pretty nifty!

In Chapter 4, I briefly discussed some tools to help you determine how much solar energy your home is capable of receiving. The previous solar radiation map is a starting point, but you want to know how your home's orientation, altitude, and surroundings enhance or limit the sunlight. This is especially important because you will want to size, price, buy, and install a system that is the optimum size for your existing home. You don't want to get it in place and then find out that it's too small to do the job. Nor do you want to buy a system that's wasteful.

In addition to solar radiation, your home site needs enough space to take advantage of that sunlight. Depending on where on your site the sunlight is best, you need to have enough room to mount solar power or thermal modules.

For example, a solar power system for generating electricity to serve a standard house may be about 500 square feet in size. That's about 20 feet by 25 feet. Depending on the PV module's efficiency, it would produce from 1.5 kW to 6.2 kW. That's quite a range, illustrating that the module's efficiency (percent of sunlight converted to electricity) is vital to sizing. It's also important to price because, as you can imagine, higher-efficiency modules cost more to buy.

Here's another consideration when retrofitting your home's roof for solar power: weight. Will your home's roof safely support the solar panels and equipment needed to gather and distribute solar power? In most cases, yes. However, your building permit for the system may require that an engineering company assess the load-bearing capacity of your home's roof and make structural recommendations, particularly for older homes that may have been built before standardized building codes.

Solar Eclipse _____

System weight is a consideration if you're going to install certain types of solar thermal hot water systems on the roof. "Batch-type" solar collectors store 20 to 50 gallons of water in the rooftop collector. A gallon of water weighs about 8 pounds. Solar power systems add weight to the roof's load, so consider mounting some or all the system on a special frame above the ground or against a south-facing wall.

Planning Your Solar Power System

Several factors will influence the size of the PV system you select. For starters, consider how much of your present electricity needs your PV system should supply.

Appendix A will help you calculate the total for what power your home currently uses. If you want to meet 50 percent of your electricity needs with a PV system, you'll choose a system sized to produce and store about half your usual electricity demand.

Also consider what federal, state, and utility buy-down programs will do to help you (see Chapter 2). They may have a minimum or maximum size of system that they'll help you buy. For example, a buy-down may be limited to 125 percent of the power you purchased from your utility last year. If you used 6,000 kWh last year, they may not offer a rebate on a system that delivers more than 7,500 kWh a year. Why? Because they don't want to encourage you to use *more* energy than before. (And they may not want you to become a utility generator that competes with existing utility companies!) You can estimate the size of your solar power system online at affordable-solar.com/gt-estimator.htm.

Here's an important question in planning your retrofit (or new) solar power system: Does it need batteries? Batteries store electric power. A battery system can give your home electricity when the sun isn't out (when you need lights the most). A battery system can also serve as a backup resource in areas where power outages are frequent. If your house has public utility power, batteries are optional. If you don't have utility power, then you *need* to have batteries.

Sun Spots
Google Earth, a satellite mapping service, is being used to identify the best locations for solar power stations. In conjunction with the Natural Defenses Resource Council and the National Audubon Society, Google Earth offers online maps to pinpoint sites where solar radiation is highest *and* power stations will have the lowest impact on the local environment. For more information, visit earth.google.com.

Chapter 7 offers a more comprehensive look at battery systems. For now, consider whether you want to include a storage system in your solar plans. Remote locations, poor utility line maintenance, or mangled deregulation schemes would all be very good reasons to consider battery backup to your utility power.

Remember that retrofitting your home for solar power systems probably will require that you get a local building permit. That topic and process are covered in Chapter 4.

Some solar power systems are installed on garage roofs with exterior access to controls and monitors.

Pricing Your Solar Power System

So how much will it cost to install a solar power or thermal system? The cost of a PV system depends on the system's size and components, but also scales somewhat with the system size or rating and the amount of energy produced.

As you can see, there are numerous requirements, variables, incentives, and efficiency factors. To get a rough idea, here are some ballpark numbers:

♦ A small single-PV panel system with built-in *inverter* that produces about 100 watts of power may cost around $1,000 installed, or about $10 per watt.

♦ A medium-sized system of 2 kW (2,000 watts) may cost $14,000 to $18,000 installed, or $7 to $9 per watt.

- A larger residential system of 5 kW may cost $30,000 to $40,000 installed, or $6 to $8 per watt.

- Systems with batteries (grid-tie or off-grid) cost more. The batteries and required safety equipment add 20 to 30 percent to the equipment cost and double the installation cost.

- Typical solar power system installation costs are $1.50 to $2 per watt without batteries or $3 to $4 per watt with batteries.

def•i•ni•tion

An **inverter** converts direct current (DC) from a battery to alternating current (AC) for use by home appliances and lights. Micro inverters are more efficient—and more expensive—as they control a single panel rather than an array.

Before you call 911 for resuscitation, know that these estimates don't include deductions for any rebates or other incentives. As of 2010, federal tax incentives are available to cover 30 percent of the costs of solar installations. Also, remember that after the system has returned your initial investment in savings, it is working virtually for free. And solar power systems can keep on paying you back for 25 years or more! Think of the cost as prepaying your electric bills.

And before you get too excited about solar costs, you might price a utility line extension for new construction. Utility companies give very little in the way of free footage anymore, and most line extensions will cost in excess of *$1 per inch*. If you have to extend more than 300 to 400 yards, solar may actually cost you less initially than hooking up to the local utility.

The real point of this exercise in estimating costs is not to put you on blood pressure medicine. It's to help you know what factors are most important as you retrofit your home for solar.

Fortunately, solar thermal systems for heating hot water are more economical to install than solar power systems. And they save the power used to heat the water. However, the costs are a little tougher to calculate and investment incentives are not always available. Even so, solar water-heating systems are less expensive and can give you a faster return on your investment.

Replacing Appliances

Major appliances take a lot of electricity to operate, especially electric water heaters, electric dryers, and refrigerators. Fortunately, technology has produced some very efficient appliances during the past 10 years.

As you learned in Chapter 1, the most expensive heat source is electricity. Electric radiant heat, for example, typically costs more than three times the price of oil heat for your home. You can retrofit your home with lower-cost heating (see Appendix B). However, HVAC systems aren't the only way that heat is made in your home. Water heaters, stoves, and ovens are often powered by electricity. If you're using costly electricity for heat in your home, consider replacing these heating appliances with less costly energy sources, especially those from renewable sources.

Aside from HVAC systems, refrigerators are often the largest power user in your home. Today's typical refrigerator uses less than 650 kWh of power each year. It's often cost effective to replace an older refrigerator for a new energy-efficient unit, paid for by energy savings. Refrigerators in the store include an ENERGY STAR EnergyGuide label estimating the yearly operating cost and comparing it to the cost range of similar models. It also estimates yearly electrical use so you can calculate the most efficient size for your solar power system. EnergyGuide labels also are found on new washers, dishwashers, water heaters, air conditioners, furnaces, and other—but not all—major appliances.

Bright Idea

How efficient can a refrigerator get? The best can run on less than 1 kWh a day! The most energy-efficient models can cut normal usage by more than half. Of course, they're more expensive to purchase than brand-name units, but the energy savings offset the initial expense. You can find them through some large appliance retailers and the catalogs listed online at SolarHomeGuides.com.

Heat exchangers can be installed in existing homes to recover half or more of otherwise wasted heat from HVAC systems. Tied in to your heating system controls, they can dramatically reduce heating costs. Gas furnaces range in efficiency from 78 to 96 percent.

To find out what other energy-efficient appliances are available, go to www.energystar. gov or check the other resources online at SolarHomeGuides.com. There are even solar clothes dryers on the market!

Upgrading Insulation and Weatherstripping

Appendix B offers numerous ideas on making your existing home more energy efficient. The less energy your home uses, the less your solar power system will cost. So it makes sense to take care of insulation and weatherstripping in your home before retrofitting it with a solar power system.

Your home energy audit probably suggested where you can insulate and weatherstrip your home for greatest gain. Easy-to-reach spaces such as attics and under the floor are typically the best places to start upgrading insulation. Even installing a radiant barrier under the floor can dramatically reduce energy loss.

You may opt to have a contractor upgrade the insulation in the walls of your existing home. For most homes, the contractor drills strategic holes in the exterior walls and blows (with a reverse vacuum) insulation into wall cavities. Your local utility can recommend and may even give you a rebate for upgrading your home's insulation and energy efficiency.

There's still more you can do to your new or existing home to reduce the cost of your solar power system. For example, you can landscape for optimum solar energy, which is covered in the next chapter.

The Least You Need to Know

- Solar climate is the amount of sunlight your home site receives over a long period of time.

- Solar radiation at your home can be greater or lesser than other homes in your area, depending on microclimates.

- Replacing major appliances with more energy-efficient models is an investment in reducing long-term power costs.

- You can retrofit your existing home with solar power equipment and energy-efficient appliances to cut long-term power costs.

Chapter 6

Solar Landscaping Savings

In This Chapter

- ◆ Landscaping smartly can save energy dollars
- ◆ Discovering the environmental benefits of trees and plants
- ◆ Learning how local climate and microclimate impact your landscaping
- ◆ Exploring shading and wind protection options
- ◆ Designing a solar-friendly yard
- ◆ Selecting the right trees and shrubs

Whether you're building a new solar home or retrofitting the one you have, smart solar landscaping can dramatically cut your summer and winter energy costs. That means you can save money on utility bills *and* reduce your investment in solar power equipment.

In addition, smart landscaping can protect your home from winter and summer sun, reduce the need to water the lawn and plants, and help control noise and even air pollution. That's a tall order, yes, but solar landscaping is up to it. You'll find out how in this chapter.

Saving Money with Landscaping

Want to save $100 to $250 a year in energy costs? Simply plant three trees. Placed in the right spot, these trees can provide sufficient shade to reduce your utility bill.

Actually, carefully positioned trees can save up to 25 percent of a household's energy consumption for heating and cooling. The experts say that, on average, a well-designed landscape can save you enough in energy costs to pay back your initial investment in less than eight years. For example, an 8-foot deciduous (leaf-shedding) tree costs about as much as a large window awning for shade in the summer, yet still admits winter sunshine into your home.

Summer

You may have noticed the coolness of parks and wooded areas compared to the temperature of nearby city streets. Because cool air settles near the ground, air temperatures directly under trees can be as much as 25°F cooler than air temperatures above nearby blacktop. The process is called *evapotranspiration* (a word you may hear on the TV show *Jeopardy!*). One study found summer daytime air temperatures to be 3° to 6°F cooler in tree-shaded neighborhoods than in treeless areas.

def•i•ni•tion

Evapotranspiration is the process by which a plant actively moves and releases water vapor from trees. It can reduce surrounding air temperatures as much as 9°F.

In fact, a well-planned landscape can reduce an unshaded home's summer air-conditioning costs by 15 to 50 percent. Smart solar landscaping can pay off in summer utility savings.

Winter

Ever heard of wind chill? If the outside temperature is 10°F and the wind speed is 20 miles per hour, the wind chill is –24°F, meaning that the temperature actually feels as cold as –24°F. That's a fact. Another useful fact is that trees, fences, or geographical features can be used as windbreaks to shield your house from the wind.

One Midwest study found that windbreaks to the north, west, and east of houses cut fuel consumption by an average of 40 percent. Houses with windbreaks placed only on the windward side (the side from which the wind is coming) averaged 25 percent less fuel consumption than similar but unprotected homes. If you live in a windy climate, your well-planned landscape can reduce your winter heating bills by approximately one third. That's good news!

Trees Clean the Air, Too

In addition to the obvious benefits of improving the appearance of your home (and adding to its resale value), planting lots of trees and other growing things around your home offers numerous environmental benefits. Trees and vegetation control erosion, protect water supplies, provide food and habitat for wildlife, and clean the air by absorbing carbon dioxide and releasing oxygen.

Replacing a turf lawn with natural grasses and ground cover can benefit the environment by reducing the need for gas-powered mowers and trimmers. For example, some grasses, such as buffalo grass and fescue, grow to only a certain height—about 6 inches. They are also water thrifty.

Sun Spots

The National Academy of Sciences estimates that urban America has 100 million spaces where trees could be planted. It goes on to say that filling these spaces with trees and lightening the color of dark, urban surfaces would result in annual energy savings of 50 billion kWh—25 percent of the 200 billion kWh needed every year by air conditioners in the United States. Further, these trees would reduce electric power plant emissions of carbon dioxide by 35 million tons annually and save users of utility-supplied electricity at least $3.5 billion each year—something to consider.

Considering the Climate

As introduced in Chapter 5, weather is what happens today and climate is what happens over many, many days. The United States and Canada can be divided into four primary climatic regions: cool, temperate, hot-arid, and hot-humid. Your home's best solar landscape strategy depends on which region you live in. That means what you do to enhance solar efficiency for a home in Atlanta (hot-humid) is different from what you would do in Minneapolis (cool) or San Diego (temperate). Let's take a look at recommendations for each climate.

For a cool climate:

◆ Use dense windbreaks to protect the home from cold winter winds.

◆ Allow the winter sun to reach south-facing windows.

◆ Shade south and west windows and walls from the direct summer sun, if summer overheating is a problem.

For a temperate climate:

- ◆ Maximize warming effects of the sun in the winter.
- ◆ Maximize shade during the summer.
- ◆ Deflect winter winds away from buildings.
- ◆ Funnel summer breezes toward the home.

For a hot-arid climate:

- ◆ Provide shade to cool roofs, walls, and windows.
- ◆ Allow summer winds to access naturally cooled homes.
- ◆ Block or deflect winds away from air-conditioned homes.

For a hot-humid climate:

- ◆ Channel summer breezes toward the home.
- ◆ Maximize summer shade with trees that still allow penetration of low-angle winter sun.
- ◆ Avoid locating planting beds close to the home if they require frequent watering.

In addition, there is the climate immediately surrounding your home, its microclimate. If your home is located on a sunny southern slope, it may have a warm microclimate, even if you live in a cool region. Or even though you live in a hot-humid region, your home may be situated in a comfortable microclimate because of abundant shade and dry breezes. Nearby bodies of water may increase your site's humidity or decrease its air temperature.

Your home's microclimate may be more sunny, shady, windy, calm, rainy, snowy, moist, or dry than average local conditions. These factors all help determine what plants may or may not grow in your microclimate.

Designing for Solar Advantage

So how can you best plan landscaping to take advantage of solar opportunities? First, make sure your home is oriented and designed to admit low-angle winter sun, reject overhead summer sun, and minimize the cooling effect of winter winds.

Bright Idea _____

When building a new home in the Northern Hemisphere, align the home's long axis in an east-west direction. The home's longest wall with the most window area should face south or southeast. The home's north-facing and west-facing walls should have fewer windows because these walls generally face winter's prevailing winds. Fewer west windows means less unwanted heat gain on summer afternoons as well.

Design and orient your new house to maximize the home site's natural advantages and lessen its disadvantages. Notice the home site's exposure to sun, wind, and water. Also note the location and proximity of nearby buildings, fences, water bodies, trees, and pavement—and their possible climatic effects. Buildings provide shade and windbreak. Fences and walls block or channel the wind. Water bodies moderate temperature but increase humidity and produce glare. Trees provide shade, windbreaks, or wind channels. Pavement reflects or absorbs heat, depending on whether its color is light or dark.

If your home is already built, inventory its comfort and energy problems as covered in Chapter 5.

For both new and existing homes, use shading, wind protection, and other landscaping ideas to make your home site more energy efficient and solar-friendly.

Shading

Solar heat passing through windows and the roof is the major reason for air-conditioner use. Fortunately, shading is the most cost-effective way to reduce solar heat gain and cut air-conditioning costs.

Using shade effectively requires you to know the size, shape, and location of the moving shadow that your shading device casts. Remember that homes in cool regions may never overheat and may not require shading.

You can select trees with appropriate sizes, densities, and shapes for almost any shading application. To block solar heat in the summer but let much of it in during the winter, use deciduous trees. To provide continuous shade or to block heavy winds, use evergreen trees or shrubs.

Plant deciduous trees with high, spreading crowns (leaves and branches) to the south of your home for maximum summertime roof shading. Plant trees with crowns lower to the ground to the west for shade from the lower afternoon sun. Don't plant trees that will block south-facing walls from winter solar energy. Popular deciduous trees include oaks, elms, and maples. Ask your local nursery about specific varieties that grow best in your climate.

A 6- to 8-foot deciduous tree planted near your home can begin shading windows the first year. Depending on the species and the home, the tree will shade the roof in 5 to 10 years. (Be sure to find out how large the tree will grow before positioning it in your yard; there's more about selecting the right trees and plants later in this chapter.)

There are many related ways of keeping our homes cooler in summer and warmer in winter with smart landscaping. Here are a few:

- If you have an air conditioner, planting a tree to shade the unit can increase its efficiency by as much as 10 percent.

- Trees, shrubs, and groundcover plants can also shade the ground and pavement around the home. This reduces heat radiation and cools the air before it reaches your home's walls and windows.

- Use a large bush or row of shrubs to shade a patio or driveway.

- Plant a hedge to shade a sidewalk.

- Keep in mind that fewer west windows mean less unwanted heat gain on summer afternoons.

Solar Eclipse

Can you dig it? Make sure you know where any underground wires, cables, and pipes are before digging so you can avoid them. Call 811, the federally mandated call-before-you-dig telephone number to find out. They can help you identify where utilities are buried on and near your property so that you don't damage them—or break a law. For more information, visit call811.com online.

- Vines can shade walls during their first growing season. A lattice or trellis with climbing vines, or a planter box with trailing vines, shades the home's perimeter while admitting cooling breezes to the shaded area. Or try using a trellis for climbing vines to shade a patio area.

- Shrubs planted close to the house will fill in rapidly and begin shading walls and windows within a few years. However, avoid allowing dense foliage to grow immediately next to a home where wetness or continual humidity is a problem.

Well-landscaped homes in wet areas allow winds to flow around the home, keeping the home and its surrounding soil reasonably dry.

Wind Protection

Wind can reduce your home's energy efficiency as well. Properly selected and placed landscaping can provide excellent wind protection and cut energy costs. In addition, these benefits will increase as the trees and shrubs mature.

The best windbreaks block wind close to the ground by using trees and shrubs that have low crowns. Evergreen trees and shrubs planted to the north and northwest of the home are the most common type of windbreak. Trees, bushes, and shrubs are often planted together to block or impede wind from ground level to the treetops. Or evergreen trees combined with a wall, fence, or earth berm (natural or man-made walls or raised areas of soil) can deflect or lift the wind over the home.

A windbreak will reduce wind speed for up to 30 times the windbreak's height. For example, a 20-foot windbreak can reduce the wind's speed for up to 600 feet. However, for maximum protection, plant your windbreak at a distance from your home of two to five times the mature height of the trees. That's 40 to 100 feet away from the house for a tree that will mature to about 20 feet in height. Of course, you don't have much control over windbreaks on a small residential lot.

If snow tends to drift in your area, plant low shrubs on the windward side of your windbreak. The shrubs will trap snow before it blows next to your home, increasing heat loss.

> **Solar Eclipse**
>
> Be careful not to plant evergreens too close to your home's south side if you are counting on warmth from the winter sun! Their leaves and needles can block solar rays when you most need them.

In addition to placing more distant windbreaks, planting shrubs, bushes, and vines next to your house creates dead air spaces that insulate your home in both winter and summer. When planting, be sure there is at least 1 foot of space between full-grown plants and your home's wall.

Summer winds, especially at night, can have a cooling effect if used for home ventilation. However, if winds are hot and your home is air-conditioned all summer, you may want to keep summer winds from circulating near your home.

Planning Your Landscape

Before you start landscaping for energy efficiency, first develop a plan. The components of your plan could include deciduous trees and plants, coniferous trees and plants, earth berms, walls, fences, sheds, and garages. Here's how to create a landscape plan before you plant around your existing home or before you begin construction on a new house.

> **Solar Eclipse** _____
>
> Landscape-planning software is available to help you select and place appropriate trees and other solar aids. Punch! sells a home and landscape planning package (punchsoftware.com). Many professional landscapers use GardenSoft (gardensoft.com), as it includes PlantMaster, a plant database. Google SketchUp (sketchup.google.com) offers a basic three-dimensional design program for free that can be incorporated into Google Earth, a mapping program.

Use paper and colored pencils to begin designing your landscape. There are also inexpensive landscape design software programs available at building material and computer retailers. First, sketch a simple, scaled drawing of your yard. Locate its buildings, walks, driveways, and utilities (sewer, electric, gas, cable, and telephone lines). Note the location of all paved surfaces—streets, driveways, patios, or sidewalks—near your home. Then identify potential uses for different areas of your yard: vegetable gardens, flower beds, patios, and play areas.

Draw arrows to show sun angles and prevailing winds for both summer and winter. As you sketch, circle the areas of your yard needing shade or wind protection.

Indicate with arrows how you want views to be preserved or screened. Mark routes of noise pollution you wish to block. Also highlight areas where landscaping height or width may be restricted, such as under utility lines or along sidewalks.

Notice yard areas that suffer from poor drainage and standing water. Some trees and shrubs will not grow well in poorly drained areas; others will. Note existing trees and shrubs. If they provide valued shade or windbreak, plan for their replacement when they become old or sick.

Perhaps you want more defined property boundaries or less traffic noise. Consider a "living fence" of dense trees, bushes, or shrubs. Depending on its location and application, this hedge can be customized to be tall, short, wide, narrow, open, or dense. Privet is a species of shrub that grows in most parts of the United States and can serve as a living fence.

Areas of lawn not used as picnic or play areas can be converted to planting beds or *xeriscaped* areas. Converting a traditional lawn to alternative, water-conserving grasses or other forms of xeriscaping saves energy and reduces water consumption.

def•i•ni•tion

Xeriscaping is a landscaping technique that uses vegetation that is drought resistant and able to survive on rainfall and groundwater when established.

Maybe you live in an urban area where yards are small and neighbors close. Your neighbor's yard may be the best place for trees to shade your south-facing windows. Your yard may be the best location for their windbreak. Bringing your neighbors into your plans could benefit everyone involved.

The more you identify your goals and familiarize yourself with your yard's features— current and proposed—the better your chances for success with your landscaping projects.

Selecting Trees and Shrubs

Trees and shrubs come in all shapes and sizes. How you select your trees and shrubs and how you plant them will directly affect your home's comfort and energy efficiency.

Trees and shrubs have a life span of many years and can become more attractive and functional with age. But poor planning of landscape improvements often creates trouble. Ensure proper plant placement and minimal maintenance before you plant!

Shapes

Tree shapes are very diverse. The density of a tree's leaves or needles is important to consider. Dense evergreens, such as spruces, make great windbreaks for winter winds. If you're looking just to impede summer winds, choose a tree or shrub with more open branches and leaves. Such trees are also good for filtering morning sun from the east, while denser trees are better for blocking harsh afternoon summer sun.

Growth

Should you plant slow-growing or fast-growing tree species? Although a slow-growing tree may require many years of growth before it shades your roof, it will generally live longer than a fast-growing tree. Also, because slow-growing trees often have deeper roots and stronger branches, they are less prone to breakage by windstorms or heavy snow loads. And they can be more drought resistant than fast-growing trees.

Consider growth rate, strength, and brittleness when locating trees near walkways or structures. Ask whether the mature tree's root system is likely to damage sidewalks, foundations, or sewer lines. The smaller your yard, the more important it is to select a tree with manageable roots.

Buying

Landscape professionals can help you choose and locate new trees, shrubs, or ground cover. Share your drawings and ideas with your local nursery or landscape contractor. As long as you define your intended use and available spaces in which planting is actually possible, a competent nursery or landscape specialist will be able to help you make decisions. He or she will probably know the local climate and what trees and shrubs will flourish in your yard.

Bright Idea

After considering the placement of your trees and consulting landscaping and nursery professionals, go back to your drawings or plans and add the new information on species, shape, and mature-size spacing. This provides a final, prepurchase review to make sure that all elements will work well together—in the short- and long-term.

When planting trees, shrubs, hedges, or bushes, find out how large the mature specimen will grow. In all cases, determine spacing by the mature sizes. For those plants close to your house, leave at least 1 foot (30 centimeters) of extra clearance between the full-grown shrub and the wall of the home. This will prevent heavy pruning or damage to home siding in the future.

When you're ready to purchase your trees and shrubs, avoid buying damaged specimens. Thoroughly inspect the trunk, limbs, leaves, and roots to make sure the plant was handled carefully during growing, digging, and shipping. Reject plant stock with signs of insects or disease such as cocoons, egg masses, cankers, or lesions.

After you purchase the plants, be sure to keep tiny roots damp and shaded at all times. The plants will not survive if the roots inside the root ball are allowed to dry before planting.

Contact your county extension agents, public libraries, local nurseries, landscape architects, landscape contractors, and state and local energy offices for additional information on regionally appropriate plants and their maintenance requirements.

You've gone a long way in this section on saving your energy. Next we get more specific about selecting the best solar equipment and systems to reduce your home's energy costs.

The Least You Need to Know

- ◆ Well-placed trees can save you up to 25 percent of your home's heating and cooling bill.

- ◆ Smart solar landscaping can reduce your home's air-conditioning costs by up to 50 percent.

- ◆ Plant landscaping that works with your local climate and microclimate, not against it.

- ◆ Plant trees for solar shade as well as wind protection.

- ◆ For efficiency, plan your solar landscaping on paper and talk with local nurseries to make sure selected plants meet your goals.

Part 2

Solar Energy Solutions

Wow! Solar power really *is* an option! That's good news. And there's more good news. Solar electric generation is just one of many smart options. There's passive solar, solar water heating, solar space heating, wind power, hydropower, and even fuel cells.

Technology is applied science. And technology has really been applied during the past few decades to energy options. There are smart controllers that manage home energy. There are PV modules that actually track the sun across the sky, absorbing as much light as possible. There are batteries that last longer than a Honda.

So let's take a peek at what technology has been busy doing lately to warm and light our homes with the power from the sun.

YOU'RE COMPROMISING MY SOLAR INTAKE.

Chapter 7

Solar Electric Generation and Storage

In This Chapter

◆ Turning sunlight into electricity

◆ Learning the components in a typical solar power system

◆ Selecting the right inverter for your solar power system

◆ Figuring out which batteries to use

◆ Learning about the other stuff your solar power system needs

◆ Installing solar power systems

Buying a solar power system is similar to paying years of utility bills in advance. Of course, after it's paid off, it begins paying you back. That's the good part.

The not-so-good part is that you have to learn about photovoltaics, crystalline silicon, lead-acid batteries, and other scientific stuff. Fortunately, I'll explain all this and more in this chapter, so let's get started!

Understanding Solar Electricity

Photovoltaic (PV) technology converts sunlight into electricity. However, it *doesn't* use the sun's heat to do so. Then how does the magic happen?

def•i•ni•tion

A **solar** or **PV cell** is the smallest semiconductor element within a PV module to perform the immediate conversion of light into electrical energy. Output is direct current (DC).

Let's begin at the beginning. PV produces electricity directly from the electrons freed by sunlight striking the semiconductor materials in the PV cells. The basic building block of PV technology is the solar cell. *Solar* or *PV cells* are wired together to produce a PV module, the smallest PV component sold commercially. PV modules range in power from about 10 watts to 300 watts.

PV modules produce direct current (DC). Your home uses alternating current (AC). What to do? You can either use only DC loads or you can convert them. An *inverter* is a special piece of equipment that changes DC electricity into AC. If you don't need the PV electricity right then, you can either store it in batteries or ship it off to someone who needs it. Let's consider these options one at a time.

Direct-current (DC) solar power system.

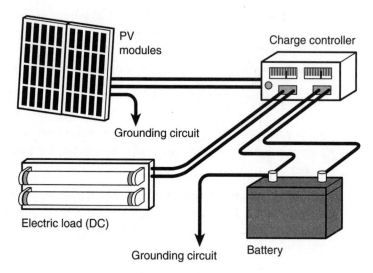

Direct-Current (DC) System

PV modules

Charge controller

Grounding circuit

Electric load (DC)

Grounding circuit

Battery

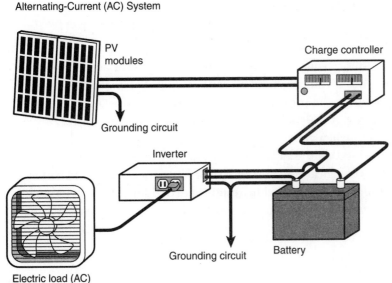

Alternating-Current (AC) System

Alternating-current (AC) solar power system.

PV modules

Charge controller

Grounding circuit

Inverter

Electric load (AC)

Grounding circuit   Battery

Batteries Not Included

The power-distribution system is often referred to as the *grid*. Remote, *off-grid* solar power systems typically use batteries to store electricity for later use, such as when the sun isn't shining. In addition, about 10 percent of grid-tied systems use batteries for backup power in case their utility goes down—which happens frequently in some areas.

def•i•ni•tion

The **grid** is an electrical utility distribution network consisting of the wires that transport electricity from a power plant to your home—and all the equipment in between. **Off-grid** electrical systems are those that don't use outside electrical utilities; they are stand-alone electrical systems, such as a solar or wind power system that serves only your home.

You can install batteries in your solar power system to store PV electricity until needed. These batteries serve the same function as the one in your car, which stores electricity developed by the engine and alternator until needed to start the car or run the CD player. Solar batteries hang on to the PV electricity until needed to operate lights or appliances in your home. The batteries are installed in a solar power system *after* the PV modules and *before* the inverter. Batteries in your solar power system can make sure you have power even when the sun isn't out—or it's hiding, or you need more power at the moment than your PV modules are delivering.

Should you include batteries in your solar power system? The answer depends on what you want your system to do. If you have local power outages, a battery system can power your life until the utility company delivers again. If your home is off-grid—not connected to the local utility grid—you'll want batteries to power lights for reading and other activities at night when your solar power system is sleeping. If you'll be selling power back to the local utility, a battery array may pay for itself. However, remember that there's an ecological issue, because solar batteries are lead-acid batteries, and the manufacturing and use of lead-acid batteries isn't good for nature. Even so, it may be better than the alternative of relying on fossil fuels for backup because you have no way of storing solar power. I'll tell you more about batteries later in this chapter.

Net Metering

So what's this about shipping power to other folks? If your solar power system is connected to the utility grid, and you have an agreement with the power company to do so, your system can send electricity to the grid for use by others. It's called net metering.

Laws in most states now require utilities to allow net metering with approved residential customers, meaning that your solar electric generating system complies with the utility's requirements and you've signed an agreement. Chapter 12 offers more specifics and how-to's on net metering.

In many of these states, the utility must pay you the retail rather than the wholesale price for your power. That means your solar power system can actually produce a little income to offset costs. No, you won't get rich—the power company will make sure of that. But this extra income can help you make a decision to invest in solar power. Utilities may credit you at the retail rate so you can use the power later, but they will not pay more than the avoided cost—the cost of the fuel they don't have to burn—in cash. Some utilities will honor your credits as long as you own the system, but others zero out your balance annually. Make sure you know the rules of your utility partner (see Chapter 12).

Want another financial incentive? In some areas, you can sell your solar power to the utility during peak hours at one rate, then buy it back during off-peak hours at a lower rate. Contact your state's utility department (see SolarHomeGuides.com). Additional financial incentives for solar power, such as tax credits and rebates, were covered in Chapter 2.

Here's how to calculate electricity bill savings for a PV system. First, determine the system's size in kilowatts. Next, using the map, select the *energy* production factor for your location. Then plug those numbers into the following equation:

Annual PV System Energy = (PV kW) × (kWh ÷ kW-year)

Annual Energy Bill Savings = (kWh per year) × (Residential Rate)/100

def•i•ni•tion

Energy is a measurement of power over time and is usually measured electrically as watt-hours (Wh). A 100-watt module operating for one hour will have produced 100 Wh. In 10 hours, it will have produced 1,000 Wh or 1 kilowatt-hour. Amp-hours (Ah) are another measurement of energy. Battery manufacturers use this measurement to rate the energy storage in a battery. A 220 amp-hour 6-volt golf-cart battery has 1,320 Wh (1.3 kWh) of storage (220 Ah × 6 V = 1,320 Wh). Confused? Don't worry. Just remember that PV modules are usually measured in watts, charge controllers in amps, and batteries in amp-hours.

For example, a 2 kW system in Denver, Colorado, at a residential energy rate of $0.12 per kilowatt-hour will save about $480 a year. Here's the math:

2,000 kWh per kW-year × $0.12 per kWh × 2 kW = $480 per year

That's about $40.00 a month in savings.

I'll talk more about net metering later in this chapter as well as in Chapter 12.

System Components

There's a lot going on in the world of PV. Let's take a look at the technologies, the applications, and the issues so you can make an informed choice when selecting your system.

Components in a typical PV solar power system with optional batteries.

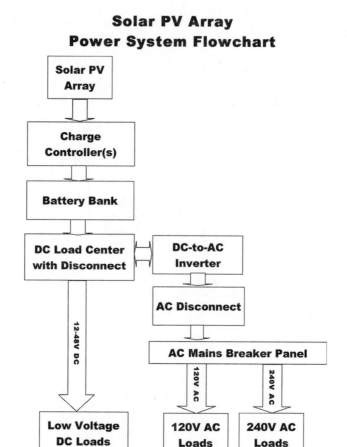

Solar PV Array Power System Flowchart

Solar PV Array

Charge Controller(s)

Battery Bank

DC Load Center with Disconnect

DC-to-AC Inverter

AC Disconnect

AC Mains Breaker Panel

12-48V DC

120V AC

240V AC

Low Voltage DC Loads

120V AC Loads

240V AC Loads

Sun Spots

The San Francisco Airport has installed UNI-SOLAR photovoltaic laminates (PVL) on one of its support buildings to test the product. It's a flexible, nonreflective, thin-film amorphous silicon cell that is manufactured and installed in the roofing material itself. It works similarly to other PV cell materials, yet it's part of the building. The UNI-SOLAR PVL solar shingles won the *Popular Science* Grand Award, Best of What's New, and *Discover* magazine's Technological Innovation Award.

PV Modules

PV modules are a major component of all home solar power systems. They usually make up 50 percent of the cost of an off-grid system and 70 percent of what you'll spend on a grid-tie system. Most PV cells today are made from crystalline silicon (c-Si) using a variety of production methods. The raw material, sand, is impure, so manufacturing processes must remove impurities and defects. The result is called solar-grade silicon feedstock.

Typical solar panel.

To make the silicon even better at gathering and converting sunlight, it is doped. That is, boron or phosphorus is added to adjust the frequencies of light that the silicon responds to. Alternatively, a coating can be applied.

Thin-film photovoltaic cells use layers of semiconductor materials only a few micrometers thick. The layers are attached to an inexpensive backing such as glass, flexible plastic, or stainless steel. Complete PV modules can also be encased in a shell to protect cells and to enhance production.

Typical thin-film PV panels used as roofing.

How does a crystalline PV work? You can think of PV cells as direct-current generators powered by the sun. When light photons of sufficient energy strike a solar cell, they knock electrons free in the silicon crystal structure, forcing them through an external circuit (battery or DC load) and then returning them to the other side of the solar cell to start the process all over again. The voltage output from a single crystalline solar cell is about 0.5 V (volts) with amperage output based on the cell's surface area. For example, a 6-inch square multicrystalline solar cell puts out about 7 A (amps).

Typically 30 to 36 cells are wired in series (+ to –) in each solar module. This produces a solar module with a 12 V nominal output (~17 V at peak power) that can then be wired in series and/or parallel with other solar modules to form a complete solar array to charge a 12, 24, or 48 V battery bank.

How efficient are solar cells? That's the question you'll be asking suppliers as you trade cost for efficiency. More expensive modules offer a higher efficiency factor than less expensive modules. As a ballpark estimate, most cells will range between 8 to 20 percent efficiency. That is, 8 to 20 percent of the energy they receive from sunlight will be turned into electricity. Thin-film cells are in the 8 percent efficiency range and crystalline products are in the 15 to 20 percent range. Unless space is an issue, don't get hung up on efficiency. Instead, pay attention to the dollar per watt cost and the reputation of the manufacturer. Also look for modules that have a UL-1703 (Underwriters Laboratories) rating.

Will PV work in your location? Solar energy is universal and available virtually anywhere. However, some locations are better than others for turning sunlight into electricity. *Irradiance* is a measure of the sun's power available at the surface of the earth, and it averages about 1,000 watts per square meter. With typical crystalline solar cell efficiencies around 14 to 16 percent, that means you can expect to generate about 140 to 160 watts per square meter of solar cells placed in full sun. *Insolation* is a measure of the available energy from the sun as "full sun hours." Obviously different parts of the world receive more sunlight from others, so they will have more full sun hours per day. The solar insolation zone map in Chapter 1 will give you an approximation of the full sun hours per day for your location.

def•i•ni•tion

Irradiance is a measure of the sun's power available at the surface of the earth and it averages about 1,000 watts per square meter. **Insolation** is a measure of the available energy from the sun as "full sun hours."

A decade ago, the basic PV building blocks were 50-, 75-, and 100-watt 12-volt modules. Now system designers are using larger modules in the 150- and 200-watt range. Is bigger better? Not necessarily. The main advantages of bigger modules include faster installation time on large arrays and lower dollar-per-watt cost. The disadvantage of bigger modules is that they are often designed to work with grid-tied inverters and not battery banks. For battery-based systems, the more expensive controllers are a requirement as they can adjust the not quite 24-volt output to match the battery bank. For grid-tie systems without batteries, the odd voltage of the larger modules is not an issue.

A dozen years ago, all modules had junction boxes on the back. Today, most modules larger than 100 watts have quick-connect wires or pigtails. When you are wiring a large high-voltage array (300 to 600 volts DC), quick connects are a delight and save about 15 minutes of installation time per module. For small 12- and 24-volt arrays, the advantage of quick connects isn't as important, as you end up having to pay a little extra for the extension wires to get back to the combiner box.

There are many ways that PV technology is applied to making electricity from sunlight. Concentrating PV collectors, for example, use lenses and mirrors to focus the sunlight onto solar cells. Building-integrated PV systems are made with dual purposes such as to collect sunlight *and* serve as roofing or other building materials. Stand-alone systems are made to, well, stand alone. That is, they supply power to remote sites where no other electric service is available, such as microwave towers on mountain tops.

Sun Spots

The National Center for Photovoltaics stays up nights figuring out new ways to harness the sun for electric power. It creates, develops, and deploys PV and related technologies with lots of scientists and engineers working in an impressive laboratory. Find out what it's currently up to at National Center for Photovoltaics, National Renewable Energy Laboratory, 1617 Cole Blvd., Golden, CO, 80401, or on its website at nrel.gov/pv.

BIPV Modules

The latest type of solar electric panels is called building-integrated photovoltaic (BIPV) panels or modules. Rather than separate panels mounted on a frame atop a roof, BIPV panels are integrated into a building as the roofing or glazing material. How does that work?

Typical building-integrated photovoltaic (BIPV) panels installed as roofing.

BIPVs work just like traditional solar panels, except they are thinner. Most BIPVs use amorphous silicon mounted on industrial fabric rather than crystalline silicon under glazing. They typically weigh less than 1 pound per square foot, so they don't add much load to the roof—an important benefit in some applications. In addition, BIPV products don't look similar to solar panels, which makes them more attractive to some home builders. Of course, it's tough to brag about your solar home if you have to explain why it doesn't look like a solar home.

The three types of BIPV products are shingle/tile, roofing membrane, and architectural. Shingle/tile BIPVs are installed similarly to composite roofing shingles or tiles. Roofing membrane BIPVs are installed similarly to rolled roofing. Architectural BIPVs are installed as glazing or windows, which makes their installation more difficult and more expensive.

The primary disadvantage of BIPV is that, because they are mounted directly onto the roof or wall, there is less air circulation around them and they run hotter. PVs don't really like to get hot and are less efficient when they are. So expect some reduction in output depending on the design and installation. However, an entire roof surface of BIPV can make a lot of electricity.

Selecting Batteries

Batteries are a necessity for remote and backup home power systems. Batteries make up about 10 percent of the cost of a system that uses them. Batteries store electricity for use at night or for meeting demand during the day when the power source isn't keeping up with demand. Without batteries, you're not able to turn on a light when it's dark outside.

> ### Sun Spots
>
> A deep-cycle 12-volt battery is one that has a full charge of 12.75 volts and delivers a consistent voltage as it discharges. For efficiency, keep the state of charge at or above 60 percent, typically about 12.35 volts, for wet-cell batteries. Gel-cell batteries are more efficient when operated at or above 70 percent, 12.45 volts, of full charge.

You could use just about any type of 12-volt car battery to store DC electricity. However, car batteries are designed with thin plates so they can give a rapid discharge to crank over your starter motor. In a deep-cycle application, they will only last a year. To provide electricity during long periods, your home power system needs deep-cycle batteries. These batteries, usually lead-acid, have much thicker lead plates and are designed to gradually discharge and recharge 80 percent of their capacity hundreds of times. Car batteries are shallow-cycle batteries that discharge only about 20 percent of their capacity. Drawing lower will very often damage the battery.

There are a variety of deep-cycle batteries—one called flooded and the other sealed. Let's talk about flooded batteries first.

Flooded batteries are generally less expensive and last longer than sealed batteries. Tip a flooded battery over and the electrolyte will spill out. The least expensive are golf-cart batteries at about $100 each. These are great for smaller systems of 800 watts of PV or less and will last three to five years. Marine deep-cycle batteries are fine if you only need three or four batteries, but will only last about two or three years. Middle-range expense deep-cycle batteries are designed for use in electric floor sweepers. Sometimes called L16s (they used to be 16 inches tall), they cost about $300 each. Dollar-per-watt-hour, they are more expensive than golf-cart batteries, but they will last five to eight years. L16s are bigger batteries, so they are good for PV systems up to 1,600 watts. High-end flooded batteries can last as long as 10 to 12 years and can be used for systems as large as 6,000 watts. For batteries capable of being banked this size, expect to pay $700 per battery.

Flooded lead-acid batteries do give off gases, so make sure your system is designed with an adequate vent to the outside. Zephyr Vent (zephyrvent.com) makes a neat line of battery vents.

Sealed batteries can be as much as three times the cost of high-end industrial batteries, but they are usually about 25 to 50 percent less than their flooded cousins. Generally, sealed batteries have a 20 percent shorter cycle life than comparable flooded batteries. The big advantages are that they require no maintenance and they don't have to be vented outside. Maintenance may not be a big issue for your system. For flooded batteries, you have to add distilled water (_never_ tap water) every three to six months. You will also have to run a controlled overcharge or equalization charge to balance the cell voltages. Some of the sophisticated charge controllers (discussed next) will equalize your batteries for you. Wear old clothes, because even tiny acid splashes will dissolve your jeans at the next wash cycle. Do the maintenance-free batteries sound better now?

All lead-acid batteries are temperamental when it comes to temperature. Like Goldilocks, they want it not too hot and not too cold. All lead-acid batteries work best at 77°F, so keep them indoors if possible. If indoors is not an option for you, tell your supplier so it can adjust the size of the battery bank accordingly. Even though deep-cycle batteries are designed to be discharged down to 20 percent capacity, they don't like it. The shallower the cycle, the longer a battery will last. As a rule of thumb, don't cycle a battery bank deeper than 50 percent.

Here are a few more rules of thumb for selecting solar system batteries:

- ◆ A battery bank should be sized for five days of load.

- ◆ Avoid adding new batteries to an old battery bank. The old batteries will not rise up. Instead, they will pull the new batteries down.

- ◆ Use no more than four parallel strings of batteries. The fewer strings, the better. The more strings, the harder it is for the cell voltages to stay in balance.

- ◆ Keep the connections and battery tops clean. Corrosion will rob your power.

- ◆ Learn to use a hydrometer to test the battery's specific gravity.

- ◆ Only use distilled water to fill batteries.

- ◆ Remember that battery acid is hazardous. Wear safety glasses and gloves when handling batteries.

- ◆ Treat batteries with respect. In the wrong conditions, they can explode.

- ◆ Traveling? Sealed and gel batteries are also classified as nonhazardous, so they are far less regulated for commercial transportation. This makes them easier to ship out of the country if you are planning a solar power system elsewhere.

The batteries you choose should have a combined capacity greater than the need. The smartest approach is to get advice from your power equipment and/or battery provider on batteries that will supply your long-term needs.

Solar Eclipse

Lead-acid batteries contain a solution of about one part sulfuric acid to two parts distilled water. Flooded lead-acid batteries can give off explosive hydrogen gas when recharging. Make sure that the batteries are located in a well-ventilated space away from other system components, people, and pets. Read and follow the manufacturer's instructions.

Charge Controllers

Charge controllers regulate the flow of electricity within the battery system. They're critical to the health of a battery-based PV system, and yet they usually only make up about 5 percent less of the cost of a system. The main function of charge controllers is to stop the PV array from overcharging your battery bank.

Recently manufacturers have designed sophisticated charge controllers that have Maximum Power Point Tracking (MPPT) circuitry in addition to the voltage regulation circuitry. What MPPT means to you is an extra 10 to 20 percent energy from your PV array. Expect MMPT circuitry to double the cost of the controller; it can be well worth the extra expense. These stand-alone units typically cost between $25 and $700, depending on your system's ampere capacity and what features you want.

Your choice of a controller depends on your application. Look for a controller with pulse-width modulation (PWM) and temperature compensation (TC) and consider the extra expense of MPPT. Expect to pay $5 per amp for a simpler controller with PWM and TC and $10+ per amp for a more sophisticated controller with PWM, TC, and MPPT.

Typical charge controller used in solar power systems.

Some of the controllers with MPPT can also allow high-voltage arrays with lower-voltage battery banks. This can be very useful when long runs from the array to the battery bank are unavoidable.

Some controllers have low-voltage disconnects (LVDs). LVDs will disconnect the load from the battery and allow the battery to charge back up. As charging back up can take days and people don't want to be without lights, most designers don't use

LVDs. Instead, they recommend end users learn to read the system voltage meter and moderate their consumption accordingly—in other words, either cut back or fire up the generator.

Selecting Inverters

Inverters are devices that change DC electricity into AC electricity. As mentioned, the DC could be coming from one of a variety of power sources. It can also come from batteries because they store electricity as DC. Your car's battery, for example, stores 12 volts DC—unless you're driving a 50-year-old classic with a 6-volt system.

Typical inverter used in solar power systems.

Inverters sound like simple devices, and they are. However, technology has really enhanced them during the past 20 years to where they do much more, and they do it more efficiently. Most inverters made for the United States convert 12-, 24-, or 48-volts DC and produce 120-volts at 60-*hertz* AC. Other countries prefer an AC output of 220 volts at 50 Hz. Good-quality inverters make up about 25 percent of the cost of an off-grid (battery-based) system and 10 percent of a grid-tie (battery-less) system.

def•i•ni•tion

A **hertz (Hz)** indicates the number of times that AC alternates in a second. DC can be stored, but can't travel very far on a wire without loss. AC can travel much farther, such as from a power plant to your home, so most appliances are AC. The two standards, 50 Hz and 60 Hz, were established long ago, and neither is really better, just different.

Small inverters can power individual appliances. However, solar and other power systems that want to power many appliances need larger inverters. Fortunately, commonly available inverters can provide up to 5,000 watts of AC electricity. The quality and type of AC current that an inverter produces depends on the waveform, frequency, and voltage.

Waveform

The waveform of the alternating current your system produces is important to the appliances it powers. A waveform is the form or shape of the wave that the electric current looks like. Backing up a bit, AC alternates around a single point, first positive, and then negative. The reference line is 0 volts. If drawn, the waveform line would go above the reference line for a while, then back and down below the reference line in a shape that looks similar to an *S* sleeping (see the following illustration). The line goes as far above the reference line as below it.

The height of the waveform above and below the reference line is called its amplitude. The amount of time it takes to go from the line up, then down, then back to the line is called the frequency. Those are the basics of a waveform.

Components of a waveform.

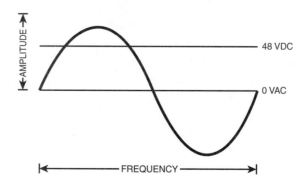

The input is DC, and it can be drawn as a straight line somewhere above the 0-volt reference point. Obviously, a 48-volt DC line would be drawn higher above the reference point than a 12-volt DC line. So the inverter's job is to get that DC input to alternate above and below (positive and negative) the 0-volt reference point. And it must do so at the amplitude and frequency needed for your appliances—12 volts DC in to 120 volts at 60 Hz AC out, for example.

In an ideal world, the output waveform should be a sine wave, the sleeping *S*. That's what appliances prefer. But, as you can imagine, turning a straight line into an *S* takes some work. It's more expensive than converting the straight line into a square wave.

What's a square wave, you ask? In the previous drawing, it looks similar to two adjacent squares, one above and one below the reference line. A square wave is the intermediate step between DC and sine-wave AC. It's cheaper to produce. Some appliances can run nearly as well on square-wave AC as on sine-wave AC. Heating appliances can do this. But many appliances, such as stereos and TVs, really need the good stuff—sine-wave AC—to work properly.

Confused yet? I hope not! We're going to take another step and introduce a waveform that's halfway between a square wave and a sine wave. It's called a modified or quasi sine wave. Most appliances can run on AC from a quasi-sine-wave AC inverter. The advantage here is that these inverters are simpler—meaning cheaper—than pure sine-wave inverters. Actually, square-wave inverters just don't exist on the market anymore. Virtually all the smaller and/or lower-cost inverters available today produce modified sine-wave power.

However, fan motors and refrigerator compressors will run louder and hotter on modified sine-wave power. Higher-end electronics may not be able to filter out the dirtier waveform. The results could be that the TV screen may have lines in it, the stereo may hum, and the washing machine may not be able to run through its cycles. Newer-model submersible impeller pumps without relay boxes or with solid-state relays will not work. Nor will high-end, super-efficient furnaces. They all prefer electrical power from pure sine-wave inverters.

Here's the bottom line: Buy the least-expensive power inverter that will do the job of delivering the right type of electricity to your home's appliances. Ask questions as you buy solar power equipment. You'll now know what the salespeople are talking about.

Frequency

I mentioned AC frequency a moment ago. U.S. appliances are built to run on a frequency of 60 Hertz (Hz) or cycles per second. Most other countries prefer

50 Hz. Who cares? Your clocks care! Anything with a timing device in it relies on the frequency of incoming AC to keep track of the time. It counts 60 Hz, then advances the clock by 1 second. Just remember that unless you're in Asia or Europe, you want your inverter to produce an output frequency of 60 Hz.

Voltage

I also mentioned voltage in talking about waveforms. Most inverters manufactured for the North American market supply 120 volts at the output. Some can be connected in series to produce 240 volts for things such as submersible well pumps.

Alternatively, a step-up transformer can be installed on those appliances to turn 120 Vac into modest amounts of 240 volts AC. Appendix A covers inventorying your home's appliances to figure out whether you have any that require 240 Vac.

Power Rating

One final question to ask when buying an inverter: Is the power output continuous or surge? The answer is important because electric motors in your home (fans, blowers, blenders, refrigerators) that go on and off during the day need as much as six times the normal operating power to get started—it's much like getting out of bed on a Monday morning! The inverter you select must be rated to handle the extra load. Otherwise, some of your appliances may not start up.

Solar Eclipse

Be careful plugging battery chargers into a system with a modified sine-wave inverter. Many chargers, such as those for a battery-operated drill, use a temperature sensor to tell when the battery is charged. The modified sine wave confuses the temperature sensor, and the charger won't turn off. Batteries have been known to melt! Your charger or inverter owner's manual may not mention this problem. If you must charge with modified sine-wave power, check your charger carefully to make sure it turns off by itself after an hour or so. If it doesn't, you have a manually controlled battery charger. If you don't turn it off, you, too, will melt batteries.

So make sure that the inverter you select is able to run every device you plan to connect to it—and then some. Certainly you'll be adding electric tools and appliances in the future.

Inverter Types

As you begin shopping for an inverter, you'll discover various types. Which one is the best? The answer depends on the application. A rotary inverter uses DC electricity to power a DC motor that turns an AC generator. Rotary inverters produce a pure sine-wave output and automatically deliver electrical load based on demand. The downside is that they have very low efficiency, don't handle surges well, and they can't adjust to changes in frequency.

More popular are electronic inverters. Two types are available. High-frequency switching units use all solid-state components for lighter weight and lower cost. However, they have limited surge capacity and generally don't last as long. Transformer-based units are larger, heavier, more surge capable, and generally have longer life expectancies, but they are more expensive initially.

Solar Eclipse

Grid-tie inverters typically are installed to serve groups of 6 to 12 PV panels. However, the output of individual panels may vary, so the inverter loses some efficiency to compensate for the average outputs. New micro inverters are installed one-per-panel for optimum output efficiency. A set of micro inverters is more expensive than a group inverter, but can offer increased output and overall savings. Ask your solar equipment supplier for the latest information on micro inverters.

There's also what's called an *intertie* inverter. These are used on systems that intertie to the utility grid, also known as grid-intertie or simply grid-tie. It synchronizes power between the incoming electricity grid and what's produced by the home system, so it's also called a synchronous inverter. If the generated power is more than the house needs, the unit sends excess power to the utility grid. If the solar or other house power system can't keep up with demand, the synchronous inverter pulls power from the utility line, much like water seeks its own level. (Chapter 12 offers more information on selling excess power.)

def•i•ni•tion

An **intertie** system is one that links an independent power producer, such as your solar power system, with a public power system so that they can draw from each other. An intertie system is also commonly known as a grid-tie system and will be covered in greater detail in Chapter 12.

If you're buying a power-distribution system, make sure that the inverter included in the package matches your home's power needs and will intertie with the utility grid.

Battery-Charging Inverters

We covered batteries for your power system earlier in this chapter. Note that inverters are available that include a DC source battery charge controller. This type of unit manages not only power between the utility grid and your home power system but also the electric charge stored in batteries.

It works like a traffic cop. It watches what power is needed by the house and what's available from the house's power system, storage batteries, and the utility grid. It then manages the flow of power as needed to meet demands. If the house power system can't keep the batteries charged, it gets electricity from the utility to charge them. Pretty nifty!

Intertie Inverters

If you're planning on tying your home power-generation system into the public-utility grid, you'll need to install an inverter that is approved by the utility for intertie or grid-tie systems. There are two types: direct and battery.

A direct intertie inverter feeds electricity directly to and from the incoming utility line. (Batteries are not included.) There's less equipment to control, so the cost is less. A typical nonbattery intertie inverter costs $1,500 to $3,000. An intertie inverter that must also control a battery system will, obviously, cost more—about $4,000 for a typical unit.

Building to Code

The National Electric Code (NEC) has one job: to ensure safety in all systems that generate, store, transport, and use electricity. That's a big job. It includes codes that are specific to solar and other home power systems. That's good. Whoever installs your home power system (you, a dealer, or contractor) must follow NEC equipment requirements so that the system will be approved by local electric code officials. (Some states require that a licensed electrician install any electrical system.)

However, some local code officials aren't familiar with PV and other power-generation systems. The solution is to start early in the building permit process (see Chapter 4) finding out who will do the inspection and whether he or she is up-to-date on your type of system. If not, begin the education process. Invite the inspector to watch what you or the dealer is doing before the system is closed up in the wall or roof system. Most will be open to learning.

Bright Idea

A plain-English translation of the NEC codes for photovoltaic power systems is reprinted in the latest edition of *Solar Living Sourcebook* published by Gaiam/Real Goods (see SolarHomeGuides.com).

What Else Will You Need?

In addition to requiring an inverter, batteries, and controller, your home power system will need cables, some fuses, and some protection. Let's take a look.

Fortunately, wire for solar, wind, hydro, and fuel-cell power systems looks like wire for utility power—because it's exactly the same wire. Electricity doesn't care what it travels on. What's important is that the wire is rated for the load and the application for which you're using it. The amount of current it can safely carry depends on its size; the larger the wire, the more it can carry. To confuse things a little, larger wire has a smaller gauge number than smaller wire. That is, a 10-gauge wire is bigger and is designed to carry more current than a 16-gauge wire.

Where you plan to run the wire also dictates the type of wire you should use. The NEC code will get specific. In the meantime, know that some wire is intended to be run through walls, other wire through the ground, and still other to lie in the sun all day.

AC systems require AC outlets. If you're planning to use DC appliances and lights, you'll need DC outlets and adapters. It's best to use an electrician to install or at least to plan and oversee the installation of any new wiring.

Fuses and circuit breakers are important to the safety of electrical systems—and to the folks who plug things into them. Any wire attached to a power source must be protected from overcurrent. There are numerous fuses, disconnects, ground-fault protection, and lighting protectors available. Whoever designs your power system should be following code, including fuses and other protections.

Selecting Your Solar Power System

What are the components of a solar power system? PV power generation systems are made up of interconnecting components, each with a specific job to do. One of the major strengths of PV systems is modularity. As your need grows, individual components can be replaced or added to provide increased capacity.

Selecting System Components

System components typically include the solar array, optional battery bank and charge controller, inverter, and distribution parts.

The solar array consists of one or more PV modules that convert sunlight into electric energy. The modules are connected in series and/or parallel to provide the voltage and current levels needed by the system. The array is usually mounted on a metal structure and tilted to face the sun.

The optional battery bank contains one or more deep-cycle batteries. A battery stores the power produced by the solar array and discharges it as needed. The charge controller makes sure that the battery is recharged by the solar array and prevents overcharging.

The inverter converts DC power from the solar arrays into AC needed by most appliances and household loads. A home that uses only DC lights and appliances, such as an off-grid house or RV, doesn't need an inverter.

What else? That depends. Additional equipment may include a rack for the modules, an array combiner box, cabling, fuses, switches, circuit breakers, and a meter. If an *intertie* or net-metering system is installed, it will require a meter that can travel in both directions. For greatest solar efficiency, PV modules can be mounted with motors to actually track the sun across the sky.

Sizing Your System

As you can imagine, the size of your solar power system depends on your electrical needs. Appendix A shows you how to calculate your home's current energy needs. Appendix B offers numerous suggestions for reducing dependency on electricity so your home doesn't need a large solar power system. In addition, you've decided how much of your energy needs you want or need to have supplied by a PV system. You may be aiming for 50 percent, 75 percent, or all your power from solar.

For instance, maybe last year your house and its occupants used 6,000 kWh of electricity, but an energy audit and energy-efficient measures cut that need by 25 percent. You estimate that your home's energy needs are now about 4,500 kWh of electricity a year. Further, you've decided to install a system that can cut that in half—and have room for future expansion. You want to take advantage of rebates and tax incentives as well as net metering. So what size system do you need?

Fortunately, solar power systems are becoming more and more consumer-friendly. When you know the size of the system you need, you can begin shopping based on size and equipment. For example, one solar equipment supplier offers a grid-tie system, without battery backup, designed to produce 2 kWh per day for about $16,000. The major cost components of this system will include 10 to 14 PV modules, an inverter, and racking. Minor cost components include disconnects, lightning protection, and wire.

A grid-tie or off-grid system *with* batteries may cost about $24,000, plus about $6,000 to $8,000 in labor. (Costs can be reduced by rebates, as discussed in Chapter 2.) The major cost components of this system include 10 to 14 PV modules, an inverter on a power panel, racking, and 16 to 20 L16-type deep-cycle batteries. Minor cost components include circuit breakers, disconnects, PV array combiner boxes, inverters and battery cables, and lightning protection.

Grid-tie systems with or without batteries manage the power generated by the solar modules, supplementing it with power from the utility company as needed. These systems have numerous safety features that not only protect your home and appliances, but also protect any public utility workers who think they turned off the power to lines on which they're working. In fact, your agreement with the local utility will require that you install an intertie or grid-tie system with these safety features.

A 4 kW solar power system will run about twice the price of the 2 kW system, less rebates.

Sun Spots

A good quality solar module or panel measures about 26 by 60 inches and just under 2 inches thick. It will produce 125 or more watts of power at a price of about $4.60 per watt—down from about $5.40 per watt in 2001. (Installation materials and labor are additional.) The manufacturer's warranty is 25 years. Look for the Underwriter Laboratory (UL) certification on the module. For states that offer solar power rebates, look to see which modules are approved for rebates. The dsireusa.com website can get you to your local rebate program.

Direct intertie systems, without battery backup, make up 90 percent or more of grid-tie applications. They allow you to sell excess solar power to the utility as it is produced. System prices range from about $8 to $10 per kilowatt installed, with labor costs being about $2 to $3 per kilowatt. I'll cover solar power systems for RVs, supplemental power, and emergency power more fully in Part 3.

Keep in mind that rebates, tax credits, and other discounts may be able to cut these prices by as much as half, depending on the system size and where you live. Installation charges often are eligible for rebate money as well.

Of course, if you're your own utility company, supplying power to your residence alone, off-grid, your system doesn't need to be as complex. Full stand-alone systems are available or you can get suppliers to design one for your needs. Besides requiring an inverter/power panel, PV modules, batteries, and cables, a build-your-own system should include the following:

- PV combiner box
- DC ground fault protection
- Lightning protector
- Safety and overcurrent protection

Batteries or no batteries is a standard question. Again, 90 percent or more of grid-tie systems *do not* have batteries. Ask yourself these questions:

- Do I want to check the batteries every three to six months?
- Do I want to buy and change out batteries every five years or so?
- Am I willing to pay an additional 40 percent for the system?
- Will the rebate cover the extra cost incurred by the batteries?
- Do I think power outages are a serious enough issue for me to pay the additional costs?

If the answer to each of these questions is yes, then go ahead and include batteries in your system. And when a passing storm knocks your neighborhood's power out for an evening, there are some bragging rights to being the only lighted house on an otherwise dark block!

Installing Your Solar Power System

Should you attempt to install your own solar power system? If you have the skills to build or wire your own house, then maybe. But find out from your local building authority what you can and cannot do. You're installing an electrical system that, in many areas, requires a building permit and an electrical inspection and certificate. A local electrical contractor—preferably one with solar power system experience—may be required to install the system.

If you really want to take it on, work with your supplier and electrician and see what needs to happen. For a system as described in this chapter, figure on the cost of labor to be about $2,000 to $3,000 per system without batteries and $3,500 to $4,500 with batteries, depending on where you live. Most of the work will be installing the power panel. If you're handy, you may be able to cut costs by helping with the installation of PV modules and running or trenching cables.

Solar Eclipse

Think of electricity as being alive—with teeth! Make sure it's fast asleep (off) before attempting to work on electrical circuits. Don't take someone's word for it that the circuit is off. Check for yourself. Make sure the correct circuit breakers are off and then test the circuit with a voltmeter or other circuit tester (available for a few dollars at most hardware stores) before working on electrical systems.

How are PV modules mounted? Of course, you want them oriented so they receive the greatest amount of solar radiation throughout the year. The permanent angle is equal to your home's latitude in degrees. For example, for a home in Boulder, Colorado, at 40° latitude, you would mount modules on a permanent frame set at an angle of 40° to level.

The PV module mounts can be fixed or tracking. Fixed mounts are much easier and cheaper to build and install. Tracking mounts can be manually or mechanically moved. If your modules are installed where they can easily be adjusted seasonally, the mounts can be tipped up 15° for winter (lower sun) or down 15° for summer (higher sun). At the example home in Boulder, the mounting would be tipped to 55° in winter and down to 25° in summer.

Smart tracking systems add expense but can actually follow the sun as it travels from east to west across the sky each day. However, they can recoup their cost in increased efficiency.

Racking PV Modules

PV modules are designed to be mounted and pointed at the sun. You can mount racks on the roof or the ground. Roof-mounted racks are usually made of aluminum and flush mount to the roof. If your roof is flat or the pitch is not enough, most manufacturers provide legs (at additional cost) to increase the angle.

Roof-mounted solar panel rack.

If you are squeamish about putting holes in your roof and have the extra real estate, consider a pole-mounted rack or a tracking rack.

Depending on the season, tracking racks will give you an additional 15 to 40 percent more energy over fixed racks, but they cost more than twice as much. How do you decide? For grid-tie systems with rebates involved, a tracker may not be cost effective. This is because most rebate programs pay by number of watts installed, not by the amount of electricity generated. Even though a tracking 1 kW system will produce 20 percent more energy annually than a fixed-array system, many rebates and tax credits stay the same. Know your rebate and credit requirements.

Pole-mounted solar panel rack.

Azimuth and Declination: What's the Angle?

You will pay a lot for your PV modules, so you will want to face them square to the sun. To calculate azimuth or the angle of the PV array from horizontal, the rule of thumb is to take your latitude and add 15° for the optimal winter angle. For the summer angle, subtract 15°. For example, Albuquerque, New Mexico, is at about 35° north. The optimal winter angle would be 50° from horizontal and the optimal summer angle would be a flatter 20°.

You also need to be aware that magnetic declination solar south and magnetic south are not the same. The magnetic fields of the Earth vary depending on your location and slowly change over time. For example, the declination for Albuquerque, New Mexico, is 10° east, so the compass needle is pointing slightly to the west. When siting the array, you'll want to have the array about 10° due east of magnetic south.

Most good maps will have magnetic south shown. One website to visit is ngdc.noaa. gov/geomagmodels/Declination.jsp.

There are two general types of trackers: active and passive. Briefly, active trackers use low-speed motors and are slightly more expense and slightly more accurate at tracking the sun. Passive trackers are gravity drivers that use the shifting weight of an inert gas to follow the sun. They are slightly less accurate and slightly less expensive.

Solar technology is improving every year and costs are slowly coming down as more people buy them. So even if you don't buy a system today, keep watching the marketplace. It's getting better.

Chapter 17 offers tips on selecting a solar power system installation contractor, and Chapter 18 shows you how to do it yourself. For more information on residential electrical systems and how they fit into the home construction process, read *The Complete Idiot's Guide to Building Your Own Home, Third Edition* (Alpha Books, 2007), especially Chapter 22 on electrical systems.

You now know how electricity is generated from sunlight and how you can harness it to power your home. Next, let's look at how you can take a big energy load off your solar power system by using the sun to heat water.

The Least You Need to Know

- ◆ Photovoltaic technology converts sunlight into electricity that can replace fossil-fuel power.

- ◆ In most states, you can utilize net metering (selling excess solar power to utilities) with an intertie system.

- ◆ System components typically include the solar array, optional battery bank and charge controller, inverter, and distribution parts.

- ◆ An inverter changes direct current into alternating current as required by your appliances. Choose an inverter by its waveform, frequency, voltage, and power rating—and your budget.

- ◆ Some inverters also serve as system controllers, battery chargers, and intertie with the utility grid.

- ◆ The National Electric Code (NEC) includes specific codes for installing solar and other home power systems. You'll also need wiring, fuses, protectors, and some other hardware, depending on the system you're installing.

- ◆ Whether you can install your own solar power system depends on local building codes and permits.

Chapter 8

Wind and Water Power

In This Chapter

- ◆ Finding enough wind to make electricity
- ◆ Selecting a wind turbine system
- ◆ Using water to generate electricity
- ◆ Picking an efficient hydropower system
- ◆ Figuring the economics of wind and water power

Solar energy isn't the only renewable resource you can use to generate electricity. Wind and water flow also can do the trick.

This chapter offers you some renewable energy options if you live where you can take advantage of them. City dwellers on small lots typically can't capture the wind or enough water to make it worthwhile. However, country folk—and those who plan to join them—can use technology to build productive power systems to supplement solar power.

Harnessing the Wind

In some locations, wind can be a nuisance—unless it's harnessed to produce electricity. Then at least it's a valuable nuisance. If you're living on a larger parcel of land (more than an acre), as about a quarter of Americans are, you might be able to turn the wind into power. For many rural home locations, wind power is an excellent, cost-effective, and renewable power source.

Technology has advanced wind power systems so that locations with little natural air movement can generate at least some of the electricity a home needs. And it can be cost effective. Depending on your wind resource, a small wind energy system can lower your electricity bill by 50 to 90 percent. Combine this with a solar power system, and you may never have to pay a utility bill again—as long as the sun shines and the wind blows.

How much wind is necessary? Maybe not as much as you think. Wind is a renewable resource, just like the sun and the flow of water. A wind turbine power system can be effective with an average annual wind speed of 8 miles per hour; average means 24 hours a day, 7 days a week. And that's the minimum. Actually, some of the newest systems can operate with even less, though the cost per kilowatt-hour is relatively high.

Because of changes in terrain over a large parcel of land, you may be able to find a point on your property where the wind moves rapidly enough to install a cost-effective generation system. If you're looking for a new home site, you can put wind on your list of desired features. To measure local wind conditions, visit a science or weather equipment store for wind-speed equipment. (Most larger cities have science and weather equipment stores, some of them in larger malls.) Most electronic weather stations can measure wind speed and direction. You can buy a handheld digital windometer for less than $50. Alternatively, wind socks are available that indicate speed by how full they become with wind.

Bright Idea

You can view the *Wind Energy Resource Atlas of the United States* on the National Wind Technology Center website at nrel.gov/wind/. The Department of Energy (DOE) sponsors the Windpowering America website at windpoweringamerica.gov, as well. If you don't have access to the Internet, contact the DOE (see SolarHomeGuides.com).

The U.S. Department of Energy and other agencies have produced wind resource maps that show the estimated yearly electricity production available from a small wind turbine. The maps are based on the average wind speed, but you'll want a location that gives you consistent wind speeds if possible. Otherwise, you'll want a battery system for storing generated power. (You may anyway.)

The highest average wind speeds are usually found along the seacoasts, on ridge lines, and on the Great Plains. If you don't know local wind conditions but live near an airport, ask the airport manager for the info. Even the smallest airports track local wind speeds and direction for pilots. However, airport winds can be about 20 percent greater than the surrounding area. That's because the measurement is made 20 to 30 feet above the ground, where wind speeds are greater than at ground level, and because airports are flat with fewer obstructions like trees and buildings to slow winds down.

A wind turbine looks similar to a weather vane and a small airplane combined—which is what it is. The weather vane part rotates to turn the propeller into the wind. The prop then spins as the wind passes over the aerodynamic blades. As an analogy, whereas an airplane pulls itself through the air using engine power, a wind turbine gathers the wind's power and turns it into electricity.

The best location on your property for a wind turbine is away from anything that will slow the wind down and near anything that will speed it up. That makes sense. Trees and buildings absorb, deflect, and ruffle up much of the wind's energy. Your turbine needs to be 30 feet higher than any obstruction within a 200-foot radius or it's going to get beat up, suffer low output, and die young. Hills can channel the wind to make wind speed at the ridge higher than in the surrounding valleys.

As you learned from the earlier airport wind calculation, the higher the turbine, the greater the wind's velocity. There's a practical as well as economic limit because the poles on which the turbines are mounted get more expensive with every foot of height.

Selecting a Wind Power System

Wind turbines are the primary (read: most expensive) component of a wind power system. They are the working end. Most wind turbines are horizontal upwind machines with two or three blades. The amount of power a turbine can produce depends on the diameter of the blades or rotor. That's called the sweep area, and it means the quantity of wind that the turbine intercepts.

Right behind the rotor is the alternator or generator. It converts the rotor's rotation into electricity. Behind it is the body and the tail, similar to an airplane's tail, designed to keep the turbine pointed into the wind. Finally, the tower holds everything off the ground where the wind is best.

The tower is typically at least as high as 30 feet plus the rotor radius. It should be even higher if there are obstructions within 300 feet that would slow down the wind. Towers can go to 100 feet or higher. They cost more than shorter towers but can increase power output sufficiently to make it a worthwhile investment. In many locations, there's about 40 percent more wind power at 100 feet than at ground level. Taller towers ordinarily are the cheapest way to increase output.

Typical wind turbine for generating electricity.

Turbine towers are either freestanding or guyed (that is, they use wire or cable supports). Most home wind power systems use guyed towers because they are less expensive and easier to install and maintain. But how the heck can you get a 30- to 100-foot tower up? Most towers are designed for simple tilt-up, tilt-down installation. You assemble everything safely at ground level and then raise the tower with help from friends and equipment. Tilt-down towers can be installed by one or two persons following manufacturer's instructions. They are also handier when it's time for maintenance. Of course, that means you need a flat space around the tower that's greater than the tower's height.

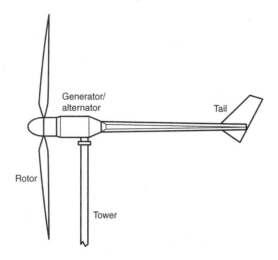

Basic parts of a small wind electric system.

Generator/
alternator

Tail

Rotor

Tower

As with other renewable energy systems, you'll need more than the generating equipment. You also need wiring and maybe batteries to store electricity. Fortunately, they are the same as those needed for solar and water power systems. That means you can tie your wind turbine's output into your renewable energy electrical system to keep costs down. Of course, make sure that the system is sized to accept the additional power.

A wind generator (right) can supplement solar power (left) for 24-hour electricity.

How much will a wind turbine power system cost? A small system, called a micro turbine, can be purchased and self-installed for about $1,000. It can put out about 400 watts of power at 28 mph wind speeds, but only about 30 watts at 10 mph. It's intended more for remote locations. Large turbine systems can run up to $40,000 installed. Yikes! Fortunately, in Chapter 2, you learned how to cut the cost of energy investment dramatically with rebates and tax incentives. Note that although there are some incentives for wind systems, they are not as readily available as for PV systems. And you can probably sell excess electricity through net metering, as described in Chapters 7 and 12.

Solar Eclipse

Don't install a wind turbine on any building that people plan to sleep in. Wind turbines transmit vibration and noises down their towers, and roofs make great amplifier membranes. Roof mounts are available, but they are only recommended for outbuildings.

For example, one popular wind turbine system with a 7-foot rotor diameter has a rating of 900 watts with a 28 mph wind. It can handle winds up to 120 mph and generate at least some electricity in winds as slow as 8 mph. The unit costs about $2,300 plus tower and installation. A bigger version (a nearly 15-foot rotor) can produce 3.2 kW at an initial cost of about $7,000 plus tower (another $800 to $2,000) and installation (the cost varies). To generate some serious electricity, such as 10 kW, a 23-foot diameter rotor can do the job.

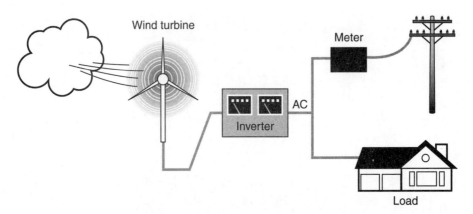

Wind turbine power can be connected to a grid just as solar power systems are.

Microhydro and Wind Generator Power System Flowchart

Components used in residential wind electric and microhydroelectric power systems.

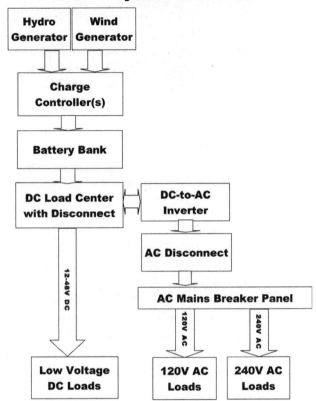

When shopping for a wind turbine system, make sure you know the unit's power curve. For most of them, you'll notice that there is an optimum range, usually between 20 and 30 mph, which offers the greatest electric output. That's important. If your site produces an average wind of only 10 to 15 mph, look for a turbine with a power curve in this range.

Towers can be relatively inexpensive. Depending on the type, expect to pay about $20 to $30 a foot for guyed towers. Stand-alone towers with no guy supports cost more. If your budget is tight, consider a roof mounting for your tower. Yes, the structure moderates the wind speed, but it can save you the cost of 20 or more feet of tower.

Using Water Power

More than two millennia ago, folks harnessed the power of water to grind wheat and do other work. Even today, many remote places throughout the world depend on hydropower systems to generate electricity so they can perform vital tasks. If your home is in a subdivision, you're probably not able to harness the power from everyone's leaky garden faucets to run your entertainment center. However, if you now live or plan to live in the country and your property will have water rights, hydropower can help.

What's really cool is that, like wind, hydropower is a renewable energy. Water isn't used up because energy is derived from its movement. Yes, there are other ecological issues (such as dam construction and flooding), but these have minimal impact when building a small hydropower system for your home.

def•i•ni•tion

Hydropower systems that can generate up to 100 kW of electricity are referred to as **micro-hydro systems**. That's about as big as you'll ever need, because a 10 kW system can typically provide enough electricity for a large home or a small business.

Only about 10 percent of U.S. electricity comes from hydropower. In the realm of renewable energy sources, hydropower ranks at the top, well above solar power. That is, we're getting much more of our utility electricity from water than from the sun. So, fortunately, if your home is near a moving creek, stream, or river for which you have water rights, you may be able to install a small, efficient hydropower system known as a *microhydro system*. Let's see how.

Harnessing Water Power

Hydropower systems use the energy in flowing water to produce electricity or mechanical energy. Although there are many ways to harness moving water to produce energy, run-of-the-river systems are the most popular because they don't require large storage reservoirs. Of course, if your water source freezes in winter or dries up in summer, don't plan on year-round electricity from this single source. Look to solar or another more consistent power source.

What's a run-of-the-river hydro project and how does it work? I'm glad you asked. A portion of a river's water is diverted to a channel, pipeline, or pressurized pipeline (called a penstock) that delivers the water to a waterwheel or a turbine. The moving water rotates the wheel or turbine, turning a shaft. The shaft's motion can be used to pump water or to power an electric generator.

Is a microhydropower system right for you? The absolute answer is: maybe. You can easily measure how much sunlight is reaching your home on a given day or season, but how do you measure water flow? Actually, you must measure both the flow (the quantity of water) and the head (the speed at which it is flowing). No, you don't borrow a trooper's radar gun and point it at the river. You calculate head based on charts and instruments.

Head is based on the vertical distance that the water falls. It's usually measured in feet or units of pressure. Head also depends on the channel or pipe through which it flows. Lots of water channeled into a smaller pipe makes the water move faster, but limits how many gallons per minute you can use without suffering a pressure drop due to pipe friction. Too much pipe friction gives you a lower dynamic head. The system acts as though it has a lower head when running.

If the water falls less than 20 feet in elevation, it's called low head. Anything more than 50 feet is referred to as high head. You want high head because it has more energy, but not all water sources drop that much in elevation—naturally. So you can enhance it by forcing the water to drop farther.

So how can you tell how much of a drop a water flow has? Rather than buy loads of equipment, purchase 30 feet or more of half-inch garden hose or other flexible tubing and a funnel. Have someone hold one end of the hose at the point where you will capture water from the source. Then stretch the hose out along the stream to the point where you expect to install the water turbine. Have your partner seal the funnel tightly in the upstream end of the tubing and submerse it until stream water begins to flow into the funnel and runs from the downstream end. Run it until all the bubbles are expelled. Now lift the downstream end to the point where water doesn't flow from it anymore. Finally, measure the vertical distance between your end of the tube and the water surface. To be safe, subtract a couple of inches to compensate for the water's upstream force that shoves water down the tube.

Of course, you and your assistant can test the waters in various locations to find the one with the highest head. Your turbine doesn't have to be as close to the house as possible, but located in the optimum spot for generating electricity. You can always run a few more feet of electric wire to your house.

What about flow? What's the quantity of water you can expect to be delivered to the downstream hydro turbine? Flow is measured in gallons per minute (gpm) or in cubic feet per second (cfps). Before going to the expense of getting flow measurement equipment or hiring someone, check with the local office of the U.S. Geological Survey, the Army Corps of Engineers, the Department of Agriculture, or your county engineer, who may have maps and data on the flow for the water from which you're borrowing energy. To find these resources, try the "Government" section of the local phone book.

Sun Spots

How much water head is needed to generate hydroelectricity? Experts say that the minimum is typically about 2 feet of vertical drop or head, depending on other conditions and your budget. However, new technologies such as submersible turbines can generate electricity with a head of just more than 1 foot! Ask your hydropower equipment supplier to see the latest gadgets.

If you can't find data, you can do it yourself. Try the bucket method! First, temporarily dam the stream with logs or boards so that all the water is diverted to a foot-wide opening. Then use a 5-gallon bucket to capture and measure the flow, checking your watch to see how long it takes to fill the bucket. If the stream's full flow takes 1 minute to fill a 5-gallon bucket, the flow is 5 gallons per minute. Divide 5 gallons by your fill time in seconds, and then multiply by 60 to get gallons per minute. If your dam isn't totally efficient and is leaking slightly, visually estimate the loss and add it to the total. If it's very much, pile on some more logs or boards.

If you can't or don't want to dam the stream, you can estimate flow by first measuring the width and depth of the stream at its straightest and most uniform point. Draw these dimensions on a graph paper to look like a cross section of your stream. Next, measure off a point 20 feet upstream from your cross section and have an assistant release a float while you time its progress to your cross-section point. If it takes 10 seconds to arrive, the flow rate is 2 feet per second. If it takes 5 seconds, the calculation is 4 feet per second. You get the picture. Repeating this test numerous times will give you a good average.

Now multiply the average flow rate by the cross-sectional area of the stream to estimate the total flow. What you're trying to answer is: how much water passes a specific point in a given time? You can now answer it with reasonable accuracy.

Of course, there are many variables. The stream may be low or even dry for parts of the year. Large rocks at the bottom of the stream may significantly slow down the flow when the water level is low. In addition, you may be limited as to how much water you can divert from a stream. Water rights in agricultural areas, especially, are specifically defined. Your property's deed will tell you more.

Estimating Hydropower Output

You now know about how much water flow you have to work with. Here's how you can calculate the approximate power output to expect from a microhydropower system:

(Net head [feet] × flow [gpm]) ÷ 10

Net head is the total or gross head less any loss from friction of the pipe or channel bed. It's hard to figure, but a hydropower system provider can give you a good estimate. For now, figure that net head is 80 percent of gross flow.

So a typical calculation goes like this:

(8 × 2,000) ÷ 10 = 1,600 watts = 1.6 kW

As you can see, increasing the drop (head) or the flow can make a significant difference in the system's output.

Here are typical hydropower system components:

♦ Water delivery system (channel, pipeline, or penstock)

♦ Turbine or waterwheel that transforms flow energy into rotational energy

♦ Alternator or generator that converts rotational energy into electricity

♦ Regulator that regulates or controls the generator

♦ Wiring that delivers the electricity to your home

How much does a small hydropower system cost? A hydroelectric turbine runs $1,500 to $2,000 and can produce electricity from as small a flow as 5 gpm up to 400 gpm. It produces from 30 to 1,200 watts of DC power, depending on flow and head. Other types and sizes are available. You'll also need pipes, system controls, and wiring. Controllers will add a couple of hundred dollars to the cost. Labor (yours or someone else's) is extra.

Bright Idea

In determining whether a microhydropower system is a good economic investment for you, remember that after the system is installed, the only operating cost is periodic maintenance. Most small systems are virtually trouble-free. It's the initial investment that hurts.

So for just $2,000 to $5,000, you can install and benefit from a small hydropower system. It does require a steady flow of water but, unlike solar power systems, it works day *and* night. You can even sell excess hydropower to your local utility to increase the return on your investment, as I'll discuss in Chapter 12.

Amazing, isn't it? You can combine wind and hydropower with solar power to increase your home's energy efficiency dramatically. What else does the future hold?

The Least You Need to Know

- ◆ Even an average wind of less than 8 mph is enough to generate electricity with an efficient turbine system.
- ◆ A wind power system includes a turbine, tower, and wiring.
- ◆ You can measure your own water source to find out whether it has enough power to generate electricity—or you can hire someone to do it.
- ◆ A hydropower system needs a channel, a turbine or waterwheel, an alternator or generator, a regulator, and some wiring.
- ◆ Both wind and hydropower systems can tie into a solar power system for greater efficiency.

Chapter 9

Solar Water Heating

In This Chapter

- ◆ Finding ways of reducing wasted hot water
- ◆ Learning how solar water heaters work
- ◆ Keeping swimming pool heating costs down
- ◆ Considering a solar-heated pool

Being in "hot water" isn't such a bad thing. In fact, if you're trying to wake up, wash dishes, clean clothes, bathe a pet, or swim, it's a good thing!

It must be good because everyone uses it. Lots of hot water gets used every year by the average (if there is such a thing) family. In this chapter, you find out how to cut hot water costs dramatically by installing a solar water-heating system that fits your needs and your budget.

Cutting Hot Water Costs

Water heating is the third-largest energy expense in your home. It typically adds up to about 15 percent of your utility bill. That's a lot of money going down the drain!

Here are the numbers: A family of four, each showering for 5 minutes a day, uses 700 gallons of water a week! Here's the breakdown for a typical U.S. home: showers use up 37 percent of the home's water, washing clothes takes 26 percent, the dishwasher uses 14 percent, the bathroom flushes 12 percent, and sinks drain the final 11 percent for food preparation and drinking water.

Before turning to solar water-heating options, there are four ways to cut your water-heating bills:

◆ Use less hot water.

◆ Turn down the thermostat on your water heater.

◆ Insulate your water heater.

◆ Install a more efficient water heater.

More specifically, here's how you can both save on water and cut the costs of an installed solar water system:

◆ Repair leaky faucets as soon as the problem is discovered.

◆ Insulate your water storage tanks and pipes (don't cover the thermostat).

Insulating your home's water heater can save on energy costs and your solar investment.

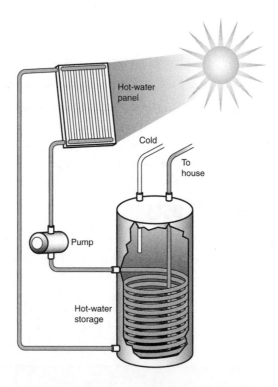

- Install low-flow faucets and showerheads for greater efficiency.

- Consider buying and installing a new, more energy-efficient water heater if your water heater is more than seven years old.

- Compare EnergyGuide labels for the most efficient model when buying a new water heater.

- Lower the thermostat on your water heater to about 115°F.

- Drain a quart of water from your water tank every three months to remove sediment that reduces efficiency.

- Take more showers than baths (the typical shower takes about half the water of a bath).

Solar Water Heaters

Solar water heaters have been around more than 100 years. They were the first application of modern solar technology. More than 1,500,000 homes and businesses have invested in solar water-heating systems in the United States and throughout the world—and most feel that it is a good investment. In fact, a solar water-heating system can be the most cost-effective solar investment you can make to meet your home's energy needs. Fortunately, solar technology has made solar water-heating systems even more efficient while making them easier and less expensive to build and install.

If your home has an unshaded, south-facing location, such as a roof, you can install a solar water-heating system for $2,500 to $5,000 in initial investment. Think of the money as prepaying for hot water.

In addition to gaining long-term financial rewards, solar water heaters don't produce harmful greenhouse gases. In fact, during a 20-year period, it's estimated that a single residential solar water heater can avoid *50 tons* of carbon dioxide emissions produced by fossil-fuel energy. That's a lot of fossils!

What should you look for in a solar water-heating system? First, watch for systems certified by the Solar Rating and Certification Corporation (SRCC), which you can find online at solar-rating.org.

What are your solar options? The first option is to replace your existing water heater with one that uses less fossil-fuel energy. During the past 20 years, technology has come up with some great ideas you may not be aware of. Let's take a look at some of the best.

If you're using electricity to heat water, heat-pump water heaters are three to five times more efficient than conventional resistive heaters. How is that possible? Heat-pump water heaters use a compressor and refrigerant fluid to transfer heat. Yes, they are still powered by electricity, but they use less electricity, so your overall energy bill will be lower.

Indirect water heaters use the home's heating system boiler to help keep water hot. It helps, but isn't as efficient as installing a solar water heater.

A demand water heater makes more sense. A standard water heater holds 30 to 80 gallons of water and attempts to keep it hot at all times—for showers and dishes, when you're sleeping, when you're away for a week—always. A demand water heater, on the other hand, produces hot water only when you need it. Hot water reaches the showerhead just as quickly with these heaters, with no standby waste.

Okay, let's get to the really good stuff: solar water heaters. All day long, the sun is giving us energy to use. How can we turn solar thermal energy into hot water? By running cold water where it can be heated by the sun. That makes sense. You can rig up some pipe on your roof and run water through it to get hot water. Or you can place a large tank of cold water in a sunny spot and let it get warm.

One of the problems with these ideas is temperature control. You certainly don't want shower water coming out of the tap at 180°F—or at 60°F. You want water delivered at a consistent temperature. Optimum delivery temperature is 115°F. I'll cover this topic after discussing how to get solar hot water in the first place.

There are two types of solar water-heating systems: *flat-plate collectors* (pipes) and *batch collectors* (tanks). Flat-plate collectors circulate water through black metal piping or plates, insulated underneath and covered on top with special glass to gather and distribute the sun's heat efficiently. Batch collectors are simply insulated tanks painted black to better absorb the sun's thermal energy. Hot water from these sources can be directly piped to the plumbing system or, better, used to preheat water for an efficient water heater.

There are other technologies being applied, but they all work on the same principles: Solar thermal energy is captured and used to heat water for the home directly or indirectly. In addition to flat plate and batch collectors, there are evacuated tubes as well as concentrating, transpired, and other types of collectors. They all have the same input (solar energy) and output (hot water).

def•i•ni•tion

A **flat-plate collector** is a rectangular box with a transparent cover, typically installed on a building's roof to collect solar thermal energy. Small tubes run through the box and carry either water or an antifreeze solution. If water is used, it goes directly to the water system. If another fluid is used, it goes through a heat exchanger to heat water. A **batch collector** (also known as a breadbox collector) uses a glass-insulated tank, painted black on the outside, to hold water. The tank absorbs and traps the sun's thermal energy to heat water inside. Mounted on the roof or on the ground, it is plumbed into the house's water system. How many collectors you need depends on available solar power and your hot water usage.

What's it going to cost to install a solar hot water system—and when will it pay back? Of course, that depends on the system you install, how much hot water you use, and how energy-efficient your home is otherwise. Here's a starting point: A 50-gallon passive batch-type heater used to preheat water for your conventional water heater will cost from $2,500 plus installation. If you figure $500 for installation, your total is about $3,000. If the system can save you $500 a year in water-heating costs, the unit pays for itself in about six years. After that, it's virtually free (with expenses for minor maintenance and eventual replacement).

Let's talk about controllers. Of course, you won't need to add an output temperature controller if you're preheating water that feeds into a conventional water heater. It has its own controls to regulate temperature before it arrives at the fixture. You will want a controller going into the conventional tank to limit the input temperature range. You don't want boiling water in your tank! Control typically means a sensor to measure the temperature of preheated water, followed by a mixer that blends in cooler water as needed to keep water below a specific setpoint. This automatic temperature control is called a tempering valve. Most have adjustable setpoints between 115°F and 150°F.

As you will learn when shopping for a solar water-heating system, there are many types. To help guide you, here are the more popular ones:

♦ **Direct systems** pump water from a storage tank through one or more collectors and back to a tank; the pump is regulated by an electric controller, an appliance timer, or a PV panel.

♦ **Indirect systems** circulate a fluid through a heat exchanger that transfers the heat from the fluid to the water.

Bright Idea _____

Want to try out an inexpensive solar hot water heater for an outdoor shower? For less than $20, you can get a low-tech Super Solar Shower (available from resources listed online at SolarHomeGuides.com) that will heat 4 gallons of water from 60 to 108°F in about three hours in the sun on a 70°F day.

◆ **Thermosiphons** use a tank mounted above collectors; as the collector heats the water, it rises to the storage tank and heavier cold water drains down to the collector.

◆ **Draindown systems** are a variation needed for collectors in cold climates; they automatically drain water out of a system before it can freeze.

◆ **Swimming pool systems** heat and circulate water for swimming pools, our next topic.

Solar Eclipse _____

If you live in a hard-freeze zone (where it gets below freezing and stays there for more than a day or two), you need a freeze-proof solar collector, or you need to mothball your system for the winter. If needed, make sure you get a freeze-proof solar collector in your solar water-heating system.

Making Your Swimming Pool More Efficient

Swimming pools offer a great way to exercise and beat the summer heat. However, installing and maintaining a pool can get expensive. Fortunately, the sun can provide the heat needed to keep your pool warm enough for a nice swim. The question of whether to install a solar pool heater is a no-brainer: Do it—the payback on most pool systems is one to two years! And that's without any rebates. Before investing in a solar water-heating system for your pool, however, make sure that your pool is efficiently filtering and circulating the water it has. Inefficiency costs money! In fact, installing a smaller, higher-efficiency pump and running less each day can save up to 75 percent in energy costs.

Which pump you choose depends on the size of your swimming pool, how much it is used, and local weather conditions. One study shows that a three-quarter-horsepower or smaller pump is generally sufficient for most residential pools. At the same time, install a larger filter and make sure that pipes are as short and straight as possible. A large cartridge-type filter is more efficient than the cheaper diatomaceous earth types. In addition, cartridges require about half as much power to push the water through.

What about circulation? You can save some bucks by simply cutting back on the amount of time the circulation pumps run. Many are set to run 6 to 12 hours a day. However, about 1 to 3 hours a day is typically all that's needed to keep water fresh. Cutting back may mean that the pool filter doesn't collect as much debris, but you can skim it off as needed or keep the pool covered. You'll save some money!

What's next? Most of a pool's heat loss occurs at the surface, where the heated water evaporates or radiates away. A pool cover offers a very effective way of keeping heat (and water) in a pool by reducing surface evaporation. A pool cover can reduce water loss by one third to one half! And each gallon of 80°F water that evaporates removes about 8,000 British thermal units (Btu) from the pool. In addition, reducing water loss reduces the amount of chemical water treatment required.

The best way to reduce evaporation and even take advantage of the sun's radiation is to add a solar or bubble cover to your swimming pool. Dark covers hold more heat in than clear or light-colored solar covers. A solar cover can pay for itself in energy savings within the first year, yet most have a life span of three to five years.

One more energy-conservation tip for your pool: install a windbreak. A fence or plants around a pool can reduce evaporation by 300 percent or more! That's money evaporating away. An effective windbreak must be high and close enough to the pool to block wind from moving across the water's surface, but it can't block sunlight. See Chapter 6 for more on effective solar landscaping.

Heating Your Pool with Solar Energy

Let's say you've made your swimming pool operate more efficiently. Now you can size and install a solar water-heating system for your pool, knowing what it needs. Actually, you'll consider two things: solar pool heaters and collectors.

A solar pool heater can be a good investment, especially when installing a new pool or replacing an older heating system. Such heating systems are one of the most cost-effective applications of solar energy. It's relatively easy to integrate a solar water heater into an existing system. The pool's water is pumped through the filter, then through solar energy collectors, before going back into the pool. The sun heats the water.

Solar domestic water-heater systems raise a small amount of water to a temperature of about 130°F. Solar pool heaters are different in that they raise the temperature of lots of water to about 80°F. So a solar-heated pool may require a slightly larger pump than a conventionally heated pool.

A basic solar heating system for an in-ground swimming pool will cost about $1,000 for a 10- by 16-foot pool (160 square feet). Add an extra solar collection panel (about $300 each) for each additional 80 square feet.

Is your pool water too hot? Solar collectors can also be used to cool a pool in hot climates or during peak summer months by circulating the water through collectors at night.

Speaking of collectors, solar pool collectors normally don't need glazing (glass) or insulation, because they operate during warmer months when solar radiation and ambient temperatures are higher and you don't need very hot output. This means that the collectors are simpler and less expensive than those for the home's hot water system. Most pool collectors are of plastic or rubber treated with an ultraviolet (UV) light inhibitor to extend the panels' life. They also weigh less than standard collectors and thus can be mounted more easily.

How big should the pool's solar heat collectors be? Much depends on the local climate, the other equipment and heat sources used, and how much of the heat you want to come from solar energy. A good rule of thumb is that the collector surface area should be about *half* that of the pool it serves. Figure a 10- by 12-foot (120 square foot) collector for a 12- by 20-foot (240 square foot) pool. If local solar conditions aren't ideal, bump that size up to 75 percent of the pool's surface; in the 120–square foot example, that's a 10- by 18-foot collector.

Solar collectors should be installed as close to the pool as possible so heat isn't lost in long pipes. If the pool is primarily used in the summer months, tilt the collectors at the angle of the latitude minus about 15°. That's a 25° angle for Boulder, Colorado, located at 40° latitude. If it's a year-round pool, build frames that you can manually adjust seasonally. Alternatively, invest in motorized frames, available from solar equipment suppliers.

Okay, we've used that lucky ol' sun to generate electricity and heat your home's water. What's next? Chapter 10 offers you dozens of ways to heat the air in your home with "free" solar energy.

The Least You Need to Know

- The average house spends more on heating water than on any other energy use.

- Solar thermal energy can be used to reduce or eliminate your home's need for fossil fuel–powered hot water.

- A wide variety of commercially available solar water heaters offer a relatively quick return on your investment.

- You can dramatically cut the costs of owning a swimming pool by using solar energy to keep it comfortable.

- Additional energy-efficient steps can save you even more money on your pool's heating bill.

Chapter 10

Solar Space Heating

In This Chapter

- ◆ Discovering how passive solar energy can heat and cool your home
- ◆ Working with the sun instead of against it
- ◆ Planning a sunspace that enhances your heating system
- ◆ Storing solar energy in your home
- ◆ Learning how to distribute and control your home's solar heat
- ◆ Cooling with solar energy

Cats have the right idea. If solar thermal energy is radiating through a window somewhere in the house, a cat will find that spot and lie down for a snooze in the sun. Cats know that the best warmth comes from the sun. Of course, on a hot day, they find a shaded spot that takes advantage of the sun-warmed air without lying directly in the hot sunlight. Cats can teach us something about solar space heating.

This chapter offers proven ideas on how to build a new home or retrofit your existing home to take advantage of solar space heating. It combines what a cat already knows with what humans have learned about harnessing solar thermal energy.

Passive Solar Basics

You probably live in a passive solar home right now and don't even know it. Passive solar homes use a room or another part of the structure as a solar thermal energy collector. Your home's windows, walls, and floors collect, store, and distribute solar energy every day. Everything under the sun does! However, your home may not be very efficient at using the sun's energy. It may be too hot on one side of the house and too cold on another. Or one room may get toasty while another is chilly. That's because the typical home isn't designed to use solar energy to its advantage.

Drive down the street of any subdivision and you'll notice that the homes are oriented to the street, not necessarily the sun. Most look as though a humongous cookie cutter passed by, stamping out houses in an orderly fashion. They were designed for the efficiency of the contractor and the utilities, not the people who will live in them. They may have energy-efficient appliances in the kitchen, but most were built to sell, not to be lived in with any great degree of energy efficiency.

The reason for this knock-'em-out architecture is economics. By placing houses in neat rows, roads are shorter, utilities don't have to go as far, and construction crews don't have to look at each home as a new construction challenge. The home is either Plan A or Plan B, which is just a mirrored version of Plan A. It's up to the painters to make the homes look different.

When building a new home, think like the sun. Consider the sun, local climate, and other conditions at the building site before you start building. If you've already built, consider how you can take best advantage of the sun without rotating your home on its foundation.

So how does the sun think? It thinks and acts based on natural laws. For those who slept through science class (and for those of us who barely remember being in school), here's a quick review of natural laws that the sun and heat follow:

♦ Heat moves from warmer materials to cooler ones until there is no longer a temperature difference between the two. A passive solar building takes advantage of this law to distribute heat by conduction, convection, and radiation.

♦ Conduction is the way heat moves through materials, traveling from molecule to molecule and from object to object.

♦ Convection is the way heat circulates through liquids and gases. Lighter, warmer fluid rises, and cooler, denser fluid sinks. These "fluids" include air. For instance, warm air rises because it is lighter than colder air, which sinks. This is why warmer air accumulates in the attic while the basement stays cool. Passive solar homes can use the law of air convection to carry solar heat from a south wall into the building's interior.

♦ Finally, class, radiant heat moves through the air from warmer objects to cooler ones. There are two kinds of radiation used in passive solar design: solar radiation and infrared radiation. When radiation hits an object, it is either absorbed, reflected, or transmitted, depending on the object. Opaque objects absorb most of the radiation that hits them—darker colors more than lighter ones. Infrared radiation happens when warmer objects get close to colder ones, such as when you are standing on a cold floor.

Okay, those are the laws. How can you make them work to your benefit and save you some money on heating your home?

Working with the Sun

Sunlight is relatively easy to put to work. In a basic design, sunlight passes through glass and warms the sunspace using a principle called *isolated gain*. The glass is either vertical (such as a window) or sloped at an angle (such as a sunroom's roof or a skylight).

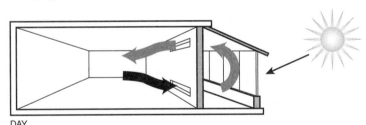

A sunroom uses isolated gain to heat the home day and night.

DAY

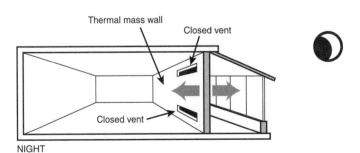

NIGHT

As cats know, it's not always easy to find a sunny spot that isn't too hot. The key is to moderate temperature swings, and the best way to do it is with massive materials such as masonry or water. Throughout the day, the mass collects solar thermal energy; then at night or during cloudy weather this thermal mass releases the heat it holds to warm the sunspace. Well-insulated windows and walls help retain the warm air. Controls such as operable windows, vents, and fans keep the sunspace from overheating. Fans and vents help circulate the warm air to the rest of the house.

def•i•ni•tion

Isolated gain uses a sunroom or other isolated area to develop and distribute solar energy.

Sunspaces can serve three main functions:

♦ Auxiliary heat

♦ Warmth for growing indoor plants

♦ Warmth for living

The design of your sunspace depends on how you plan to use it, as well as how the design fits into your new or existing home. Fortunately, there are many useful resources for planning and installing the best solar space heating system for your home and needs.

Thermal mass in the interior absorbs the sunlight and radiates the heat at night.

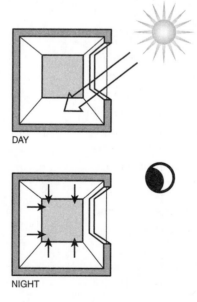

DAY

NIGHT

If its main purpose is to provide heat, you can maximize *direct gain* by using sloped glass, few plants, little thermal mass, and well-insulated end walls. If you live where winters are sunny, carefully sized thermal mass can prevent extreme overheating during the day. Most sunspaces are multifunctional rooms.

def•i•ni•tion

> **Direct gain** is the heat a structure gains directly from solar radiation. Sunlight enters the house through a collector such as south-facing windows. The sunlight then shines on masonry floors and/or walls that absorb and store the solar heat. At night, the room's air cools and the heat stored in the thermal mass is released into the room.

If your sunroom is to serve primarily as a greenhouse, remember that plants need lots of light, fresh air, water, and protection from extreme temperatures. Also consider that a sunspace dedicated to the well-being of plants may not be the most comfortable environment for people.

The third and most popular use of sunspaces is for living. They are sunrooms. They are year-round living areas, so they are designed with minimum glare and only moderate humidity. Carefully sized thermal mass can stabilize temperature extremes and improve the room's comfort level. If thermal mass is installed as a wall or floor, remember not to cover the mass with rugs, pictures, or plants. Let the mass do its job unobstructed.

You might think that designing a sunspace would be easy. It's not. For greatest efficiency, the sunspace, glazing (glass or plastic frames that trap heat), insulation, and thermal mass must all be planned in balance. They must also match the local climate and seasonal changes. You certainly don't want a sunroom that's too hot or cold to use except for a few weeks each year.

> **Sun Spots**
>
> Why include a sunspace in your new or existing home? A well-designed sunspace can provide up to 60 percent of a home's winter heating requirements. In addition, it can offer overnight warmth, summer cooling, and a great place to stretch out and read a book by natural light.

Fortunately, many architects, engineers, and designers have solar design experience—and tools—for the job. Computer software is now available for designing passive solar projects such as sunspaces. Your solar architect will use this software. If you're a computer-literate do-it-yourselfer, check the resources online at SolarHomeGuides.com, including passive solar design software.

Orienting Your Solar Space

In the Northern Hemisphere, the sun tracks along the southern sky. That means an effective sunspace must face south. Due solar south is ideal, but 30° east or west of due south is okay.

If you are retrofitting your home, consider how the sunspace will look on the south side of your house. If the south side of your house faces the street, you'll want to design it so it protects your home's privacy while looking like it wasn't an add-on.

The sun gets pretty low in the winter sky. You don't want trees or plants taller than 10 feet within about 15 feet of a solar window because they will block solar gain. Early morning or late afternoon shade is okay. The most productive solar hours are typically between 10 A.M. to 3 P.M., so trees that don't block the sun's rays to your sunspace during these hours are usually fine. Find your location's solar noon—the moment of the day that divides the daylight hours for that day exactly in half. It's the midpoint between sunrise and sunset.

If possible, locate the sunspace so that the house walls serve as one or both end walls of the sunspace. This reduces heat loss. Also make sure that the sunspace is adjacent to rooms most occupied during the day, such as the kitchen, family living areas, or playrooms.

Solar Eclipse

Clear glass transmits 80 to 90 percent of incoming solar radiation, absorbing or reflecting only 10 to 20 percent. The solar energy is then passed into the room as infrared radiation. (Sounds kind of atomic, doesn't it?) When buying windows, make sure the glass or glazing has high absorption and transmission qualities. Your solar equipment vendor can give you more specifics.

What about the glass or solar glazing? Although sloped glazing collects more heat in the winter, many designers prefer vertical glazing or a combination of vertical and sloped. There's a good reason. Sloped glazing loses more heat at night and can cause overheating in warmer weather. Vertical glazing allows maximum heat gain in winter, when the sun's angle is low, and less gain as the sun rises toward its summer zenith. In addition, vertical glazing is easier to install and less apt to leak, making it a smarter choice for the do-it-yourselfer and a solar retrofit.

Choose the best solar glazing for your home according to your needs and your budget. Glass is more popular because people are familiar with that material. However, newer plastic glazings can be cheaper, stronger, lighter, and easier to install. In addition, some of the latest plastic glazings are actually more efficient than glass at transmitting solar energy while cutting heat loss. The downside is that plastic glazing scratches more easily than glass and is harder to seal.

Better solar glazing has low-emissivity (low-e) coatings. These are thin, almost invisible metal or metal-oxide films that reduce radiant heat loss and gain while dramatically improving a window's insulation value. For example, double-glazed low-e windows are about as energy efficient as triple-glazed windows using regular glass—but they cost and weigh less.

> ### Solar Eclipse
>
> ENERGY STAR (energystar.gov) rates windows, skylogiths, and other glazings by two primary performance ratings. U-Factor measures thermal conductivity. Solar Heat Gain Coefficient (SHGC), called G-Factor in Europe, measures thermal transmission. Think of U-Factor as the decimal fraction of inside heat that passes out through the glazing, and the SHGC as the fraction that passes from the outside in. In both cases, the lower the numbers, the more efficient the glazing.

Special double-glazed windows can also benefit from filling the space between the panels with something other than air. Argon, sulphur hexafluoride, carbon dioxide, and other gases increase the insulating value. Technology continually enhances solar glazing, so ask your supplier or contractor about the latest and greatest. Just remember that it needs to be not only effective, but cost-effective.

Storing Solar Heat

I've mentioned thermal mass but haven't gotten too specific. Let's get down to it. Water is the most efficient thermal mass because it holds the most heat per unit of volume. Homeowners and solar designers have used everything from plastic jugs to 55-gallon drums to hold water as thermal mass. More efficient are sealed columns filled with water and chemicals to minimize mildew. They use the *indirect gain* method.

Though they store only about half as much heat as water, masonry masses can serve other purposes (in floors and walls) and thus are popular thermal masses. The most

def•i•ni•tion

An **indirect gain** passive solar home stores thermal energy between the south-facing windows and the living spaces. The most common is a Trombe (pronounced without the *e*) wall directly behind the window glazing. It collects the heat and passes it into the room

effective are of solid brick, concrete, or stone, 4 to 6 inches thick—the correct thickness for a wall. To enhance the storage of thermal energy, surfaces should be painted black or dark blue. Even a deep red color has an absorption of more than the required 70 percent.

First question: Where should the thermal mass be? In the sunspace's floor and/or the north, east, and west walls. It will collect and store both direct heat from the sun as well as heat from the air in the room.

Second question: How much thermal mass is needed? If the mass is masonry, for every square foot of south-facing glazing, figure about 3 square feet of 4-inch-thick masonry. For a water mass, figure about 3 gallons for each square foot of glazing. For example, for a 100-square-foot south-facing glazing, plan on 300 square feet of 4-inch masonry or a 300-gallon water mass wall. These are just guidelines, so get a solar architect to give you the specifics for your home and location.

A thermal mass or Trombe wall collects and distributes solar heat.

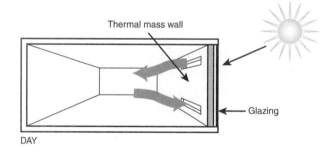

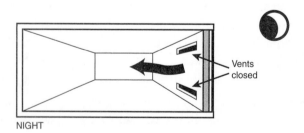

When you've paid good money to trap solar heat in a sunspace and its thermal mass, you don't want to let it get away easily. That means insulating the heck out of the sunspace. Insulate the space's roof, floor, and walls to keep the energy in. Also plan for window coverings and other movable insulation to trap the warm air in the sunspace after Sol has set or on days when he can't be seen.

Distributing and Controlling Solar Heat

There are a couple of ways to distribute warm air from your sunspace to other parts of the house. It can enter the heating system's duct work for distribution or it can move passively. Warm air rises. By designing doors, windows, hallways, and room vents to take advantage of this fact, the air warmed in the sunspace will travel on its own through the house. A strategically placed ceiling fan or two can help push it along.

Also consider a thermosiphon. In a thermosiphon, warm air rises in the sunspace and passes into the adjoining space through an opening high on the wall. Cool air from low in the adjoining space is drawn into the sunspace to be heated. How big of an opening is needed in a wall to take advantage of thermosiphoning? The minimum for a single opening should be about 8 square feet for every 100 square feet of glass area. So a 12-foot long solar glazing wall that's 8-feet tall should have an opening that's at least 2 by 4 feet. Less total opening space is needed if one opening is high and one is low. In that case, the same wall needs only two openings of at least 2½ square feet each if they are 8 feet apart. That's a rule of thumb, easily confirmed or contradicted by passive solar design software measuring your home's conditions.

Bright Idea

How can you take advantage of passive solar design if you live in a cold climate? First, make sure that your building site has no obstructions to the south. Second, choose a design with a long south wall that faces within 15 degrees of true south. Third, include ample thermal mass in your home and consider an earth berm on the north side. Fourth, maximize energy-efficient windows on the south side and minimize those on the east and west sides, with the fewest on the north side of your home. Also install a dark-colored roof that will absorb the greatest amount of winter solar energy. Finally, of course, maximize insulation. Stay warm!

Maybe you've done your job *too* well, and it's getting hot in your sunspace. How can you tell? Plants and people are wilting! The aquarium is boiling! The cat left the room!

Overheating can kill plants and make the sunspace unlivable. To control overheating, you can install operable vents at the top of the sunspace, where temperatures are the highest, and at the bottom, where they are the lowest. You can open and close vents manually as needed or by using thermostatically controlled motors.

If it's impossible to get the warm air circulating through the house on its own, install fans with thermostatic controls to get things moving. Alternatively, you can install climate controls on movable window shades.

Cooling with the Sun

You can get more than heat from the sun. You can also cool your house with it. Actually, the movement of solar-heated air will cool parts of your home. Many passive solar designs include natural ventilation for cooling. Casement or other operable windows for solar gain can also be fitted with vertical panels, called wing walls, on the windward side of the house. These panels can accelerate the natural breeze in the interior to keep the air cooler.

Another passive solar cooling device is the thermal chimney. It works as a fireplace's chimney to vent hot air from the house out through the roof. A solar architect can show you how it actually works and how to control it without losing too much energy.

You also can produce a thermal chimney in your home's attic. Most attics trap hot air. By replacing the roofing tile at the ridge or top of the roof with special venting ridge tiles, you give the attic's hot air somewhere to go—outside. The specially designed ridge tiles or caps allow rising air to exit the attic without allowing rain or snow in. Best of all, you don't have to install a whole new roof to put a thermal chimney in it. Alternately, you can install roof vents to keep attics cooler.

Bright Idea _____

What should homeowners in hot climates do to take advantage of passive solar design? In warm, humid climates, forget thermal mass and, instead, open up the crawl space under the home so that air can flow around the structure. In arid climes, install thick walls to buffer against the sun. Make your home as compact in shape as possible to present the least amount of wall to the southern sun. Build your outdoor living space (such as decks and patios) on the north side of the residence. Plant trees on the east and west sides to block morning and afternoon sun. Also plant trees nearby to absorb the heat and to radiate cooling moisture. Cool ideas!

The Least You Need to Know

- Using the natural laws of solar energy can save you thousands of dollars in future utility bills—and keep you as comfortable as a cat.

- Direct gain uses energy directly from the sun; indirect gain uses thermal mass in the living space; and isolated gain uses a separate air space to store thermal energy.

- Solar glazing is specially designed to take advantage of solar thermal energy and transfer it to your living space with minimum loss.

- Sunrooms can use convection to distribute solar heat without fans.

- Solar energy can also be used to cool your home by encouraging natural ventilation and airflow.

Part 3

Solar Power Systems

See how it works? The sun shines energy onto Earth and a bunch of man-made gadgets turn it into electricity. Nifty!

This part shows you how all those solar components go together into solar power systems. There's one that's right for you. Availabilities include solar power systems to power the entire home, to act as a supplemental or emergency power source, or to power your microwave on a camping trip. We'll cover everything from solar cookers to big systems that will be the envy of your local utility.

Now that you've learned how the components of a solar power system work, you're ready to see how they work as a system—and power your life.

Supplemental Power Systems

In This Chapter

- ◆ Using solar and other energy sources for supplemental power
- ◆ Learning how generator-inverter systems work
- ◆ Using the sun to power outdoor lighting
- ◆ Using the sun to power DC appliances and lights
- ◆ Needing solar power for remote needs

Not every homeowner needs—nor wants—a complete solar power system. The total cost may be too high for your budget. Perhaps there isn't enough local sunlight to energize a full system. Or your home may already have a primary renewable power source. Or maybe all you want is to get power to a water pump, outdoor lighting, or other system. There are several good reasons.

This chapter offers ideas and specifics on how to select a supplemental solar power system. It also covers other power systems that can work with your solar power system to power your home.

Using Supplemental Power

One alternative to investing in a complete solar power system is to use solar energy as a supplemental power system. Let it power your outdoor lighting, supplement power from your local utility grid, or add solar power to your wind or hydropower system.

Typical hybrid utility intertie (grid-tie) system with solar PVs, a wind turbine, and a fossil-fuel generator.

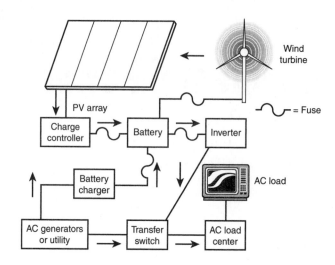

Genverter Systems

Some homes just don't get enough sunlight for a full solar power system. Yet they are off-grid and can't depend on the local utility company. Nor are wind and hydro systems an option. What to do?

Solar Eclipse

Thinking about adding a generator to your power system? Make sure it's portable—or at least can mount on a portable trailer. If your generator needs service, it's cheaper to take it to a mechanic than to have the mechanic make a house call.

The most common power source for homes off the utility line is a gas, diesel, or propane generator. A generator is a mechanical device used to produce DC electricity. Power is produced by coils of wire passing through magnetic fields inside the generator. Combining a generator with a solar power system is a better, more environmentally friendly source than a generator alone. Fortunately, diesel generators now can be operated using biodiesel, a renewable fuel made from vegetable oil—including used restaurant cooking grease. If you don't mind the smell of french fries, biodiesel is a good option.

Some generator power systems operate on demand only. That is, in the evening when lights are needed or throughout the day as a refrigerator's compressor needs power, the generator is turned on to furnish power. For some houses, this can mean that the generator is on up to 16 hours a day producing kilowatts of power when only watts are needed. Not very efficient! Alternatively, a generator system can be on just a few hours a day to charge a bank of batteries that power the home throughout the day and night. It's a smarter option.

Ultimately, an even better system relies on solar power to charge the batteries while the generator supplements solar to keep battery power at needed levels. An automatic control system can even run the generator in the evening when power demands are highest. Appliances will get power directly from the generator, whereas excess power will go to charge the batteries.

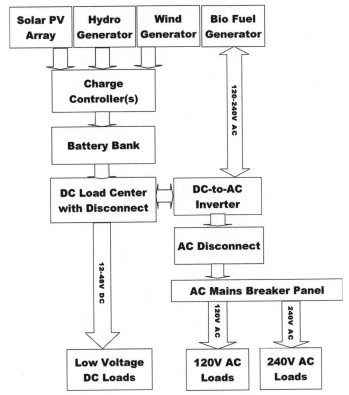

Components of a typical supplemental power system.

The system described is called a generator-inverter-charger-battery, or "genverter" system. It can supplement a solar-inverter-charger-battery or solar power system. Using a battery bank and including solar energy can dramatically reduce the generator size required to help power your home.

Switching between generator, solar, and battery power can be manual or automatic. The most efficient system uses a single controller that not only manages the power sources but also serves as the system's inverter, changing DC to AC. Some power control units can even manage loads for DC as well as AC appliances.

Components

What components will you need for a genverter system? The inverter/controller is the most important—and expensive—component. You'll want one that can handle the power resources you've selected, including the generator, solar, wind, hydro, grid, or whatever. It must be sized to handle the highest anticipated load in kilowatts. Make sure it can manage anticipated DC as well as AC loads.

You'll also need a bank of batteries with cables. How many depends on your system requirements, so refer to Chapter 7 on storing and distributing power for more info.

Other components you'll need include a monitor and an AC distribution panel. The AC panel is probably already in place because it's your home's main panel. The monitor reads voltage and amperage from the battery charger to the inverter. It also stores and reports cumulative data so you can check operating history and manage the system better.

> **Sun Spots**
>
> Greg Dunbar, one of the technical reviewers for this book, tells of moving to the country a couple of decades ago and installing a generator system to supplement solar power. Alas, so did a half-dozen other pioneers. Although all the homes in the valley to which they moved were spaced thousands of feet apart, the sound of generators carries well. During winters, when solar power was unavailable, everyone started a generator to power the home. Soon, all were wondering why they had moved to the noisy country instead of the relatively quiet city!

Cost

What's a genverter system going to cost? If you're simply adding a generator to your existing solar power system, probably not much more than the cost of the generator and wiring. Of course, if you have to resize the system with a new inverter/controller, the cost goes up. A small battery bank (four 24-volt batteries), 2.4 kW inverter, AC panel, monitor, and a fused disconnect will set you back about $3,000. Add to that the cost of the generator.

Electric generators range from small 3 kW units to all-you-need 15 kW generators. The rating is the *maximum* power output. Generator manufacturers suggest that you double your required wattage to come up with the maximum unit you need. Of course, they're in the business of selling generators. You may not have to double your needs, but the unit should provide at least 150 percent of your requirements. The "rated" watts are typically 10 to 20 percent less than the "maximum" watts.

You can purchase a small, portable generator for about $500. However, one that will help power your house will cost much more. A 10 kW stationary generator, for example, will cost about $4,000 plus shipping and wiring. Diesel generators of 15 to 20 kW start at about $8,000. Most households need at least 5 kW to charge batteries and run the washing machine or well pump simultaneously. Generators of more than 10 kW are expensive to run. Don't go bigger than you really need or can use. Generators run most efficiently at about 70 to 80 percent of full load.

How do you choose the right generator for the job? Here are some questions to consider:

♦ What is the total wattage of appliances and equipment that I need to operate?

♦ Will the generator be used with a solar or other power system?

♦ Should the generator be stationary or portable?

♦ Should the generator have a manual or automatic starter system? (Automatic is best unless the generator isn't used often.)

♦ What's the best fuel for this generator: gasoline, diesel, biodiesel, liquid-petroleum gas (LPG), or propane?

♦ How will fuel be delivered and stored for lowest cost and optimum running time between refills?

♦ Do I need more than one power outlet on the generator itself?

In adding up the total wattage of equipment you need to power, double the wattage of anything that has a motor or compressor that turns on. Remember to plan for the future. It will get here very soon!

Bright Idea _____

If you're not sure of an appliance's wattage, use the power formula (from Appendix A): volts × amps = wattage. Check the manufacturer's plate on the appliance (typically on the back or bottom) for the amps. Most household appliances are 110 volt, but manufacturers figure wattage based on the top limit, 120 volts. So a 7.5 amp toaster is 900 watts (120 × 7.5 = 900). Most small appliances draw 1 kW or less of electric power. A water heater is typically 3 kW to 4 kW.

Outdoor Solar Lighting

One popular method of using solar power at home is outdoor lighting. In fact, it's the first place many people start when looking at solar power. Outdoor lighting offers both security and beauty, so it's an important use of electricity. Because it is outside, it's the perfect application for solar electricity. And it's an inexpensive way to try solar power.

Outdoor PV lighting systems use small PV modules that convert sunlight into electricity. The electricity is stored in batteries for use at night. They can be cost effective relative to installing power cables or step-down transformers for relatively small lighting loads.

Several companies now market units for marking or decorating driveways, walkways, and patios. Most of these devices are totally self-contained units that need only to be staked into the ground in a sunny location. Others have the lights separate from the PV module so that it can be placed in a sunny location. Units vary in size and function from small ⅛-inch red glowing pathway markers to pole-mounted patio and high-beam security lights.

Outdoor solar lighting is also being used by governments to add lighting where it's more expensive to run electrical wiring. For example, many roadside emergency phone systems are powered by PV modules mounted atop a telephone post. Solar lighting is used at municipal parks, campgrounds, rest areas, highway signs, and even on billboards.

Home outdoor PV lighting systems are available in hardware, lighting, and discount stores. You can also buy them through environmental companies that sell from catalogs and on the Internet. Most parts of the country have sufficient sunlight to power outdoor home lighting. Even so, make sure the spots where you plan to install the lights aren't too shaded to capture enough sunlight. If they are, consider a system where the PV module is separate from the light and can be placed for optimum energy collection.

Most outdoor solar light units list a specific number of hours of sunlight needed to charge the batteries for overnight lighting. Some only require four hours of direct sunlight, while others need eight hours to recharge. A short charge means that the lights won't be on early in the morning when it's still dark outside. In addition, completely draining the batteries each night will dramatically shorten the life of the batteries.

Remember that outdoor solar lights aren't intended to turn night into day. To keep PV modules small (and costs down), most outdoor solar lights use very small bulbs and refracting lenses to maximize output. Typical units are intended for lighting pathways. If you're trying to light up a driveway or doorway for security, you'll need larger PV modules.

Batteries inside outdoor solar lighting units are nickel cadmium, sealed lead-acid, or lead-acid. Most batteries can be removed and replaced as needed. However, some lighting units use built-in batteries that can't be replaced. Low batteries mean a new lighting unit. Make sure the solar lighting units you purchase have removable batteries.

Solar Eclipse

Winter in many locations means less daytime sunlight. Clouds get in the way. That means outdoor solar lighting won't get as much solar energy to recharge batteries. The total charge may be cut by 30 to 50 percent. It's a good idea to select outdoor solar lighting based on how much sunlight is expected during *winter* months.

Outdoor solar lighting is comparable to anything else: You get approximately what you pay for. Small driveway marker lights can be purchased at large hardware stores for $10 to $20 per light. Stand-alone porch lights range from $25 to $50. Better-quality solar-powered garden path lights cost $50 to $100 each. A solar-sensor porch light that is motion activated to turn on when someone comes near will run around $100. Beyond that, a PV module can be installed to supply power to a wired string of solar outdoor lights.

DC Appliances and Lighting

As covered in Chapter 7, direct current (DC) is electric current that flows in one direction only. Solar, wind, and water power systems develop DC; batteries store DC. Alternating current (AC) is electric current that alternates in direction. AC can travel farther across wires than DC, but cannot be stored. An inverter converts DC into AC. Your supplemental power system budget can stretch farther if it doesn't need an inverter to convert DC solar power into AC for your home. How can this happen? By installing appliances and lighting that run on direct current rather than alternating current.

Many home appliances that are available for AC circuits are also available in DC models. Due to fewer models being available, prices are typically higher. Even among manufacturers that make both an AC and a DC model, the DC version is usually higher in price.

Small stand-alone DC/AC solar power system.

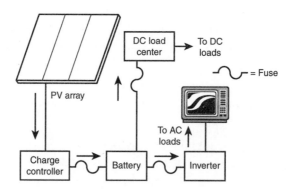

For example, an energy-efficient 16-cubic-foot DC or AC refrigerator can cost about $2,500—twice that of a typical refrigerator. It is designed and manufactured to be highly efficient, drawing less power than comparable units sold at major appliance stores. All you need is two 75-watt PV modules to power the DC refrigerator. Although the initial cost is higher, the operating cost is lower. Of course, prices will come down as more people buy these more energy-efficient appliances.

DC freezers are available, too. Chest models are more popular than upright freezers because they are typically more efficient. One super-efficient model claims that operating costs are just 5¢ a day. In addition, it doesn't use freon or other chlorofluorocarbon (CFC) refrigerants that damage Earth's ozone layer.

Sun Spots

Because fluorescent lighting needs only a quarter of the electricity of incandescent lighting, most DC lights are fluorescent. They also give more light (measured in lumens) than standard lights. Light emitting diodes (LED) offer very low-cost, long-life lighting. LEDs use one third the power of fluorescents to get the same amount of light. Red, green, yellow, and blue are easy to get, but white LED technology is a challenge.

DC can power your home lighting as well. However, DC lights are more expensive than AC lights. A good quality 12-volt DC light "bulb" can cost $20 or more. Fortunately, it typically lasts longer than an AC bulb. DC lights are more popular for recreational vehicles and other low-use applications. They can also be used for emergency lighting systems.

Remote Power

Another practical application of solar technology is powering remote equipment such as pumps. These units are especially popular on large ranches where livestock water pumps are located far away from electrical service. A submersible pump is powered by a PV module installed above ground level. Solar-powered water pumps are rapidly replacing wind-powered water pumps on the plains because they cost one third as much and are far easier to install.

Solar-powered pumps can also move water from a spring or pond to a stream or a tank. In most cases, the pumps use DC electricity, so the DC from the PV module can be applied without an inverter. You can use small solar power systems to power remote well pumps, too.

Solar Eclipse

You can take solar power systems anywhere—even in remote locations. For example, a foldable, 34-watt PV panel can be used anywhere the sun is available to power a mobile radio, a video camera, and other electronic devices. Or it can recharge 12-volt batteries. It weighs less than 5 pounds and it folds down to the size of a book for easy transport! The cost is about $700.

Farmers also use remote solar power systems to power fan blades that keep birds off their crops. Others use large field fans to minimize the effects of freezing temperatures on delicate crops. PV modules are also put to work at remote greenhouses, saving the cost of running wiring for greenhouse lights or fans.

You may not be a farmer, but there are many applications for remote power that PV modules and solar technology can solve for you. Think about it.

What's next? Many people who want solar or other power systems use them as emergency backup. That's the topic of our next chapter.

The Least You Need to Know

- Gasoline, diesel, and propane generators are a popular source of supplemental power for off-grid homes.

- A genverter system can cost-effectively supplement your home's solar power system.

- Many homeowners start their solar experience with outdoor lighting systems.

- DC appliances and lighting are available, but can be costly to purchase.

- Solar power systems are ideal resources for remote equipment such as well pumps and other powered devices that are too far from electrical service.

Grid-Tie Systems

In This Chapter

- Deciding whether net metering is smart for you
- Understanding the interconnection process
- Signing an agreement to sell power to a utility
- Buying and installing a grid-tie solar power system

You've been buying electricity from the local utility for years. In this chapter, I tell you how you can *sell* your excess renewable energy power to the utility. Better yet, you learn how to deposit it into the utility's "bank" and draw it out when you need it.

This chapter isn't for everyone. It's not for solar homeowners who live off-grid. They can't *truck* their excess power to the local utility. It's about installing a solar system and selling *excess* electrical power back to the utility. Due to the cost of systems, most people do not buy large systems to "sell back." And utilities usually only pay full retail rate for your electricity until your meter hits zero.

How Net Metering Works

As you learned in Chapter 2, the Federal Public Utility Regulatory Policy Act says that individuals and businesses that generate excess renewable-generated power can sell it to the local utility at avoided cost through a program called net metering. *Avoided cost* is the minimum amount an electric utility is required to pay an independent power producer, equal to the costs that the utility calculates it avoids in not having to produce that power. It's usually substantially less than the retail price charged by the utility for power it sells to customers. Avoided cost is essentially wholesale pricing. How would you like to get residential retail pricing for the electricity you sell to the utility? Of course you would. That's net metering, and it's good stuff.

Residential solar power systems can be oversized and the excess electricity can be sold to the public utility.

Net metering can dramatically decrease the long-term costs of your solar power system. The Database of State Incentives for Renewable Energy (DSIRE) is a comprehensive source of information on state, local, utility, and selected federal incentives that promote renewable energy. For a good up-to-date listing of net-metering states and the particulars of those individual state programs, check DSIRE's website at www.dsireusa.org.

Is your system eligible? More than 35 U.S. states have net-metering programs that allow you to sell electricity to utilities at residential power prices. In California, for example, Public Utilities Code section 2827 says that all utilities in the state must offer the option of interconnecting on a net-metering basis to residential and commercial customers with PV or small wind systems that produce 10 kW or less of power.

> **Bright Idea** _____
>
> If your state doesn't have a net-metering program, contact your state energy office (listed online at SolarHomeGuides.com) about becoming an advocate and getting laws passed in your state legislature to make it available.

How does it all work? As an eligible customer, you interconnect with your utility and feed your surplus electricity to the utility grid. You can use an equivalent amount of electricity later without additional cost to you.

Normally, your electricity meter spins forward when electricity flows from the utility into your home. Net metering allows the meter to also spin *backward* when your system produces surplus electricity that is not immediately used. Think of it as "banking" your excess electricity on the utility grid.

You could set up two meters, one for incoming power (from the grid) and one for outgoing power (to the grid), but it's simpler to have one meter that moves both forward and backward. The decision of how many meters is made by the utility company and included in your interconnect agreement.

What are the advantages of a grid-tie system? Because there are typically no batteries in the system, there is no battery maintenance, the costs are less than a battery backup system, and grid-tie systems without batteries are more efficient and simpler to install.

What's the downside of a battery-less grid-tie system? If the power grid is down, you won't have electrical power.

A grid-tied battery backup (BBU) system functions exactly as a standard grid-tie system, except that the inverter connects to a battery bank. The solar panels charge the battery bank and excess power is sent back to the grid. If the grid goes down, the inverter disconnects from the grid, draws power from the battery bank, and connects to a Critical Load Center. This center supplies backup power to refrigerators, freezers, and a small number of lights—but no AC loads!

The battery bank can be sized relatively small as compared to an off-grid system, realizing that the backup power will be limited. One disadvantage to this system is that the inverter efficiency is about 91 percent compared to a standard grid-tie inverter of 93 to 95 percent efficiency. Traditionally, a BBU system costs about 20 percent more than a direct-connect standard grid-tie system due to inverter and battery costs.

Diagram of typical components in a grid-tie system that doesn't include DC storage batteries.

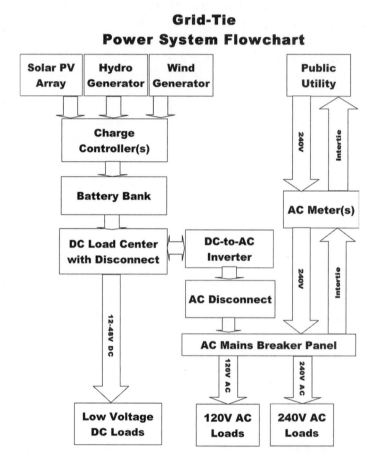

Grid-Tie Power System Flowchart

So what are the disadvantages of a BBU grid-tie system? These systems, as with off-grid battery systems, require periodic battery maintenance. Also, they take more money and time to install than systems without batteries.

Typical grid-tie inverter.

Why would folks at the utility do this for you? First, because the law says they must; second, because thousands of minigeneration systems similar to yours can save the utility from having to build new power plants. Your system becomes a *Small-Scale Renewable Energy System (SRES)*. However, don't expect the utility to make it easy for you.

def•i•ni•tion

A **Small-Scale Renewable Energy System (SRES)** is a system with less than 100 kW of capacity that converts renewable energy (solar, wind, water, biomass, biofuels, and so on) into electricity. A residential solar power system is an SRES. Power systems installed in business and industry also fit the capacity criteria. Together, these systems can replace larger fossil-fuel power systems.

Net metering gives you more value from your home-grown electricity by offsetting your future electricity (retail) purchases rather than selling your excess electricity at avoided cost (wholesale). For example, if you sell your excess electricity to the local utility at 3¢ per kilowatt-hour, then have to buy some back later at 12¢ per kilowatt-hour, you're not making much. However, if you "bank" the surplus on the grid and get it back later, you're both buying and selling at *retail* price.

How your utility deals with billing will vary from state to state, and sometimes from one utility to another. Generally, credit from one month—such as June, for instance—can be rolled over to the next month, or the next. At least once a year, the utilities are required to charge you for the *net* energy consumed by your house during the previous 12 months. Depending on the interconnect agreement you sign, credits may be sold at wholesale or the utility may not pay for them at all.

Exactly how this all works depends on the agreement you sign with the local utility. Your home's electric generation system *must* be certified as a Qualified Facility and you *must* agree to do certain things before the utility *must* buy power from you. However, solar power system contractors and suppliers know about local requirements and can help you with the paperwork and red tape. It helps them sell more systems.

In fact, based on the interconnection agreement you sign and the state's net-metering laws, you can probably afford a larger solar power system than you otherwise could. The system is not only reducing your power bill, it's actually generating some income from any surplus, even though it is at wholesale rates. That means you can size and manage the system to generate a surplus for sale. Again, make sure that your system meets the utility's requirements and doesn't exceed its production limits. The utility wants assistance meeting local power needs—it *doesn't* want competition.

How to calculate cost savings for net-metering systems.

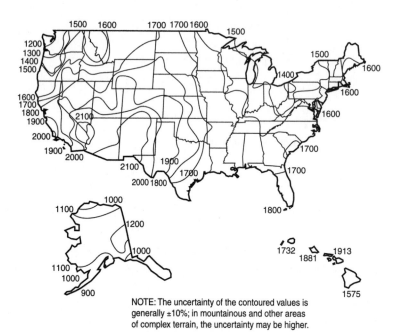

NOTE: The uncertainty of the contoured values is generally ±10%; in mountainous and other areas of complex terrain, the uncertainty may be higher.

The Interconnection Process

What's needed to interconnect your solar power system with the local utility grid? Many utilities have streamlined the process to make it easier for customers to interconnect with the least red tape. Others are still back in the stone (or fossil fuel) age. You'll find the more modern ones may even have an Internet website that guides you through the interconnection process.

A typical interconnection process will include these steps:

1. Complete the application form.
2. Furnish a system diagram and project details.
3. Read and sign a copy of the interconnection agreement.
4. Furnish proof of insurance coverage.
5. Furnish a copy of the approved building permit for the system.

In some locations, the interconnection process will go quickly while in others it may take months. The interconnection process depends on who's managing it, how much pressure is put on the managing department by economic and political powers, how well the department is staffed, and how many other folks are doing what you're doing. Hope for the best, but plan for the worst.

Understanding the Interconnection Agreement

Setting up with your utility a two-way connection that was previously one-way requires that you enter into an interconnection agreement and a purchase-and-sale agreement. Many utilities have developed standardized interconnection agreements for small-scale PV systems. These agreements may be a single contract with your local utility or separate contracts with your utility and your electrical service provider.

The interconnection agreement defines the terms and conditions for connecting your system to the power grid. Included are the technical requirements your system must meet to ensure safety and power quality. The agreement also will spell out your obligation to get all necessary permits, to maintain the system, and to be responsible for the system's safe operation.

The agreement also defines the type of interconnection you and the utility will have. Residential customers usually have a net-metering system in which one meter tracks both incoming and outgoing power. Commercial and industrial customers are often required to set up a dual-metering system, with one meter for incoming power and another for outgoing. It also spells out the utility interconnection standards.

Utility interconnection standards (UIS) tell you what you can and cannot do as you set up a two-way connection with the utility. Mostly, they ensure that the power you deliver to the utility matches requirements and won't cause a system hazard or injure utility workers. That makes sense.

Solar Eclipse

Call your homeowner insurance agent to make sure that there are no clauses that exempt claims from grid-intertie systems. This is new stuff to most insurance companies and you don't want to find out too late that your system isn't covered. Ask questions now.

The most important part of the UIS covers inverters. As you remember from Chapter 7, inverters convert the DC electricity generated by PV arrays into AC electricity used by loads in your home. Grid-tie inverters do even more, managing and conditioning power. They manage and condition power and include protective relays, disconnects, ground-fault protection, and other safety components.

The point here is to make sure that the grid-tie inverter you buy meets the standards required by your utility's interconnection agreement. Most do. Two commonly used standards are from Underwriters Laboratories (UL) and the Institute of Electrical and Electronic Engineers (IEEE). All utilities require UL 1741 certification for grid-tied inverters. Most will also want a lockable disconnect switch between the inverter and main power panel mounted next to the service meter. Grid-tie inverters are available in sizes from 3 to 7 kW. Plan on spending about $800 to $900 per kilowatt for a grid-tie inverter; a 4.3 kW unit will cost about $3,600. Shipping and installation are extra.

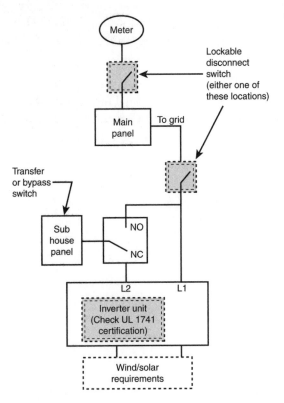

Typical interconnection plan.

Getting Permits

In most locations, you'll need permits from the local building department before installing a PV system. That means you'll need to know—or hire someone who knows—local electrical code requirements. It probably will be based on the National Electric Code (NEC) for residential solar power installations. It's called Article 690.

Before installation, you or your contractor should find out about building permit requirements. Do so at the city or county building department that has jurisdiction for your property. The more you know before installation, the more easily the permit and inspection process will go.

Local building codes may be more stringent for power systems that are being connected to the local utility grid. Inspectors may take a closer look at the installation because they don't want to get into trouble with the utility by approving something that isn't up to snuff. It's also true that your system may get a harder look if it is the first solar installation your inspector has seen. Just make sure that someone (you, your electrician, your contractor, or your supplier) knows the local electrical code well and has installed equipment that meets the UIS requirements.

What you're aiming for is called a sign-off. It's a copy of your building permit with the signature of the inspector who made the final inspection and approved it for use. You can't even switch the system on until you get this sign-off. You'll also need it to get any rebates or buy-downs (covered in Chapter 2) for the purchase and installation of your system.

Buying System Components

The next step is to purchase the components you need for your system. Chapter 16 offers specifics. Components for a typical grid-tie power system (6.4 kWh for five hours of sunshine) include:

◆ 14 130-watt solar PV modules

◆ Module interconnect cables

◆ Module power combiner

◆ Roof or ground mounting racks

◆ Inverter (sized for system)

◆ Miscellaneous components: conduit, electrical tape, connection nuts, bolts, anchors, caulk, etc.

You often can earn a discount for purchasing all components through a single reseller. In addition, you may get assistance in applying for tax credits and rebates (see Chapter 2).

Installation

Installing an interconnection, grid-tie, or net-metering system is similar to installing other solar power systems. The difference is the inverter, which will be a direct connect with or without a battery backup. Depending on the interconnect agreement, a second electrical meter may be required. Fortunately, most homes built during the past couple of decades already have a bidirectional watt-hour meter or electrical meter, so no upgrade is necessary.

The inverter is the key player. In the grid-tie game, there are two types of inverters. They are either designed for intertie with the local utility grid with no battery backup or they are designed to intertie with the utility with battery backup. These inverters are quite different and not interchangeable.

Even folks who don't plan to intertie soon often spend the extra money for a grid-tie inverter— just in case. It's often cheaper and easier to upgrade now than to retrofit later.

For most systems, installation requires placement of the PV array on a roof or requires ground mounting plus installing of the controls in a more accessible location. Most solar power products come with installation instructions. In addition, refer to installation guides produced by federal and state energy departments. Instructions for do-it-yourselfers are included in Chapter 18.

> **Sun Spots**
>
> The inverter you buy will also depend on whether you're installing a battery bank. If you plan to install a battery backup in the near future, consider adding the functionality to your inverter now. Your solar equipment contractor or supplier can give you the specific dollar differences and potential benefits.

Here are some suggested steps for installing a grid-tie solar power system following specifics in prior chapters:

- Size the system for your production needs and budget.
- Verify that the site you select has clear and adequate access to the sun.
- Eliminate tree shading that will reduce system efficiency (see Chapter 6).
- Consider snow and ice buildup in winter.
- Purchase the equipment for your planned system.
- Be sure to follow all mechanical and electrical safety rules.
- Ensure the system is installed according to local electrical and building codes and NEC Article 690 electrical codes.
- Get the system inspected and passed by the electrical inspector.
- Get a final interconnect inspection by your utility company.
- Receive written authorization to commence interconnect operation.
- Turn on your new grid-tie solar system and produce electricity!

The Least You Need to Know

◆ The law requires utilities to offer interconnection to small-scale renewable energy systems.

◆ Net metering allows you to bank your solar power system's excess power with the utility and get it back when needed.

◆ Make sure you know the exact terms before signing an interconnection agreement with a utility company.

◆ Solar and other renewable power equipment must meet certification requirements to allow intertie with a utility grid (grid-tie).

◆ Start the building permit process early so you know the requirements needed for the final sign-off.

13

Off-Grid Systems

In This Chapter

- ◆ Considering a complete solar power system for your home
- ◆ Learning what's included in a stand-alone system
- ◆ Getting an off-grid system
- ◆ Monitoring your solar power system

For some people interested in renewable energy power, the only option is a stand-alone system. There are no utility lines nearby, or it is prohibitively expensive to extend them to their home site. The good news is that thousands of homes are completely energy-independent: off-grid. They don't need no stinkin' power lines. And they can enjoy all the gadgets that their city cousins rave about. They have choices! The rule of thumb is that if you are building more than a half mile from power lines, solar probably is a smart option for you. This is because the utility companies are going to charge you $25,000 to $30,000 to run lines overhead to your property. If they have to go underground, expect that cost to triple! For that kind of money you can install a solar power system.

However, off-grid solar is not for everyone. Do you really want to have to maintain the batteries and possibly a generator? Maybe a $30,000 line extension is better suited to your lifestyle than a $20,000 solar system.

What's a Stand-Alone System?

A solar power system is one or more solar electric components that are engineered and sized to work together. Most are built around the basic component of a solar power system, the single PV module. One or more PV panels electrically connected together are a PV array. Next comes the kit of one or more PV modules plus related hardware, such as mountings and connectors. If you haven't already done so, read Chapter 7 and go over the major components of an off-grid system.

An off-grid PV system typically includes PV modules, optional batteries, and an inverter.

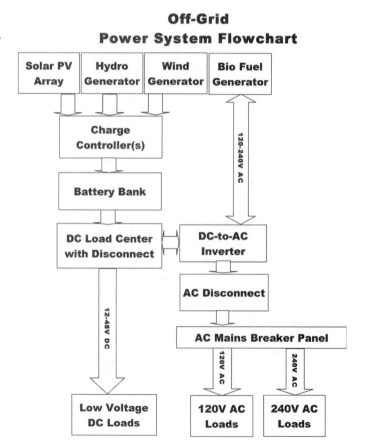

Off-Grid Power System Flowchart

A stand-alone system is designed to produce and distribute solar power to your home. It's often called an off-grid system because the house isn't otherwise connected to the local electric utilities power grid.

The major components of a stand-alone solar power system are PV modules, an inverter, a charge controller, a PV module rack, and batteries. Typically, PV modules make up 40 to 50 percent of the system cost, an inverter is 20 to 25 percent, charge controller is 5 percent or less, racking another 5 percent, and batteries about 10 percent of the total system price. Equipment will cost approximately $8,000 to $10,000 per kilowatt. Installation is more complex than with grid-tie systems, so installation costs are typically twice the price at $3,000 to $4,000 per kilowatt. Often off-grid systems are in the boonies, so you may expect to have to pay the installer drive time. Many off-grid installers of remote systems expect to have to drive up to four to six hours for an installation and they are going to be at your place for a week or more. Expect the relationship to be long-term, as you have a power system and it will need maintenance. Optionally, learn how to install (see Chapter 18) and maintain (see Chapter 19) your off-grid solar power system.

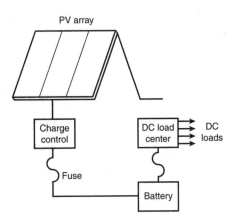

The stand-alone solar power DC system includes few components. An AC system adds an inverter.

Some solar power systems must rely on an electric generator to keep sufficient power in the house. The generator offers a backup source for when the sun doesn't shine enough to provide household power or recharge system batteries. Alternatively, installing a generator in the solar power system means you don't have to size the PV modules for worst-case conditions. In the sunny Southwest, you may be able to get away without a generator, but expect to run very lean for a week or two in December and January. As you move closer to the Canadian border, such as Idaho and Montana, count on running on a generator more often. You'll learn more about generators in Chapter 14.

Efficiency Is a Virtue

Solar is expensive. The best way to reduce your initial costs is to use the most efficient appliances money can buy. For every dollar you spend on an energy-efficient appliance, you can expect to save $3 to $5 on the cost of a PV system. Read Appendix B for information on the yellow EnergyGuide labels and other ways to reduce your home's energy needs.

After lighting with fluorescents and LEDs, start looking at very efficient refrigerators (see Appendix D and SolarHomeGuides.com for supplier resources). A standard side-by-side 19-cubic-foot refrigerator may use 2.5 kWh per day. Even in the sunny Southwest, that is going to cost you $5,000 worth of PV equipment to run. An energy-efficient 19-cubic-foot refrigerator using 4 inches of insulation and dual compressors will use about 1 kWh per day. This means it will cost you about $2,000 worth of PV equipment to run it. The downside of some super-efficient refrigerators is they cost $2,000 to $3,000. Think of the purchase as a long-term investment.

That is why some people opt for a propane refrigerator. Now you've saved several thousand dollars in PV equipment. Propane refrigerators range from $1,000 for an 8-cubic-foot unit to $2,000 for an 18-cubic-foot model. Propane refrigerators are not efficient, but propane is comparatively cheap. Expect an 8-cubic-foot unit to use 1 to 2 gallons of propane a week, and an 18-cubic-foot unit to use 2 to 3 gallons a week. If you calculate costs over a 10-year span, you would have been better off getting an efficient electric refrigerator. The downside of propane is that you must either have it seasonally delivered in tank trucks or fill smaller propane tanks in a nearby town—neither of which is an efficient option.

AC or DC?

Houses on the grid use mostly 110-volt appliances and some 220-volt AC appliances. In the 1970s and 1980s, many off-grid back-to-the-landers used 12-volt DC appliances. That was because the inverters were inefficient and unreliable (recall that inverters turn DC to AC). Twelve-volt appliances were readily available for the RV and automotive market. People would run 12-volt lights, blenders, TVs, hair dryers, and more. They were expensive and not always the best quality, but they worked. By the mid-1990s, inverter manufacturers resolved the issues of reliability and efficiency. Now most PV system designers recommend that the whole house be wired conventionally for 110 Vac (volts AC) and 220 Vac appliances, as modern inverters are much more efficient and cost-effective.

There are still occasions when running equipment DC (usually 12- or 24-volt) makes sense. Remember from Chapter 7 that inverters will lose about 10 percent of your precious PV-generated electricity. In a small 12-volt cabin system—say up to 200 watts—the lights and a water pump can easily run directly off the battery bank. For

larger systems, designers still recommend 12- and 24-Vdc refrigerators, as they run 10 to 12 hours a day. But be aware that plugging a 12-volt appliance into a 120-volt outlet is forbidden and usually accompanied by a pop and smoke puff. If you are using DC equipment, the designer should provide you with plugs and receptacles that will not accept 120-volt equipment. If you are using 12V or 24V lights, make sure the light switches are designed to use DC. Usually the DC switches will make a loud snap indicating the heavier-duty contacts.

> **Solar Eclipse**
>
> Don't plan on saving money by using automotive batteries in your off-grid system. It will work, but not for very long. Even marine batteries don't have longevity when used in a solar power system. You need deep-charge batteries as recommended by your solar power system's supplier.

12, 24, or 48 Volts?

Regardless of whether you use DC appliances, you need to decide which solar power system voltage to go with: 12, 24, or 48 volts. If you are in a mobile application, the decision will be made for you as you have to go with the system voltage you inherit. Most RV and marine systems are 12-volt and few are 24-volt.

For most remote home systems of less than 500 watts, many experts recommend that you use 12 volts. From 500 to 1,000 watts, use 24 volts. For more than 1,000 watts, use 48 volts. Ten years ago, most systems were 12 and 24 volts. Now system designers are using 48 volts even for 800-watt systems. There is no right answer as to which voltage to use. Smaller systems are still using 12-volt appliances. As long as we have RVs and boats, there will be lots of 12-volt appliances. There are fewer 24-volt appliances, but you can still get the important ones, namely lights, refrigerators, and pumps. You'll find that 48-volt appliances are harder to find (see Appendix D and SolarHomeGuides.com).

The reason for the trend to 48 volts is line loss, the amount of electrical power lost in the wire. The higher the voltage, the easier it is to accommodate for line loss. A 1,000-watt array 50 feet from a 12-volt battery bank is going to use a *4/0* copper cable as thick as your thumb and cost $6 per foot. Bump up the system voltage to 48 volts and you can use an *AWG #4* cable as thick as a pencil at less than $1.50 per foot.

def•i•ni•tion

Wire and cable sizes are indicated by a standardized wire gauge system called American Wire Gauge (AWG). The sizing ranges from #40, the smallest, to #0000— also known as **4/0** or "four-oh"—the largest. The larger the wire, the more electrical current it can carry.

The main disadvantage of higher DC voltages is that you have to buy your PV modules and batteries in larger units. If you want to add to a 12-volt system, just add in one more 12-volt module. If you want to add to a 24-volt system, you now need to buy two 12-volt modules and put them in series for 24 volts. For a 48-volt add-on, you now need to add four modules at a time.

Wiring a battery system for 12-volt output.

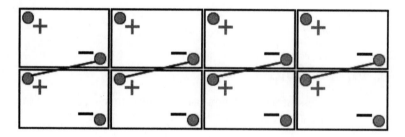

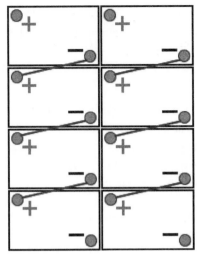

Wiring a battery system for 24-volt output.

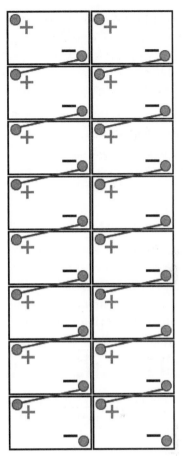

Wiring a battery system for 48-volt output.

Systems with Batteries

Most off-grid power systems require a battery system within. The batteries can keep you from buying utility power when the sky is dark. The batteries also serve as a backup power source.

Unfortunately, a lead-acid battery isn't environmentally friendly and it needs periodic maintenance. The best lead-acid batteries for solar power applications are only about 80 percent efficient and they contain toxic substances. New research improves them, but they are the best that technology has to offer right now.

Stand-alone power systems that use batteries can be purchased as full systems, needing only local wiring and installation to be put to work. They include the PV modules, an inverter/controller, mounts, interconnection cables, and related hardware. The inverter for a direct intertie system is a special model that can both handle intertie to the utility grid and manage the battery system.

A midsize system includes 20 PV modules with mounting hardware, all cables and fuses, the inverter unit, and batteries. How many batteries you need depends on how you're planning to use the battery system. A midsize system may use a bank of six batteries at an additional cost of $2,000 to $3,000 installed. If the home gets "average" solar radiation (5.5 hours a day year-round), it will deliver about 11.6 kWh a day. That's about 75 percent of the typical house's power needs. The package price is around $25,000 plus batteries, installation, and finished wiring. Figure on a total of $35,000.

A larger system with 30 PV modules, the inverter, and everything else (including eight batteries) will run up a bill of about $35,000 to $45,000 including installation. Subtract any rebates or incentives you can get. Add $3,000 to $5,000 for a larger battery bank—even more if you want to go with top-of-the-line batteries that can last more than 20 years with proper maintenance.

The Small Off-Grid System

You can capture enough solar power with a half-dozen PV modules to fully power a small house that has no other electrical connection. Of course, output depends on how much sun the home is getting.

For example, a stand-alone system with four PV modules of about 50 watts each that gets five hours of direct sunlight a day can, theoretically, provide about 1 kWh of power a day. Actually, the modules and system may not be 100 percent efficient. Use the module efficiency factor from the manufacturer to calculate net output. Add in batteries as needed and you have a basic system.

Another system that can provide 1 kWh per day will include a 240-watt solar electric ray, a 1.5 kW inverter with battery charger, enough batteries for a five-day reserve, a controller, and related wiring and safety equipment. Approximate cost (before rebates) is about $5,000.

You can get a system that's four times the size for about three times the money ($15,000). Included is a 4 kWh per day system with 960 peak-watt modules, 16 batteries, a charger, and a controller with wiring.

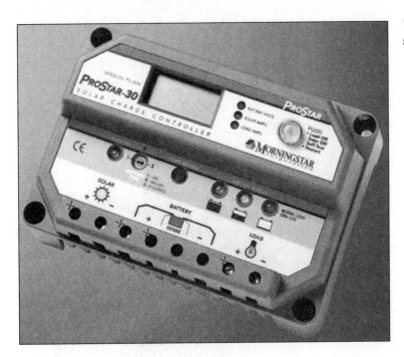

Typical charge controller with meter.

These are examples and guidelines. There are *so many* variables when selecting and installing a solar power system that you really need advice that's specific to your conditions, budget, and economic opportunities. Check Appendix D or SolarHomeGuides.com as well as your local telephone book under "Solar Products—Dealers and Services" for more information.

Sizing Your Off-Grid System

Calculating the size—and cost—of your off-grid solar power system is relatively easy. Here's what you need to know:

- How much electricity you use each month in kilowatt-hours (from electric bills)

- What percentage of the house requires solar power (off-grid without generator = 100 percent)

- How many peak sun hours your home site gets (taking into account how these change with the seasons)

Using these numbers, you can calculate the minimum system size online at affordable-solar.com or with the help of a solar contractor. You also can use the site's power load calculator to see how much you'll save in system costs by simply switching from incandescent to fluorescent lighting or by using ENERGY STAR appliances.

Monitoring Power Production

Technology is amazing! Not only are you about to gather energy from the sun, wind, and water and convert it into electricity, but you can also use technology to manage it. The latest inverter/controllers manage the process of making and storing power. They can also monitor your system. For example, many solid-state inverter/controllers have monitoring systems that can tell you how much power is currently being produced, how much has been produced during a specific period, and how much has been delivered to the utility and/or stored in batteries.

You can also watch it all on your computer! Software is available that monitors and displays system information on PV modules, inverters, battery status, and other data, both current and historical. With it you can see how efficiently your solar power system is working and determine whether there's anything you can do to increase productivity. Maybe you can shut down part of the system when it is not needed, or you can decide whether more PV modules would be a good investment.

In addition, a monitoring system can manage solar tracking motors on the mounts so that the PV modules follow the sun across the sky. Don't expect this technology to be cheap, but it can help you manage a larger home power plant.

Fortunately, you don't have to spend big bucks on a solar power monitoring system. Simpler systems that include voltmeters and ammeters can be installed and mounted in your system for less than $100. Keeping track of your power system can save you money. I'll cover system tracking and maintenance in Chapter 19.

Next, let's consider emergency power systems.

The Least You Need to Know

◆ A solar power system is one or more solar electric components that are engineered and sized to work together.

◆ Some solar power systems are easily installed, while many need additional sizing of battery banks to match home needs.

◆ Generators and even local utility lines can supplement a solar home's power requirements.

◆ Monitoring your solar power system can help you keep it running more efficiently.

14

Emergency Power Systems

In This Chapter

◆ Knowing the difference between an emergency and an annoyance

◆ Planning your power system for an emergency

◆ Finding alternatives to more electric power

◆ Selecting and installing backup power systems

Y2K! It's a term that reminds us of emergencies that don't arrive. Throughout the 1990s, there was much talk about the beginning of the year 2000, everything from inoperable computers to the end of civilization. That was more than a decade ago. Didn't happen.

For those of us who remember it, there were the bomb shelters of the 1950s and 1960s leading up to the Cuban Missile Crisis of 1962. Some U.S. cities saw near panic as people emptied store shelves and headed for safety. Fortunately, disaster didn't happen then either.

What about the next one? Or what about the time when the local utility has a major blackout or brownout and your home is without power? That's when an emergency power system can come in handy. This chapter offers ideas to help you plan for "what if." It helps you decide how much, if anything, you need to invest to get through power emergencies with renewable energy.

Planning for the Worst

If the sun falls out of the sky, your solar power system won't work any longer. However, that won't be the *worst* of the subsequent problems! So let's list some of the things that could go wrong, things we can all agree are emergencies:

◆ The utility company goes bankrupt and there's no one willing to take over power generation. (Hey, it could happen!)

◆ Local utility services are disrupted due to inclement weather, a natural disaster, sabotage, excessive use, or mismanagement.

◆ Your solar power, wind power, or hydropower system is broken and can't supply you with electricity.

On the other hand, here are some *non*-emergencies that fit on a nuisance list:

◆ Your home's power goes off during the final episode of your favorite TV show.

◆ Power goes out overnight and the breakfast milk is spoiled.

◆ The lights flicker and your computer needs to be restarted and digital clocks reset.

◆ Someone hits a nearby power pole and you are without electricity for a few hours.

You get the picture. There are power emergencies and there are annoyances. Fortunately, it's easy and not all that expensive to prepare for annoyances. It's the emergencies that threaten life, health, and economy that require more planning—and more money.

What's an Emergency?

The first step in emergency preparation is defining your version of an emergency. Winters may offer emergencies where you live. If power goes out during a Miami winter, no one will freeze to death. But if it goes out during a Minneapolis winter, you could have a *real* emergency. What are the chances?

Most regions of the country draw inclement weather and natural disasters of one kind or another, including hurricanes, tornados, ice storms, floods, earthquakes, and blizzards. Even though local power companies know about and prepare for emergencies caused by these natural phenomena, they can't *guarantee* uninterrupted service. It's up to you to analyze the risks and take appropriate action—or sit in the dark.

If the local power service is frequently interrupted, a backup system may be a good investment, as a long-term outage could become an emergency. For example, if you're 12 miles from the closest power pole, you may want a backup power generator for bad weather protection.

If you live in areas where clouds can move in for months at a time (such as Seattle), your solar power system may need an emergency backup system. You might at least want to consider staying connected to the public power grid.

Of course, the duration of the power outage is important. A closed refrigerator can keep foods from spoiling for 6 to 24 hours or more, depending on its insulation. If an outage lasts much longer than that, you'd better start eating stuff. An evening without electricity can be cozy—once a year. But once a week can cut into your lifestyle and become a real inconvenience—perhaps still not an emergency, but possibly a health or economic hazard.

Then there's the cost. How much will an emergency power system cost to plan, install, and operate? There are lots of variables here. If you're simply adding batteries to your solar power system, the cost may be minimal. But if you need to install a full solar power, wind power, or hydropower system as emergency backup, the cost could be many thousands of dollars.

Solar Eclipse

If your business is in your home, you should especially consider what sources you have for emergency power. Land-line telephones will probably work, but you won't be able to send or receive faxes or check your e-mail, both of which require 120-volt electricity. VoIP (Voice over Internet Protocol) phones will work only if there is electrical power and an Internet connection.

So the first step in developing your home's definition of an emergency is to consider these questions: What can't you live without and for how long? When does a nuisance become an emergency? Think about it for a while and ask others in your living group to come up with what would constitute a true emergency in your home.

What Do You Need?

How much power must your emergency system provide—and for how long? Finding the most accurate answer can save you money. Because refrigerators and freezers use more power than most home appliances, they are a prime consideration when designing an emergency power system. A standard refrigerator can use up 3 kWh to 5 kWh of power a day. A generator that can keep the fridge operating may cost as much as the appliance. So it's wise to invest in the most efficient refrigerator and/or freezer you can. It will mean your emergency power system doesn't need to be as powerful.

Alternatively, you can have a small backup refrigerator that can run on batteries, propane, or some other power source that isn't so interruptible. It should be large enough for the necessities. Or you may prefer a propane freezer to keep your investment in TV dinners from spoiling during an outage.

Next comes heat. If you're living in Buffalo, New York, and there's a winter power outage, heat will be high on the list of things you don't want to do without for more than a couple of hours. In Tucson, Arizona, the reverse is true if the outage occurs during the summer months; having no air-conditioning in August may be a major problem. You can size your emergency power system for such events. Or you can plan on alternatives, such as using a woodstove or propane heater for heating or battery-powered fans for cooling.

The same is true for lighting. Rather than buying a generator or installing batteries to keep the home lights burning, consider candles, propane cylinder lights, battery lanterns, or other resources. Having several powerful flashlights on hand is a good idea, too. They may save you from needing to buy an oversized generator or battery bank.

Cooking, of course, is also an issue when the power goes out. There's always going out to eat, but that's going to get old fast—not to mention expensive. Rather, if you need to plan for emergency cooking, consider a small propane cylinder cookstove or even a solar oven. Both are relatively inexpensive—compared to a generator—and will serve your basic needs during an emergency.

So, what else can go wrong? You can lose communications. Fortunately, standard telephones have their own built-in power, which means they work even when your home power is out. Cordless phones may not work without battery backup. However, if you depend on them for your health or livelihood, backups are available. Consider a cell phone if you live where even telephone service goes out during an emergency, such as an ice storm.

If you're in the country and power goes out, you may not get water from your well. Water pumps usually run on electricity. A backup could be a solar-powered water pump, an uninterruptible power supply (or UPS, which we'll talk about in a moment), or even a hand pump just in case the water delivery system stops.

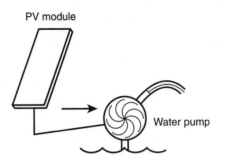

PV module

Water pump

A PV module can power a remote water pump, saving wiring.

After you determine your emergency power system needs, you can better select from the many options that are available. Check catalogs such as those listed in Appendix D and SolarHomeGuides.com for additional ideas and products for emergency preparedness. You can get everything from a water filtering system to a portable solar oven.

Calling for Backup

Your emergency power options depend on your needs, your primary power source, and your budget. Fortunately, you can select and install a backup power system for just a few hundred to a few thousand dollars.

UPS

Let's start small. If you're most concerned about a computer going down, get an *uninterruptible power supply* (*UPS*). These are battery systems installed between the power plug and your PC. When everything is going along well, the power is serving your PC *and* charging the UPS. When the power goes out, the UPS takes over and the PC never knows the difference. Alternately, you can switch from a desktop to a laptop computer. Most laptops have a built-in battery that can power your web surfing for two to five hours. If more time may be needed, consider having a standby battery unit as well—or minimizing your surfing.

def•i•ni•tion

An **uninterruptible power supply (UPS)** is a power supply capable of providing continuous uninterruptible service; it normally contains batteries to provide energy storage.

A UPS has a time limit, however. You may get 6 hours, 12 hours, or even 72 hours of battery life, depending on which you buy. The longer the life, the higher the cost. The life also depends on how much juice your PC needs. Also, turning off the printer or other connected hardware (such as a scanner or fax) when the UPS is needed will increase the number of hours you can run your PC.

A UPS can be used for other important household appliances. If you have frequent outages—or think you might—and don't want to lose that freezer full of prime steaks, consider a UPS for it. Get the appliance's power requirements from the manufacturer's plate (typically on the back) and shop for a UPS that will exceed requirements for whatever period you think you'll need it.

UPS units are also popular with those who have home health equipment that cannot be without power, such as an oxygen system or a dialysis machine. Some of these units have built-in backup batteries, but their life span may be shorter than the outage. At just a hundred dollars or so for smaller units, a UPS is good insurance. Get them at larger hardware or computer equipment stores. Be aware that the batteries in all UPS units will need periodic replacement. Three years is about average; five years is the maximum. Don't expect your 10-year-old UPS to function without routine maintenance and battery replacement.

Generators

Many folks install generators to increase the available power because their solar or other power source just doesn't deliver enough juice. Others install generators as backup for emergency use only. The difference between the two is function and size.

A small-to-medium-size backup generator can be purchased and installed for less than $1,000. The keys to buying the best backup generator for the situation are your emergency power requirements and the generator's fuel source. A light-duty generator is about 6.5 kW or less in power at 3,600 revolutions per minute (RPM). Large commercial generators and quieter models run at half the speed (1,800 RPM). Generally, the slower the speed, the longer they last. Generators are definitely in the "you get what you pay for" category, so don't skimp if your power depends on it. Do follow the maintenance schedule and change the oil by the book.

Earlier chapters guided you in sizing solar and other renewable power systems. So by now you have a pretty good idea of what power you really *need* if something bad happens to your primary power source. For example, you may decide that an "emergency" is more than 24 hours without electricity, at which time you'll need 1.2 kW of power for at least five days. In this case, a backup generator may be your best choice.

Emergency Power System Flowchart

Components of an emergency or backup power system.

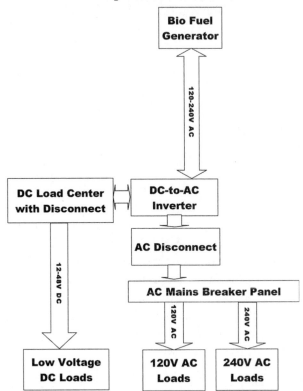

Bio Fuel Generator

120-240V AC

DC Load Center with Disconnect — DC-to-AC Inverter

12-48V DC

AC Disconnect

AC Mains Breaker Panel

120V AC   240V AC

Low Voltage DC Loads   120V AC Loads   240V AC Loads

Sun Spots

Those Californians who seemingly erred by buying generators for Y2K were ready for the rolling brownouts that followed (thanks to Enron). Soon, snickers evolved into polite requests from their neighbors and friends to plug in. However, when the brownouts were history, friendly requests turned into demands to "turn that noisy thing off!"—until the next emergency.

You can purchase a small 2 kW pull-start gas-operated backup generator for about $500. If power goes out, you fill the tank, start it up, turn off any unnecessary circuit breakers, and plug it into the main power panel. If you're powering only a couple of vital appliances, you can run a power cord from the generator to the appliances. Of course, you want to keep the noisy, smelly generator outside and away from the house.

A few words of warning: A fossil-fuel or biodiesel generator is powered by an internal combustion engine. That means thousands of explosions are going off inside it every minute. Make sure the generator you select has an automatic shutoff in case of overheating. Also, be sure that there are no fuel leaks or faulty wiring that can start an *external* combustion!

A larger 5 kW or 10 kW backup generator will nick your wallet for $2,000 to $5,000 installed, depending on whether it has autostart (which requires a battery), has lots of electrical outlets, or has a large fuel tank, and how quiet you want it. The quieter generators typically are more expensive.

What fuel should you use? Again, it depends on how much power you need and for how long. If you're buying a small, once-a-year backup generator, gasoline is the most popular and readily available fuel source. But remember gasoline loses volatility (goes bad) after a month or two even with a chemical stabilizer added to it. So drain out the gas after use or expect a sticky, nonstarting mess next winter. If you need more power or longer running time, diesel fuel or biodiesel is less expensive than gas. Though not quite as easy to get, it will last a year or more in a storage tank. The preferred fuel for long-running generators is propane. It burns cleaner than fossil fuels, though it can be more expensive, depending on the quantity purchased. Propane lasts a long time; it can be delivered in bulk; and, if you are heating with propane, the fuel can do double duty—triple duty if you are using a propane refrigerator. Propane generators are a little more expensive. Check around; prices will vary.

Additionally, your fuel choices may be limited. Biodiesel or natural gas may not be available in your area. Or a fossil-fuel generator may make too much noise for quiet neighborhoods.

Legally, your local building code may not allow you to wire your generator system into the main power panel in your home. You probably need a licensed electrician for this job. However, you can save some money by getting the generator in place and ready for the electrician.

Battery Banks

Generators are great workers—when they work hard. They're happiest when they deliver about 80 percent of their capacity. A 2 kW generator prefers to deliver about 1.6 kW. It's not very efficient to use a generator to deliver 1 kW or less of backup power. Batteries, however, aren't as picky.

We've talked about batteries before (in Chapter 7). However, selecting and sizing a *battery bank* is different for a backup power system than for an off-grid application.

If you're installing a solar or other renewable power system, a battery bank makes sense as a backup. Even if you're not ready to invest in a battery bank for your solar power system, spend a few extra bucks on an inverter that includes a battery charger and controller for the day when you do add batteries. You probably will.

How many batteries? Again, determine what load you'll need the batteries to cover and buy enough to at least meet that power goal. It's better if batteries exceed your power needs so they don't run low and damage the cells. Also, you'll probably want to increase the load someday. But don't install 24 batteries when 12 will do the job just fine. It's a waste of money. Your solar power system provider and/or your local utility can help you select the most cost-effective backup battery bank.

def•i•ni•tion

A **battery bank** is a group of batteries wired together to store power in a solar electric system. It allows you to use the stored power at night, on cloudy days, or to run more power than the array can produce at one time.

Bright Idea

Batteries are available as 2-volt, 6-volt, and 12-volt. Prices typically are based on how much electric current (amps) a battery can store. Check with local hospitals and others who must have backup batteries; they sometimes sell used (but still good) batteries for a fraction of the new cost.

Should you choose 12-volt or 24-volt? The nominal voltage of your system depends on the system size. Small to medium systems with mostly DC loads can use 12-volt system output. However, the PV modules and loads can't be far from the battery bank because of high line loss. Medium to large systems typically require 24-volt output to cut line loss. For big systems, consider 48-volt system output.

Whether your system voltage output is 12-volt or 24-volt, you'll probably use either 12-volt or 6-volt batteries. Smaller systems can use 12-volt batteries; as battery capacity (and weight) goes up, the batteries tend to be sliced into 6-volt sizes, so they're still manageable physically. Connecting batteries in series (positive to negative) increases the output voltage. Connecting them in parallel (positive to positive, negative to negative) increases the output current.

Connecting 6-volt and 12-volt batteries for 12-volt and 24-volt output.

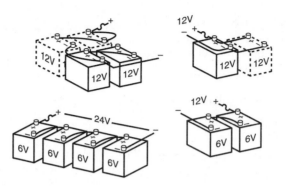

Other Renewable Backup Systems

If you're thinking about a backup source for your home's solar power system, consider other renewable resources. Chapter 8 offered more information about wind power and hydropower. Deciding which option is right for you will take some knowledge of what other renewable resources are available in your piece of the world. For example, observation may tell you that, even if the sun doesn't shine on a specific day, there's always wind on a nearby high spot. Or your property may get lots of stream water during the winter, when the sun isn't as efficient for you. So consider a wind turbine generator or a small hydroelectric power system. These can provide emergency power when the sun doesn't shine.

If you have other renewable backup power systems available, combine them with a battery bank for greatest efficiency. Then the wind or water can help keep the solar power's battery bank charged. It can give you enough juice to get through any emergency. If not, there's always a backup-backup generator!

Want to use solar power for your *other* home? Chapter 15 offers dozens of ideas for adding solar and other renewable power sources to your recreation vehicle, cabin, or other residence. It also offers ideas for apartment dwellers who want to take their solar power system with them from place to place.

The Least You Need to Know

◆ An emergency is an event that can cause health or safety problems if electric power is interrupted.

◆ It's important to first define what constitutes a power emergency for *your* home.

◆ Consider lower-cost power sources to meet potential emergencies.

◆ Size your emergency system based on current and future needs.

◆ Select the most cost-effective (and ecologically friendly) emergency power system for your home.

Chapter 15

Portable Power Systems

In This Chapter

- ◆ Taking solar power on the road
- ◆ Providing solar power for boaters
- ◆ Having solar power for apartment dwellers
- ◆ Cooking with solar energy
- ◆ Designing a portable PV system for use in remote locations

Solar power on the go! Nope, you don't have to have a stationary site for your solar electricity system. It can be mounted on a travel trailer, motor home, or boat or it can be one that you pack up and move with you from apartment to apartment. It can even be small enough to carry wherever you go!

This chapter offers information and ideas to help you become even more energy-independent. Imagine taking many of the comforts of home with you yet being miles from the nearest electrical outlet. You can make it happen—with portable solar power systems.

Taking to the Road: Solar RV Systems

I've owned a number of recreational vehicles (commonly known as RVs) over the years, shunning RV parking lots for remote sites where no one but tenters usually camp. I've used generators and batteries to make living more independent, but many people today are replacing fuel burners with solar power systems.

Most folks who RV are looking for a way to have dependable electricity while enjoying nature where trees are more plentiful than power receptacles. Solar power systems offer the nearly perfect solution. RVs already run on 12 Vdc. Most don't need much power compared to the typical house. They usually have enough roof space to mount PV modules. And they are less expensive—and quieter—than a generator.

Because batteries are charged when traveling, RVs depend mostly on the vehicle's alternator as the primary power source. Power to charge the battery bank is also provided through a converter when plugged into the utility at home or in a campground. However, for those of us who like to spend days, weeks, or even months without driving or plugging in, photovoltaics can mean freedom.

PV modules can be mounted atop recreational vehicles for portable power.

Fortunately, a PV array can put as much power into your batteries during a day as a small gas or propane generator. Of course, generators can run at night when PVs can't. By sizing and monitoring your solar power system, you don't have to return to "civilization" until you want to. Nor do you have to put up with the noise of a fuel- or wind-driven generator.

Bright Idea

Going on a camping trip with your solar-powered RV? Remember to ask campground hosts if sites are available that offer unobstructed solar access for your PV modules. Alternately, you can use a portable PV rack that you can place up to 100 feet away from your rig.

Most RVs can get sufficient power from one to three PV modules. Of course, the exact number and power rating depend on how much electricity your home-on-wheels needs. As with estimating home power needs, you need to total the wattage of all appliances and lights you use each day as well as the average number of hours used. You want watt-hours (Wh) or kilowatt-hours (kWh). A chart for estimating power needs is included at the end of this chapter.

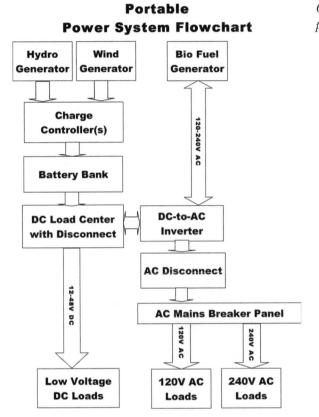

Portable Power System Flowchart

Hydro Generator · Wind Generator · Bio Fuel Generator · 120-240V AC · Charge Controller(s) · Battery Bank · DC Load Center with Disconnect · DC-to-AC Inverter · AC Disconnect · 12-48V DC · AC Mains Breaker Panel · 120V AC · 240V AC · Low Voltage DC Loads · 120V AC Loads · 240V AC Loads

Components of a typical portable power system.

Unfortunately, RV air conditioner systems take a lot of power. If you need to run them, you'll probably have to start an onboard generator to supply large amounts of AC power. Microwaves don't take as much power to operate, but they need AC from an inverter or an AC power utility plug. Most RV refrigerators can run on AC, DC, or propane. Microwaves require AC electricity.

Another part of your power calculation is estimating how much solar radiation you'll be able to collect on the road. That is, if you winter in Arizona's desert, you may get eight or more hours of quality solar radiation. If you're planning a winter trip across Canada, however, available sunlight will be less. If you don't really *know* where you'll be (you nomad, you!), plan for a worst-case scenario. Your system can always turn itself off if you get too much solar power for the day.

One good thing about mounting PV modules on an RV roof is that the RV can be turned to capture the best solar radiation. Most installers mount modules flat on the roof. This means you will get less juice from the sun but it is much more convenient, as you don't need to risk falling as you clamber up and down your RV to adjust the angle of the PV array. If you prefer to park under the trees but still want solar power, consider a portable ground-mounted PV array and enough cable or extension cord to get the power to your RV.

Mobile and stationary PV installations use the same equipment (PV, controller, and batteries) except for the inverter. A mobile application inverter is designed to work with a floating ground (the zero or ground wire isn't attached to a ground point, such as a pipe in the ground). Inverters for homes are designed for a static ground (connected to a ground point). If they sense a floating ground, they see a ground fault signal and shut down. Only buy a marine or RV-rated inverter for your mobile application.

Portable ground mounts can be used to generate PV electricity nearly anywhere.

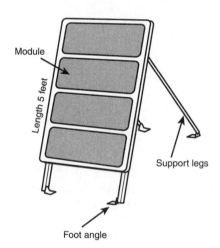

When mounting portable PV modules, make sure you set them to the optimum angle.

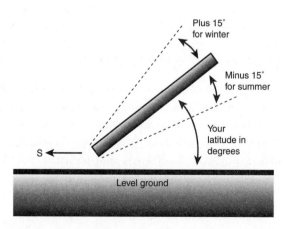

For example, a basic solar power system for your RV will look like this:

- 130-watt PVC module

- Charge controller

- Mounting kit

- #10 AWG wire

That's it. There's no inverter, so the costs are kept down. However, it only powers 12-volt appliances and lighting. Price? About $1,000. The system can be installed in just a few hours.

Of course, you want to plan your entire electrical system—not just the solar part—if you plan to travel to the boondocks very much. That is, your battery bank should be sized for long-term visits to the world without utilities. The same goes for your fresh- and waste-water systems. Most RVs are built for a weekend or up to a week away from services. If you're planning longer, make sure your RV power and services are up to it. Fortunately, an RV without a generator has room for more tanks or equipment.

Solar Eclipse

Remember to turn off unnecessary lights and other power users in your RV. Think about energy efficiency (see Appendix B) in your home away from home just as you would in your regular home.

Also look at alternatives for any electrical equipment in your RV that takes lots of power. Consider fans instead of an air conditioner. Try a solar oven or do your cooking over an outdoor campfire. Planning ahead can help you stay on vacation longer.

Taking to the Water: Solar Power for Boaters

Another popular recreation vehicle is, of course, the boat. It's used for sailing, water skiing, cruising, fishing, and just relaxing on the water. *Outdoor* activities. That means the sun is shining—you hope—and you can take advantage of it! Many boaters rely on small, portable solar power systems to furnish electricity and to recharge batteries. They're similar to the ones that land-bound RVs use.

For example, a marine solar power kit will be similar to the RV kit (discussed in the preceding section) except that it may have two 80-watt PV panels that can more easily fit on the foredeck or cabin roof. Cost will be about the same: $1,000.

Boaters and RVers also use solar showers. A specially designed bag is hung where the sunlight can heat up the water inside. When ready, open the spigot and enjoy warm water that doesn't need fossil fuel. Of course, follow directions on the unit to make sure you don't get scalded. Larger solar shower units can be built into boats and land RVs.

Cooking with Solar Power

The sun gets hot! Hot enough to fry an egg? Yes, and then some. In fact, a solar cooker can reach 600°F!

If you're looking for ways to cook away from home, leave the portable grill in the garage and try a solar cooker (also called a solar oven). A simple solar cooker is available for less than $40 and folds flat to a 13-inch square for portability. The kit also includes a 3-quart cooking pot. It was originally designed for distribution to developing countries where fuel shortages are an ongoing problem.

Prices go up from there. A rugged solar cooker with oven and built-in thermometer can cook most anything. Cooking temperatures range from 350 to 400°F. When preheated, the unit can cook a cup of rice in less than 45 minutes. The cost is less than $100 for a basic model, and solar cookers are available through renewable resource catalogs (see Appendix D and SolarHomeGuides.com for a list).

Sun Spots

For those who depend on fuel wood, it takes about 2 pounds of wood per person each day to cook one's food. For a family of five, that's 3,650 pounds—nearly two tons—of wood a year! In 40 of the world's poorest countries, more than 70 percent of the fuel comes from dwindling supplies of fuel wood. The good news is that with sunshine, there is a simple alternative to fire for cooking. In many developing countries, solar cookers can be used 200 to 300 days a year. In addition, solar cookers can be used to pasteurize contaminated water for drinking. They are being distributed in Kenyan refugee camps and other places around the world free of charge. Part of the purchase price of a Solar Cookit (solarcooking.org) goes toward supporting low-cost distribution in Third World countries. Solar cookers can make a difference!

Portable PV Systems for Remote and Apartment Living

Small, portable solar power systems are available for powering your remote cabin, your RV, a boat, or any other location away from power plugs. One such system can produce and deliver up to 12 amps of DC electricity. An inverter can be added to power AC equipment. Add a battery and you have a full system. The final cost depends on how many PV modules are needed, but a portable solar power system can be built for less than $1,000. Most solar power catalogs have a system like this.

Another system includes a 10-watt PV module, battery, inverter, and carrying case for less than $700. It doesn't provide much electricity, but can power a laptop computer, video, global positioning system (GPS) unit, sound recording equipment, or communication equipment from the top of any mountain—or anywhere the sun shines. A larger system costs about $1,000 with PV modules and weighs less than 100 pounds—more "transportable" than "portable."

There are also PV modules specifically designed to power a laptop computer. The cost for a basic unit is less than $200. Or you can add a solar charger to your car's battery for less than $50. Lots of neat things are coming on the solar market every month.

A portable solar power system can be used to bring backup or emergency power to your home or temporary housing such as an apartment, campsite, or remote location. If your power needs are modest, you can use a solar power system to power communications equipment from the top of Mount Everest—it's been done! Or you can use it to cut power costs in your apartment. Solar power offers many options.

In addition, portable PV systems are useful for those who want solar power but don't own their dwelling. Perhaps a landlord doesn't want tenants installing PV modules on the roof and rewiring the electrical system. For these nomads, PV systems must be portable as well as efficient.

Smaller systems can be used to power some appliances to reduce the need for utility power without permanent wiring. Larger PV modules can be installed on frames on the ground to feed an inverter, battery bank, or both. Within a few hours, the units can

Solar Eclipse

Before installing any portable solar power system, read your rental agreement carefully. Make sure your landlord, local zoning board, or neighbors don't object to your portable ecology. You may not be able to attach any solar panels to structures with screws or nails. Include your solar power equipment in your rental agreement or lease.

be disconnected and loaded up for the move—leaving the apartment or rental house undamaged.

Designing Your Portable Solar Power System

Let's take a closer look at plans for typical portable solar power systems. They will give you an idea of what you'll want in your own portable system.

One popular application is a weekend cabin. If it's built in a remote location, electric utilities may not be available or may be prohibitively expensive. So the first question to ask is: AC or DC? If your cabin has or requires only minimal electrical lighting and only a small appliance or two, a DC system may be the best. It's the least expensive because, as you've learned, solar PV cells provide DC electricity. No conversion is needed. You don't need to buy an AC inverter.

> **Solar Eclipse**
>
> Solar-powered refrigerators are now available for remote locations such as weekend cabins. With an 80-watt solar PV panel, the specially designed chest-style refrigerator has a capacity of 5.8 cubic feet (163 liters). Cost with a PV panel is under $2,000.00.

A DC-only weekend cabin system would require a couple of 12-volt PV solar panels wired in parallel (positive to positive, negative to negative), a fused disconnection, a couple of 6-volt batteries wired in series (negative to positive), and a 12-volt circuit breaker panel. The system could power a 12-volt DC refrigerator, radio, and lights. A simple system will cost less than $1,000.

An AC weekend cabin system requires the addition of an inverter that converts DC into AC. The circuit breaker also needs to distribute both DC and AC electricity safely. And you'll need twice as many batteries. Then you'll be able to plug in an AC TV or radio, maybe a low-watt microwave, a small refrigerator, and possibly a computer. Size the system for the largest expected load. Use the following worksheet to help figure out what you'll need. Plan on spending $2,000 to $4,000 or more for an AC weekend cabin system.

If you need more power than a PV system can furnish to your cabin's site, consider a generator or other backup system as covered in Chapter 14.

What's next on the agenda? Save some money and get the best equipment you can afford by learning how to buy cost-effective solar components and systems in Chapter 16.

Electrical device	Device watts	X	Hours of daily use	X	Days of use per week	÷	7	=	Average watt-hours per day
		X		X		÷		=	
		X		X		÷		=	
		X		X		÷		=	
		X		X		÷		=	
		X		X		÷		=	
		X		X		÷		=	
		X		X		÷		=	
		X		X		÷		=	
		X		X		÷		=	
		X		X		÷		=	
		X		X		÷		=	
		X		X		÷		=	
		X		X		÷		=	
		X		X		÷		=	
		X		X		÷		=	
		X		X		÷		=	
		X		X		÷		=	
		X		X		÷		=	
		X		X		÷		=	
		X		X		÷		=	
		X		X		÷		=	
		X		X		÷		=	
		X		X		÷		=	
		X		X		÷		=	
		X		X		÷		=	
		X		X		÷		=	
		X		X		÷		=	
		X		X		÷		=	
		X		X		÷		=	
		X		X		÷		=	
		X		X		÷		=	

Make sure you calculate all electric devices when planning a portable PV power system.

The Least You Need to Know

◆ Because RVs already have a DC power system, they are a good application of solar PV modules and electric power.

◆ One of the lowest-cost applications of solar energy is cooking—and solar cooking is being done around the world.

◆ Portable solar power systems can be built to move from apartment to apartment.

◆ A weekend cabin can be powered by a DC or inverted-AC solar power system that brings home to the woods.

Part 4

Solar Power Projects

So many options! And there's more. Next you need to figure out whether you will install your solar power system yourself or hire someone else to do it.

Don't be intimidated. Solar power systems are not that difficult to install—once you have a plan. Fortunately, manufacturers and suppliers know how it's done and can share their knowledge with you.

This part lets you in on how to buy solar power systems and components, and either hire a qualified contractor or figure out whether you can install some or all of the system yourself. When it's working, you'll learn tips and techniques for maintaining your solar power system for many years to come.

Chapter 16

Buying Solar Systems and Components

In This Chapter

- ◆ Figuring out what components you need
- ◆ Finding lots of sources for solar equipment
- ◆ Hiring the best equipment supplier
- ◆ Taking delivery of your solar equipment

So you're going to take the solar plunge, eh? You've decided to buy solar power components or a full system. Now what?

Good question. This chapter covers purchasing the various components in a solar power system and guides you toward finding the right supplier—and the right price. The following chapters will show you how to install or hire someone to install your solar power system.

Solar Power sans Batteries

What's included in a solar power system? As you've learned, it depends on what type and size solar power system you've selected. Systems vary greatly due to variation in size and run times of loads. The heart—the PV module—can be as small as a single 5-watt or as large as a 40-plus module array. And all the interconnections with your existing system add to its complexity.

Make sure you know exactly what components you'll need for your solar system.

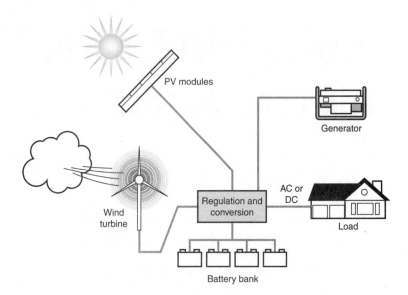

If you're buying a predesigned solar package or hiring a contractor or supplier to design the right system, your job is easier. All you need to do is ask questions such as, "Do I really need an oversized inverter if I don't expect to add to my array?" Those kinds of questions can save you bucks. And now that you've learned how solar power systems work, you know what to ask!

A typical photovoltaic system is a complete set of components, including the array and balance of system components, for converting sunlight into electricity by the photovoltaic process. However, most PV systems have common components. Only the largest systems have them all. Here they are:

◆ **PV panels or modules:** Generate electricity from sunlight. Popular brands include Kyocera, Evergreen, Sharp, Sanyo, BP, GE, Shell, and UniSolar. Voltages include 6, 12, 16, 20, 24, 30, 40, 48, and 50 volts per panel.

- ◆ **Mounting hardware:** Supports and aims PV modules toward the sun. Types include ground, roof, pole, and RV mounts. Also available are solar trackers, either active or passive.

- ◆ **Inverter:** Changes low-voltage DC to high-voltage AC. Primary types are grid-tied, off-grid, and RV/marine. Grid-tied inverters must match the 60 Hz AC phase to the grid. Popular brands include Sunnyboy, OutBack Power Systems, Xantrex, and Fronius.

- ◆ **Batteries:** Store DC electricity. Popular battery types include flooded lead-acid, absorbed glass mat sealed lead-acid (AGM), and gelled electrolyte sealed lead-acid (gel). Common brands include Concorde, Deka MK, Surrette, and Trojan.

- ◆ **Charge controller:** Regulates power to and from the batteries to prevent overcharging and overvoltage. Popular brands include Apollo Star, Blue Sky Energy, Morningstar, OutBack, PowerFilm, and Xantrex.

- ◆ **Monitor/metering:** Reports the system status (current and cumulative) and power flows. Popular power system monitoring and metering products are produced by Bogart Engineering, Fat Spaniel Technologies, Magnum Energy, Midnite Solar, OutBack, SMA, and Xantrex.

- ◆ **Generator:** Provides backup to AC power. Popular brands include Baldor, Briggs & Stratton, Cummins/Onan, Generac, Honda, Kohler, Powermate, Proforce, Reliance, Robin Subaru, Vox, Winco, and Yamaha.

- ◆ *Breaksers/fuses:* Protect the system against electrical overload.

- ◆ **Wiring:** Connects the components so electricity can flow.

def•i•ni•tion

> Breakers and fuses are devices used to protect electrical equipment from short circuits. **Breakers** turn off the circuit if excess power attempts to pass. **Fuses** are made with metals that are designed to melt when the current passing through the fuse is high enough. When the fuse melts, the electrical connection is broken, interrupting power to the circuit or device.

Wire is selected by size and insulation. AWG (American Wire Gauge) is the standard measure of wire in the United States and Canada. Wire sizes range from 0000 (thumb size) to 60 (human hair size). Larger numbers indicate smaller wire size. The wire is insulated or wrapped with plastic. (For wire sizing, visit affordable-solar.com/wire. charts.htm.)

That's the gist of it. You may hear some of these components called by other names, but their functions are the same. Remember to keep notes in your Solar Home Book on what components your system needs and where to get them.

Sun Spots

PV cells can be made from several processes or technologies. Types of PV cells you'll hear about include crystalline silicon, poly-crystalline silicon, amorphous silicon, cadmium telluride, copper indium gallium, and diselenide. They all do the same job: produce electricity from sunlight. As you shop for PV modules, ask manufacturers and suppliers why one type should be selected over others. Some use more environmentally friendly manufacturing processes, some are less expensive per watt, others are easier to manufacture, and still others are expected to last longer.

Solar Equipment Resources

In some locations, finding a PV provider can be as simple as picking up the telephone book. Make sure the supplier or contractor has solar electricity experience. Some providers you may hear about have furnished or installed solar water heating systems but may not have a clue about solar electricity. Or they are electrical contractors who have read about PV but have yet to install a solar electric system.

If you're online, check the Solar Energy Industries Association (seia.org) for a list of solar service providers.

Bright Idea

Want to save even more money on your solar power system? Find some other folks interested in buying approximately the same system at the same time and try to get a volume discount. The group could be a neighborhood or a solar power club you form for the explicit purposes of sharing information and savings.

Another potential resource for solar power equipment and experience is your local utility company. Those who encourage residential solar power systems (many of them) have developed contacts within the local solar industry. These contacts can be useful to you as you buy and install your system.

Where can you buy components for your solar power system? Most places are listed in the yellow pages of your local or regional telephone book. Typical headings include "Solar Products—Dealers and Services" and "Solar Products—Mfrs and Whsle." In addition, some large hardware stores have solar power equipment and packages. Many have at least the mounting, wiring, fuses, and other materials.

If you can't find a dependable local source for solar power equipment, consider making some telephone calls and going online for regional and national suppliers. You'll find many resources in Appendix D and online at SolarHomeGuides.com.

Finding Good Suppliers

In general, the most cost-effective way to find and hire good equipment suppliers is to …

1. Find a large pool of potential suppliers.

2. Choose the most qualified from that pool.

3. Negotiate the best terms you can.

4. Hire the most qualified suppliers for the fairest terms.

Common sense, right? However, finding a large pool of qualified suppliers and asking the most telling questions can be easier said than done. You'll need a variety of components and materials for your solar (or other) power system. They include PV modules, inverters, batteries, controllers, monitors, wiring, safety equipment, and structural support. Where are you going to get all this stuff when you need it and at the lowest price?

Start calling the solar power system suppliers you found in your local phone book and which you can find in the resources listed in Appendix D and online at SolarHomeGuides.com. Then select the three or four best suppliers for your primary materials (modules and controllers). If your system is large or you have numerous potential suppliers, contact each supplier about bidding on your project. Suppliers will need specs and plans for your power system.

You may have more than one supplier. The PV modules, for example, may come from one supplier and installation from another. The best rule is to know what you're buying and get fair prices from the best available suppliers.

Before selecting your primary system supplier, interview one of the salespeople who may handle your account. You want to know about quality, pricing, discounts, delivery, terms, and advice. Be sure to ask the following questions:

◆ Are preferred brands (if any) readily available? If not, can they be easily ordered?

◆ What are your prices on … (list a few specific products such as a 60-watt PV module or a 6-volt deep-cycle battery)?

- What discounts and terms are available?

- What discounts are available cash-and-carry?

- How can I set up an account with you and what are the terms?

- How soon can you typically deliver materials?

- Will I have a specific salesperson assigned to my account? (Such an arrangement with the sales team is usually preferred.)

- Who would I talk to if I can't come to an agreement with a salesperson?

You may *like* a specific supplier—or you may not. And the feeling can be mutual. As long as you *trust* the supplier to do what is promised, that's really all you need. Trust is an important part of all business relationships. In fact, it should be at the top of your requirements list as you look for solar power system suppliers. Do I trust this person to do what she or he says? How can you keep your trustworthy suppliers working hard for you? Apply the Golden Rule: Those with the gold rule. That is, you can use gold (money) to rule (manage) your suppliers. How?

- Make sure all agreements keep work ahead of the money; that is, appropriate payment is made *after* work is done.

- Use financial incentives as needed to keep installation moving.

- Make sure work contracts say that delays cost suppliers and contractors more than they cost you.

- Spend a dime to save a dollar whenever possible.

- Treat all suppliers as people who really want to do the best job they can.

Solar Eclipse

What can you do if you find out your supplier isn't as honest as you thought? Even well-recommended suppliers can have a bad day—or a bad employee. First, contact the supplier directly and try to work out the problem. If that doesn't work, contact any trade associations the contractor belongs to and ask for arbitration. If you're working through a state solar program, get the state involved. All that most suppliers need is a nudge to do the right thing. Just show them how it will be easier for them to solve your problem than take on a larger one.

It's important that you and your suppliers keep good records. When were items ordered? When did they arrive? Were they what was ordered and the correct quantity? Who received and inspected them? Who needs them and when? You need records with lots of details.

If you are installing a large solar power system yourself, consider using a computer and spreadsheet to keep track of materials and work. It can help you track the money and the time so you can get the best use of both.

Asking the Right Questions

To get a fair deal from a knowledgeable supplier, it is critical to ask the right questions. It doesn't matter whether you're buying a new solar grid-tie power system or a used car. Here are some good questions to ask after you've chosen a supplier:

- Do you have solar components in stock?

- What experience do you have sizing and selling solar electric systems and components?

- How long have you been in business? (This question is especially important when you are buying components with a long-term guarantee!)

- Can you recommend installation contractors in my area?

- May I talk with some of your current and prior customers?

- Do you belong to any solar equipment trade organizations?

- Can you help me estimate my solar power system needs or do you just sell equipment?

- How long will it take for my equipment to arrive at my site?

- What credit terms are available through you on solar equipment purchases?

- Are there any discounts available?

- Who manufactures the equipment you sell and what is their product warranty?

- Will I have a specific account manager for my purchase or do I place orders with the next available salesperson?

- Why should I purchase through your company?

These are good questions to ask a supplier because the answers tell you about the people you're dealing with. Price is only one component of cost. If you have to replace a defective system in three years, will the dealer and the manufacturer be there—or in Cancun?

Fortunately, because solar components are manufactured by only a few companies, you can sometimes compare pricing for the best deal. For example, many suppliers sell popular PV module models. That means you can find a qualified supplier that will stand behind the product and offer a competitive (not necessarily the lowest) price. However, don't expect discount-store pricing. There aren't *that many* suppliers yet.

Taking Delivery

You've found the best supplier and paid a fair price for your solar power system. In fact, it's on its way to you. Now what?

Depending on the size of your system and whether it is for new construction or retrofit, you'll probably need a safe and dry place to keep materials until they are installed. For an existing home, a garage or dry storage building is a good choice. For new construction, a lockable structure is good. Remember, your system costs many thousands of dollars. It's an investment—one you don't want to lose to theft or damage.

Alternatively, your supplier may be coaxed into holding your order for delivery just prior to the day the electrician will arrive. Or you may be able to have the equipment shipped to and stored at your electrician's shop.

Make sure you inspect the equipment for obvious shipping damage when it arrives and note problems on the shipping documents. You can also sign the documents as "Received subject to inspection." You want to retain the right to make a full inspection and submit a claim if there is any damage during shipping.

If you're using an electrical or general contractor to install your solar power system, Chapter 17 offers more specifics. If you're planning to install the system yourself, with an electrician as needed, Chapter 18 will show you the way.

The Least You Need to Know

◆ Use your Solar Home Book to list the components needed for your system.

◆ Start contacting local solar equipment suppliers, as well as ordering catalogs, to begin the shopping process.

◆ Plan what questions you'll ask of each of your equipment suppliers to make sure they are qualified and trustworthy.

◆ Have a secure location for delivery and storage of your valuable solar equipment.

Hiring the Brightest Solar Contractor

In This Chapter

♦ Deciding whether you need a solar contractor

♦ Finding the best contractor

♦ Learning the bidding process

♦ Working with your contractor

♦ Following code and understanding solar equipment standards

Imagine yourself up on the roof erecting a PV module frame and wiring the units into your main electrical system. Can you see this image? Or do you see yourself in a hospital emergency room after trying it?

The better question is: Do you need a contractor to install your solar power system? Maybe. Maybe not. This chapter helps you decide if and who. A contractor can make the job easier—for a price.

Considering Contractors

First, let's figure out whether you even need a contractor for your solar power system. You can, of course, save money if you don't need a contractor and are comfortable doing the work yourself.

A contractor can be a construction manager, called a general contractor (GC) or a specialist such as an electrical or solar contractor. For most solar electrical components, you'll need an electrician or electrical contractor to do the actual wiring. In most locations, you'll need a building or remodeling permit from the city or county as well. If you're having a solar power system installed in your home as it is being built, you'll probably have a general contractor in charge of the building process.

Building Permits

Let's look at the permit process. Not every community welcomes solar power systems. That's because they don't understand them or the advantages to the community. Their response is likely to be: "Absolutely not! Er, what's your question?" Fortunately, thousands of other folks have already gone through the permit process, maybe not in your area but elsewhere. You're not the first. An experienced supplier and/or solar contractor can take care of the permit hassle and help cut through the red tape.

Start by calling the local building department to find out who has jurisdiction and whether anybody has solar power system inspection experience. Briefly describe your system and ask about applicable code. You'll probably be referred to an electrical inspector because solar power systems are electrical.

Solar Eclipse

Some state solar rebate programs penalize do-it-yourselfers as much as 15 percent if they *don't* use a licensed contractor for renewable energy system installation. If your system is eligible for a rebate or incentive, make sure you understand and meet the requirements.

Some of the safety concerns you may face in getting a permit include the following:

◆ Exceeding roof load (the weight that a roof is designed to support)

◆ Installing unsafe wiring

◆ Obstructing side yards and setbacks (the distance between buildings and property lines)

◆ Erecting unlawful PV frames

◆ Conforming to local covenants and restrictions (the limits on what is allowed in your subdivision)

◆ Installing components too close to streets

Knowing what the permit process is can help you decide how much you can tackle yourself and how much you should or must have done professionally. In addition, local building permit departments may be able to tell you which local contractors have solar power system experience.

Licensed Contractors

A general contractor is a construction manager, keeping work flowing toward building or retrofitting a specific home as agreed. If you're having a solar home built, your general contractor will …

- ◆ Supervise all aspects of the work done at the building site.

- ◆ Hire, supervise, pay, and fire subcontractors as needed to get the job done.

- ◆ Coordinate getting building permits and any variances.

- ◆ Buy all materials and supplies needed in construction.

- ◆ Make sure that the site is inspected and approved by the building department.

- ◆ Make sure that all subcontractors are licensed and have the needed insurance (such as worker's compensation insurance).

For this effort, the GC typically gets a management fee of 15 to 20 percent of the total value of the project. The GC subtotals the costs of materials and subcontractors and then adds the management fee. Alternatively, the GC could be hired to manage the project for a specified hourly rate. Or a lump sum may be agreed upon. The *best* method of payment is the one that gives you the lowest cost while motivating the contractor to get the job done safely and on time.

> ### Sun Spots
>
> The licensing examination typically has two sections. The first is on the specific trade, such as solar power systems, and the second is on law and business topics, such as project management, bookkeeping, bidding, safety, contracts, liens, insurance, and similar topics. Candidates must pass both sections before they can be issued a contractor license.

So what does it take to be a licensed general contractor? Contractors are licensed based on knowledge, experience, and other assets. In many states, a licensed general contractor must …

- Be 18 years of age or older.

- Prove at least four full years of experience as a journeyman, foreman, supervisor, or contractor in the appropriate classification.

- Pass a written test.

- Have a specific amount of operating capital.

- Register a contractor's bond or cash deposit.

- Pay the examination fee and licensing fee, plus the renewal fee.

Workers installing a roof frame for mounting solar panels on a new home.

Recently, a national certification program by the North American Board of Certified Energy Practitioners (NABCEP) created a national credentialing and certification program for renewable energy professionals. To find a NABCEP installer, visit nabcep.org online. You can search the site by state or by zip code.

Alternatively, you may need only an electrical contractor who can plan, install, connect, and test a renewable power system for your home. Some states also license solar contractors, a specialty that incorporates both electrical and mechanical skills and experience. This is often your best bet—if you can find such a contractor in your area.

Can you be your own solar contractor? If you have experience wiring electrical systems—and local code allows it—you can save some money by doing the job yourself. Most building departments allow residential "owners" to apply for a building permit for specific projects. Or you can hire a licensed contractor to let you help with the easy stuff. You have options.

> **Solar Eclipse** _____
>
> States have licensing authority to allow or disallow contractors. Some states have a stringent testing and certification process. Others don't. Most are designed to keep out the worst, but can't really protect you from dishonest ones. That's why it's important to do your homework before hiring a contractor. Don't trust your expensive solar power system to a contractor who isn't licensed, bonded, insured, and experienced in installing similar systems. And be sure to get references!

Selecting Your Contractor

So how are you going to find the *best* contractor you can afford to build or retrofit your solar home? The search begins early. In fact, even before you've drawn up plans, you should already be looking for a qualified contractor.

Obviously, you don't have to conduct as extensive a search for a solar contractor for a $1,000 job as one for a $30,000 system. Or you may be helping to hire a solar subcontractor that will work with your new-home building contractor. Adjust the process to match the value.

Referrals are the best place to find contractors. Ask people you know who have had solar homes built or retrofitted in your area recently. Talk with local building material suppliers. Ask your lender and any subcontractors you know for recommendations.

What you're looking for at this point is a comprehensive list of contractor *candidates*. Then you're ready to weed out the bad ones. This process includes calling for qualifications and availability, then following up with interviews of the best candidates. Finally, you narrow the field down to a handful that you ask to bid on your project.

Availability is a key factor in many areas. Specialists who have solar experience may be quite busy already. In fact, if a candidate isn't busy when others are, maybe there's something you don't know about that person's work. Or it could be that the contractor is pickier about what he or she takes on. Or that the benefits of solar energy are still not well known in your area. You could be a pioneer!

How do you interview a contractor? Face to face if possible, over lunch or a long coffee break, in an office or—preferably—on the job site. Seeing a contractor at a job site can be enlightening as long as your presence isn't distracting.

Make sure to ask candidates the following questions:

- Can you tell me about your license and construction experience?
- What type of contracting license do you have?
- What is the license number? (See the following Bright Idea sidebar.)
- Can I see your contractor license?
- What experience do you have with solar power systems?
- What references can you give me?
- Can you post a performance bond (a guarantee that the contractor will complete the job)? If not, why not?
- May I see your worker's comp policy? (This protects you from job-site injury claims.)
- Can you provide proof of insurance?
- How do you go about hiring subcontractors?
- How do you plan a solar construction or retrofit project?
- Do you typically meet your building schedules?
- What lenders do you prefer to work with? Why?
- What suppliers do you prefer to work with? Why?
- What things do you need to make a firm bid on this project?
- How do you develop an accurate bid?
- Do you have any problem with my attorney looking over your standard contract?

Of course, there are many more questions you could ask depending on your house plans and how you will participate in the building process. Remember, you want to ask open-ended questions that aren't answered by a simple "yes" or "no." You want to hear explanations and find out how well the person communicates. Write down all the questions so you can ask each candidate the same ones, and make sure you keep track of the answers. The question you forget to ask may be the one you later wish you had gotten answered!

Here's one more resource: the Better Business Bureau (BBB). A well-respected consumer watchdog agency, the BBB accepts and maintains complaints and other info about all types of businesses—including contractors. Find your local BBB office in the telephone book or online (bbb.org) and ask about specific contractors.

Bright Idea

Knowing the contractor's license number will come in handy. States that license contractors will typically keep a file of complaints and resolutions that you can access if you know the contractors license number. In addition, the contractor must have the *appropriate* license; a mason contractor, for example, can't legally install your solar power system. Call your state's board of contractors (see Appendix D or visit SolarPowerGuides.com online) for more information.

Calling for Bids

You've been busy. You've found and interviewed scads of contractor candidates and selected two or three you believe you can work well with. It's time to talk money!

The bidding process is critical to you and to the contractors. You don't want them to make too much money on the project, nor do you want them to lose so much that they have to cut corners or not finish the job. Ask for bid forms from each contractor. If you can't find lots of solar contractors in your area, either look farther away or get bids from electrical contractors who haven't done their first solar job yet.

Make sure that the contractor you select has experience installing solar panels and systems.

The key to accurate bids is accurate specifications. That is, contractors don't have to guess when working with clear specifications. They know exactly how much the materials will cost, how many hours it will take for each stage, and how long it will take to finish the project. If your contractor is also a solar engineer or planner, he or she may develop the specs for you.

Be sure you know what's included in the bids. Building permit fees? Utility connection fees? Travel expenses? Site security? Cleanup charges? Also ask for a start and finish date in the schedule. It will make a difference because you pay interest on the construction or retrofit loan.

Get job responsibilities in writing on the bid. Who will call for inspections? Who notifies the lender to release money? How will changes be handled? These questions must be answered in the building contract, so ask the contractor to include them in the bid.

Be careful. Don't get cheap! If you've developed a working relationship with these bidders, you have an idea what it will take to get a fair bid. And that's what you want.

Hiring a Hardworking Contractor

Found the right contractor to build or retrofit your solar house? Great! Be sure to get it in writing. A typical contractor agreement will include some important specifics. Attached to and referred to in it will be the plans and probably the final bid. The agreement itself will include the following items:

- Contract date and parties
- Start and completion dates
- Conditions (who does what, who pays for what, who approves what, how changes are made and paid for, and so on)
- Contract sum
- Progress payments (matching the lender's draw schedule, if any)
- Terms of final payment
- Contract termination terms
- Anything else agreed upon that should be in writing

Don't sign anything under pressure. If you're not comfortable with the price, terms, or conditions, stop and think it through. Will this contract take you to your goal? What's the worst that can happen? Is it covered by the contract?

If it will make you more comfortable (and it probably will), have an attorney review the contractor's agreement prior to and during final signing.

Working with Your Solar Contractor

You've signed an agreement with a professional contractor to build or retrofit a solar home on schedule and on budget. Now what?

Maintain that relationship of trust, remembering that it is based on mutual benefits. You want a solar house, the contactor wants the money. You don't want legal or financial troubles, nor does the contractor. You want someone you can recommend to others, and your contractor wants a reference.

How can you maintain and benefit from this relationship? Communication is the key. That doesn't mean you have to talk on the phone or at the site all day. But it does mean you need to be comfortable that you know what's going on. For example, you may agree that, if you don't hear from the contractor between 5:00 and 7:00 each evening, the day went as scheduled and as previously agreed. If there is a problem that you can help solve, the contractor will let you know during that call.

The most crucial part of the working relationship is establishing how changes are approved and made. Changes *will* happen. A specific energy-efficient window is backordered. The wiring plans weren't correct and now the main panel must be changed. You decide to upgrade or downgrade the PV modules before installation. Who approves changes? Who designs the change? Who pays for it?

There are three periods when changes occur, especially during construction of a new solar home. When changes are made, it impacts who makes the change and how much it costs:

- During planning, when simple design changes lead to more research and some redrawing

- During installation, when some time and materials are lost

- After installation, when more time and more materials are lost

Bright Idea _____

If you're not home much, make sure you have a telephone answering system or service where the contractor and others can leave detailed messages. Or exchange cell phone numbers. In fact, you and the contractor may not speak face to face to each other for days or weeks.

The preference is to make all changes during design, of course. They are less expensive at that stage. Design changes can even save you some money. You may decide that the PV modules you selected are not as efficient as newer, less expensive models, for example, so you change the order before it's shipped.

Changing the location of PV modules or of a passive solar wall during construction will be more expensive. And changing it *after* installation can be quite costly. It can even delay other construction steps.

The moral, of course, is to review the plans carefully and have others review the plans many times, looking for potential changes, before finalizing the plans. The other moral is to keep good communications going with the contractor so that you can effectively participate in needed changes.

And remember that any change you make to a new home design impacts other parts of the house. Even changes in a retrofit can cause changes elsewhere. Adding PV modules may mean upgrading the inverter, for example. It can get complicated.

Builder Beware!

Someday we may all live in an ideal world. Meantime, there are folks out there who will take advantage of other people's lack of specialized knowledge.

So what can go wrong in hiring and dealing with general and solar contractors? Here are some troubling things that can happen:

- Poorly written or verbal contracts allow contractors to walk away with other people's money.

- Verbal promises aren't kept.

- Contractors substitute inferior materials and pocket the difference.

- Contractors receive hiring fees from winning subcontractors.

- Unscrupulous inspectors are bribed to sign inaccurate inspections.

♦ Unlicensed and unbonded contractors and subcontractors are used, increasing owner liability.

♦ Unauthorized changes are made to plans during construction (such as installing inferior materials or equipment).

♦ Liens (loans for materials or labor) are not removed after payment, increasing owner liability.

♦ Workers not covered by worker's compensation insurance are injured at your building site.

♦ Available discounts on materials are not passed on to the owner as agreed.

You get the picture. Fortunately, learning how solar homes are built or retrofitted can save you both money and frustrations. And careful selection of a building contractor greatly diminishes surprises.

If you're serious about building a home that includes solar and other renewable energies, get a copy of my companion book, *The Complete Idiot's Guide to Building Your Own Home, Third Edition* (Alpha Books, 2007).

Solar Codes

Modern building codes cover new construction as well as retrofitting houses with solar power systems. Solar electricity is covered under electrical codes. Solar hot water systems are covered by plumbing and other building codes. For example, PV power systems are covered by parts of the *National Electrical Code* (*NEC*), adapted by most building departments. Included in the NEC are specifics for the following items:

♦ PV modules

♦ Wiring

♦ Ground-fault protection

♦ Grounding

♦ Overcurrent protection

♦ Disconnection

♦ Batteries

♦ Generators

♦ Charge controllers

♦ Inverters

♦ Distribution systems

♦ Inspections

In addition, the NEC defines and specifies installation of related wiring in your home. It's comprehensive. Your local building codes will probably incorporate all or most of the NEC.

def•i•ni•tion

The U.S. **National Electrical Code (NEC)** contains guidelines for all types of electrical installations. These guidelines should be followed when installing a PV system. Article 690 of the NEC specifically covers solar photovoltaic systems.

Solar Standards

Standards are set by the solar industry for comparing, rating, and installing solar equipment. Some are set by the American Society of Heating, Refrigeration, and Air-Conditioning Engineers (ASHRAE; ashrae.org) and others by the American Society for Testing and Materials (ASTM; astm.org). You may see these acronyms on solar equipment you buy.

Another important acronym is SRCC. It stands for Solar Rating and Certification Corporation (solar-rating.org). The SRCC administers a certification, rating, and labeling program for solar hot water collectors. It has a similar program for complete solar water and swimming pool heating systems. It's a help in comparing "apples to apples" among solar hot water energy equipment.

Additionally, the Underwriters Laboratories, Inc. (UL; ul.com) tests and certifies a wide assortment of devices and equipment including those used for solar power. In fact, many building codes require that specific electrical devices be tested by UL or to the UL standard.

Are you a do-it-yourselfer? If you've decided to act as your own contractor, Chapter 18 shows you how to install solar power systems in your home.

The Least You Need to Know

- General contractors are actually construction managers who can handle the entire new solar home or retrofit project.

- Getting bids from contractors and suppliers can save you money, but remember to consider value rather than just low cost.

- Make sure you read and *understand* any contracts your contractor or suppliers give you to sign.

- Solar equipment standards and installation codes are established to help consumers select solar power systems.

Chapter 18

Installing Your Solar Power System

In This Chapter

◆ Finding out whether you can—and should—install your own solar power system

◆ Looking at a typical solar power installation

◆ Selecting the right tools for the job

◆ Getting the lowdown on building inspectors

◆ Making sure you have adequate insurance—just in case

Are you considering installing your own solar power system? Think you can save some money by doing it all yourself? Ready to climb up on the roof and start mounting PV modules?

Don't! Don't even pick up a hammer until you've read this chapter. Here's where you find out if you *can* install your solar power system—then consider whether you *should*. In case you decide you should, we'll also cover the *how*.

Can You Install Your Solar Power System?

Hey, it's a free country, right? Well, not exactly. If you're living out in the boonies and you swear on a stack of Bibles that you'll *never* sell your house to anyone—you'll burn it down first—local authorities *may* let you build without a permit. Otherwise, fat chance.

Actually, it's not quite that bad. And there's a good reason for the hard-nosed attitude of local building departments. It's called "public health and safety." It's their job to make sure that all structures built in their jurisdictions are safe and pose no health problems to current or future habitants. They don't want anyone without experience (and probably a license or two) crawling around on a roof putting up equipment that could cause a fire today or in the future. And, of course, they want the building permit fee!

Local building codes typically require that a licensed electrician install electrical systems. Many go as far as to say that *only* licensed and experienced solar contractors can install solar power systems. In some locations, however, an owner can wire the electrical system in his or her own home without a license. It will still require an inspection by the local building department, though, so it had better be up to code. That means either taking some electrician classes or hiring an electrician to oversee the job—or both.

Larger solar power systems often aren't designed for do-it-yourselfer installation. That means they typically don't have a step-by-step illustrated instruction book. If there's any paperwork, it's written in electrician-ese and includes a schematic with lines and boxes that have no relationship to the physical placement of components. A 3-inch line could indicate a 3-inch wire or a 30-foot cable. No help there. You'll also need to know the AWG (American Wire Gauge), described in Chapter 16.

Fortunately, not everything in a solar power system is electrical. There's mechanical stuff, too. So if you're mechanically inclined, you may be able to save some money by installing the PV module frames, building a battery bank cabinet, placing the controller, and helping an electrician run wire. And it's legal to do so because the licensed electrician is ultimately responsible for your work. You're working for the electrician who's working for you.

Before you run out and buy wire strippers, consider that many of the rebate and buy-back programs (discussed in Chapter 2) *require* that a licensed solar or electrical contractor do the work. This is especially true of systems designed to sell excess power back to the local utility (see Chapter 12). The utility doesn't want one of its linemen electrocuted by your system. Nor do you.

In fact, solar rebate programs will probably require that the installer have solar, not just electrical, experience. That means a solar contractor specialty license, certification in PV systems by a group such as the Solar Energy Industries Association (SEIA; seia.org), or at least certification from the PV system manufacturer that the installer is qualified.

With a little help, many homeowners can install their own solar electric system.

Should You Install Your Solar Power System?

Okay, maybe your locality allows unlicensed electricians to install solar power systems. But *should* you? First, find out what requirements your local building department will have for approving and passing your solar power system. Then make sure there are no problems with any rebate programs you're signing up for. Then start looking for training.

Sun Spots

It may be extra trouble to fulfill local requirements to install your own solar power system. The upside is that you will be a knowledgeable owner who can maintain, troubleshoot, and repair your solar power system as well as or better than anyone. And you'll be able to do it at lower cost. So consider the do-it-yourself route if you're especially handy, on a tight budget, or live where professional installers aren't readily available. If your system goes down, you'll know who to call—you!

There are training classes available on solar power systems, but most focus on selecting rather than installing. Solar hot water systems don't use electricity, so a homeowner may be able to install such a system. But electrical systems require more training. Contact a local college or trade school to find out whether it offers classes that get you to your goal. That goal may be to meet state requirements for an electrical contractor's license. Or the school may have certification classes on solar power systems. Find out what's available.

Solar equipment suppliers can also be helpful because they work with agencies from many states and can tell you what the installation requirements are. Some have licensed electricians on staff who can answer questions and help guide you through the installation process.

If allowed, you *can* do this. So the next question is: Do you *want* to? You probably want to do at least some of the work to save money. What will you be giving up? Time. Where will you get the time? Maybe by taking off from another job or responsibility. Or from a relationship.

A solar water heating system is easier for most do-it-yourselfers to install than a PV electric system.

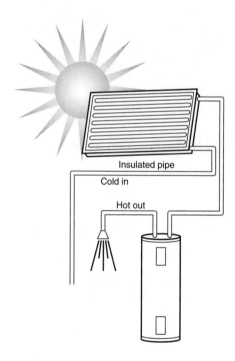

Insulated pipe

Cold in

Hot out

Actually, you're not really giving up time because you are trading it for something else. As you think about being your own solar contractor, be sure that you get a good trade.

Alternatively, there are many things that you can do to improve the quality or lower the cost of solar power. What you decide to do, if anything, should depend on your skills, time, and health. For example, you can take on any of these jobs:

♦ Picking up materials and delivering them to the construction site

♦ Assembling and installing PV module framing, possibly on a roof

♦ Cleaning up after the electrician

♦ Providing site security against theft and vandalism

♦ Keeping track of expenses, deliveries, and inspections

♦ Installing fixtures or equipment as directed by the electrician or other contractor

♦ Being a gofer as needed by any of the contractors or laborers at the job site

Remember, if your contractors and craftspeople are being paid by the hour, anything you do that saves them time also saves you money!

A Typical Installation Process

To help you decide whether this is something you want to do yourself, let's go through a typical installation. Of course, there are few "typicals" in solar power systems. That's because one person may build a complete solar home with off-grid solar power and hot water systems while another may install a solar outdoor lighting system. Each one is somewhat unique.

My version of "typical" for this example is a medium-sized residential hybrid solar power system with battery backup. In this case, "hybrid" means it also uses a generator. The system includes the following:

♦ 16 12-volt, 130-watt PV modules

♦ 4 kW inverter (85 percent efficiency)

♦ 1,000 Ah, 24-volt battery bank

♦ 6 kW, 240 Vac generator

♦ Inverters, controllers, wiring, and other secondary components

The 16 PV modules are mounted on the roof in eight subarrays of two modules each, wired in parallel and series as a 24-volt system. Output from the array is wired into a combiner box on the roof, then fed to the charge controller and PV power center. The power center then feeds the inverter, battery, and any direct DC loads (lights, appliances).

The PV power center contains safety and control equipment, including fuses or circuit breakers, a ground-fault detector, charge controls, and related components. It is mounted somewhere convenient between the array and the inverter.

The generator is installed where it is conveniently near the fuel source. It could be powered by a gasoline, diesel, or propane fuel tank from a fuel delivery truck. The tank must be located where it can easily be filled. The 240-volt generator also needs a 5 kilovolt-amp transformer that changes most or all the voltage to 120 volts for use by the house during an emergency.

Solar Eclipse

Be aware that electrical components that have been installed, especially by a do-it-yourselfer, may not be returnable to the supplier if defective. Make sure components are tested prior to installation to be sure they work.

The inverter converts the DC electricity from the PV power center to 120 Vac for the house loads. In most cases, it is wired directly into the main electrical panel for the home. In addition, the inverter includes a battery charger that makes sure the battery bank, located nearby, is fully charged for emergency use.

The balance of this typical system is the cable and wiring needed to connect everything. Your job, should you decide to accept it, is to install and electrically connect all components, following the building department–approved plans. If allowed by local code, the lender, the rebate offer, and your skills, it's a job that can be done by a homeowner. Otherwise, hire a qualified solar contractor and find another way to save some money.

Steps to a typical solar installation include:

◆ Planning the location and orientation of PV panels, controllers, batteries, wiring, and other components.

◆ Installing brackets and rails for mounting panels on the roof or other location.

◆ Wiring and installing the PV panels on the mounts. In some installations, the green wire is attached to the mounting frame as the ground. Follow the manufacturer's instructions.

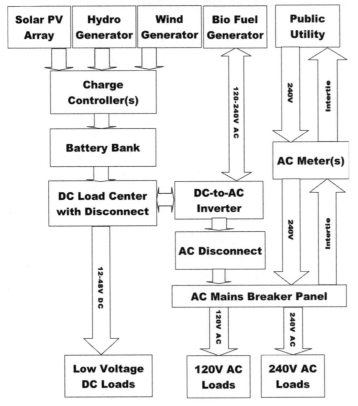

Renewable Energy Power System Flowchart

This flowchart illustrates the interconnections for a variety of solar, hydro, wind, biofuel, and public utility installations.

- Installing electrical wiring from the panels to the control center. Often, the wiring is laid in the mounting track, then into electrical conduit pipe to the controller.

- Installing the power control center and lightning arrestor with fuses and grounds.

- Wiring the controller to the battery bank (if any). Batteries are often wired into banks of 12-, 24-, or 48-volt outputs per the design (see Chapters 13 and 14).

- Installing the inverter following the manufacturer's instructions. Inverters are selected based on the battery bank input and desired output.

◆ Wiring the 120-volt output to the home's main electrical control panel. The panel may also have inputs from and outputs to the public electrical grid, depending on the design. A generator, too, can supplement the electrical service.

Your local building department will indicate at which points you must call it for an inspection. At these points, you cannot continue the installation until a building inspector has verified that the work conforms to code requirements.

The Right Tools

If you do any of the work yourself, you're going to need the right tools for the various jobs. Here's a list of the basic tools needed to retrofit a house for solar power:

◆ *Volt-ohmmeter (VOM)*

◆ Wire strippers

◆ Wire nuts and electrical tape

◆ Tape measures (25-feet and 100-feet)

◆ Carpenter's or combination square

◆ Levels (2-feet and 4-feet)

◆ Framing and finish hammers

◆ Utility knives

◆ Power saws

def•i•ni•tion

A **volt-ohmmeter (VOM)** is a device used to measure voltage, resistance, and current in an electrical device or circuit. It's also called a multimeter because it can make a variety of electrical measurements.

◆ Screwdrivers

◆ Power drill and bits

◆ Extension cords (10- or 12-gauge)

◆ Adjustable wrenches and pliers

◆ Ladders

And remember to take care of your tools. Avoid leaving them out in the weather, keep cutting tools sharp, and repair or replace frayed electrical cords.

Solar Eclipse _____

If you install your own solar power system, you'll need to follow the latest available National Electrical Code (NEC) as published by the National Fire Protection Association (NFPA). You can purchase a copy from electrical supply dealers, online bookstores, and directly from NFPA at nfpa.org. Other publishers offer books that are based on and simplify the NEC handbook. Make sure your book is the current version.

Working with Inspectors

Building inspectors can seem like both your friend and your foe, but their job is just to make sure your solar project is safe. They follow a written code that tells them what the standards are. Those standards are available to you, so you can stay ahead of the inspector by knowing what's required to pass inspection.

The inspector's job is to visit the construction site at specific events and make sure that the project is proceeding according to the plan approved by the building department. So inspectors become foes when they challenge your installation. Knowing electrical code will help you in the battle.

How can you make these foes your friends? As you get a building permit, ask about inspections and, if possible, meet one or more of the inspectors. Find out how much advance time you need to call for an inspection and what work, if any, you can continue doing prior to the inspection. Also find out what happens if the inspector doesn't sign off on the inspection. What must you do before calling for a reinspection? Who do you call? What if you dispute the inspection?

If you're financing your solar project, you may also deal with a lender's inspector. In some cases, the lender may accept the county or city building inspector's certification. Other lenders may have their own inspectors visit the site. If possible, make sure that draw schedules (payments for work completed) coincide with building inspections.

Bright Idea _____

Many building departments prefer to hire college grads who have taken extensive coursework in building codes rather than hire from the building trades. Electrical inspectors typically require more training than many other inspectors because of extensive codes. So help your inspectors by being on hand at inspection time and making sure everything is ready.

If you're serving as your own contractor, keep good records and manage your check-book accurately. If you have a computer, invest in one of the accounting software programs (such as Quicken, QuickBooks, or Money) and learn how to use it. In fact, a lender may require that you do so.

Getting Adequate Insurance Coverage

If you're doing the job yourself, your homeowner insurance may handle any injury claims. But if you're hiring workers or a solar contractor, make sure you or the contractor have adequate liability and worker's compensation insurance coverage. You don't want someone else to own your new solar home!

Building a new solar home? An insurance policy for potential losses while you're building your home (or having it built) is called a builder's risk policy and can probably be purchased through your regular insurance agent. It covers damage and injury claims based on events that occur during construction, including fire, hurricane, and theft. It *doesn't* cover the loss if a contractor takes off with your money or materials.

After a new home is finished and an occupancy permit is issued, the builder's risk policy will probably convert to a homeowner's policy and cover additional things such as all your furniture and belongings.

Your lender may require a builder's risk policy for financing. In fact, some will automatically build one into the loan package. Be careful, though, as it will probably pay only for the lender's loss, not yours. Make sure you know what it will and won't cover. If needed, add riders or additional terms to the policy to insure anything you may lose. Also, consider whether you need a rider to cover theft or vandalism at the building site. Theft of major solar components can not only cost money, but also time—which is money.

General liability (GL) insurance covers other things that can happen during construction. Which things? That depends on what insurance is purchased. For example, a PV module flies off the roof during installation and hits a neighbor's car. Who covers the cost of fixing the car? The solar contractor? Your builder's risk policy? You? A general liability insurance policy? If you are your own solar contractor, get GL insurance before starting construction. It can save you money and worry.

If you hire workers to help with your solar project, you may need worker's compensation insurance, which covers workers while on the job. The alternative is for the injured worker to sue the contractor or you! By paying worker's comp insurance premiums, you are insuring yourself against a lawsuit for these injuries. The unofficial construction rule that workers are fired just before they hit the ground doesn't really apply.

So you or a contractor have installed your solar power system and the inspector says "throw the switch!" What's next? Maintaining your system for optimum efficiency and lowest cost, the subject of our next and final chapter.

The Least You Need to Know

- Many local building departments don't allow anyone but licensed solar or electrical contractors to install most solar power systems, although owner-builders are sometimes allowed to install solar hot water systems.

- Make sure you have the knowledge and are comfortable with the process before attempting to install your solar electrical system.

- Gather the best tools for the job and know how to use them, especially electrical tools.

- Meet and work with your electrical building inspector, because he or she can make installation easier or more difficult.

- Make sure you have adequate insurance before installing or hiring someone to install your solar power system.

Maintaining Your Solar Power System

In This Chapter

◆ Monitoring your solar power system for maximum efficiency

◆ Knowing what you should be monitoring

◆ Learning tips from the pros on maintaining your solar power system

◆ Keeping track of maintenance issues in your Solar Home Book

◆ Looking for trouble: figuring out what went wrong and how to fix it

After your solar power system is installed, there's not much to do, is there? Actually, these systems are relatively maintenance-free. There are no moving parts. They're not like generators that need a periodic tune-up and fuel refill.

So what's this chapter about? It's about monitoring, maintaining, and troubleshooting your solar power system with battery backup to *keep* it running efficiently. It's about making sure that you know what's going on in your solar power system—and what to do if things go wrong.

Monitoring Your Power

Monitoring means watching. Of course, that doesn't mean you have to watch over your power system meters day and night. You can turn that job over to technology. There are three types of monitoring systems for solar power: automatic, manual, and observation.

Most larger systems include system monitors. Many grid-tie inverters, off-grid inverters, and higher-end *charge controllers* allow you to view historical data regarding your system. All these units can monitor system data on the spot and many are set up to download historical data onto your computer. The latest units allow you to view the data from a remote location via an Internet connection. You can monitor your power system from anywhere! What you are looking for are trends. Is the system performing up to specifications? If it is not, start investigating the cause and cure.

def•i•ni•tion

A **charge controller** is a component that controls the flow of current to and from the battery subsystem to protect the batteries from overcharge and overdischarge. It is essential for ensuring that batteries obtain the maximum state of charge and longest life. The charge controller may also monitor system performance and provide system protection. Charge controllers are also sometimes called *regulators*.

A centrally located solar power control center makes monitoring easier.

Think of solar power monitors as working similar to the gauges in your car. Computerized gauges take away most of the worry about efficiency. Indicator lights are either on or off and tell you when something's wrong. Or you can periodically poke your head "under the hood" to check visually what's going on.

Which monitoring system is best? Each has its merits. Computerized gauges are great, but they can't always tell you what you can see for yourself. Use them, but don't totally rely on them. Observation is good backup.

What Should You Be Monitoring?

The answer to this question depends, of course, on what your solar power system is designed to do. If it's a simple system that supplements your home's power with PV module current (no batteries), you should be monitoring PV module output. If the system includes an inverter for converting DC into AC, you'll want a meter indicating AC output of the inverter. If batteries are included, you'll want a meter that shows battery state of charge.

In addition to monitoring output for efficiency, you'll quickly want to know if something goes wrong. For example, you'll want to know quickly if there is a dangerous ground fault in the system or, better, you'll want your system to shut down appropriate circuits before any damage is done.

In fact, it's more important that your system is monitored for safety than for efficiency. It's inconvenient if you don't have enough electricity to watch Conan O'Brien. It's a major problem if a power system problem blows up your TV! Fortunately, National Electrical Code (NEC) and local building codes *require* safety features to prevent this from happening *if* equipment is installed and maintained correctly.

What do you expect to see when monitoring a solar power system? Amps and volts. Remember that a volt (V) is a unit of measure of the *force* given the electrons in an electric circuit. An ampere (A) is a unit of measure of the *flow* of electrons.

Most PV modules will be either 12-volt or 24-volt. Most appliances and other loads in the typical home are either 220-volt (stove, clothes dryer) or 110-volt (most everything else). Monitors are meters that read and report output. Some monitors also make changes in the system based on a setpoint; they are called controllers. For example, a monitor/controller may shut off the 110-volt power line if it reads more than, say, 125 volts. As you learned in the previous chapter, the meter that reads voltage measurements is called a volt-ohmmeter (VOM). (I'll get back to setpoints in just a moment.)

The flow of electrical current is measured in amperes or amps. Many circuits in your home can handle up to 15, 20, or even 30 amps of current. However, most smaller appliances and lights don't need anywhere near this much electricity. A toaster, for example, may only use 5 to 7 amps. An alarm clock may need only 40 mA (milliamps, or thousandths of an amp) to wake you in the morning.

That means ampere meters, called ammeters, in your solar power system will measure amps. An analog ammeter will use a moving needle to point to numbers on a scale. A digital ammeter will display numbers. Some meters include range switches so you can read smaller amp levels (0 to 5 amps) as well as larger ones (0 to 30 amps). A typical solar power system may include meters to measure array voltage, battery voltage, charge voltage, array amps, and load amps.

I mentioned setpoints a few paragraphs back. A setpoint is a preferred operating range. An alarm-point is a maximum value that the equipment or circuit should exceed. For example, a 12-volt battery bank's meter may have a setpoint of 11 to 14 volts within which batteries should normally be operating. An alarm-point may be 10.5 or 14.5 volts and trigger either a controller or an alarm, depending on the system.

What setpoints should you monitor for your system? Fortunately, equipment manufacturers and system designers have already figured out these setpoints for you. A PV module or array typically includes an instruction manual that tells you or the system designer what normal operating ranges should be. If you're pulling your own system together, make sure you get these figures from the manufacturer.

If your system has automatic monitoring and saves historical data, your work is done for you. You'll need to learn how to read and interpret the data that your system tracks and records. Manually monitored systems require that you keep track of readings on paper. After you've listed the components that need monitoring, along with their setpoints and alarm-points, you can develop a form for keeping track. To learn your system, take more readings than are recommended. When you know how to read it and respond, you can cut back.

Maintaining Your Solar Power System

Once installed, solar power systems require little maintenance. Here are some tips from professional installers on how you can maintain your solar power system for optimum efficiency:

- **PV modules:** Annually hose down the surface. Do this early in the day before the modules get hot. Seasonally, adjust the array for the optimal angle if the support rack is adjustable. If you are using a tracker, grease the bearings at the same time.

- **Charge controller (if used):** Does your controller have temperature compensation? If so, skip this step. For a 12-volt system, adjust the upper limit of the setpoints to 14.7 volts for the winter and lower it to 14.3 volts for the summer (or whatever the manufacturer recommends). If you have sealed batteries, consult the manufacturer's data sheet; typically, sealed batteries should not be charged at higher than 14.2 volts. For a 24-volt system, double the setpoint voltages to 29.4 volts and 28.6 volts, respectively. Double again for a 48-volt system.

- **Batteries (if used):** Visually inspect the batteries for signs of corrosion at least twice a year. Clean the battery tops as needed with baking soda but don't get any inside the cells. Scour if necessary so the connections shine. Apply proprietary electrical paste (Vaseline petroleum jelly works fine) on the terminals. Measure the cell voltages. Are they approximately equal? If your controller does not have automatic equalization, allow a controlled overcharge for six to eight hours. This will "boil" the batteries, equalizing the cell voltages and stirring up the electrolyte. Equalization is a monthly activity. In the winter, you may need to have the generator equalize the batteries, as the PV array may not have sufficient power. Recheck the electrolyte levels and add distilled water to the cells, making sure the plates are well covered. Depending on the type and quality, you should replace deep-cycle batteries every 5 to 10 years.

- **Inverters:** Check for insects, rodents, and dust. Clean if necessary. If your inverter has a battery charger, check that the charge voltage is set at 14.5 volts (or 29 or 58 volts) when using the grid or a generator to charge the batteries.

- **Electrical connections:** Check all connections from the PV modules to the inverter and tighten where necessary. Repair any wires that have become damaged or frayed. Remember that this is a live electrical system, so be cautious when handling wires and equipment.

If you are uncertain about working on your system, contact your dealer or a qualified electrician. Ask about a regular service contract.

Bright Idea _____

The efficiency of your PV modules can be reduced by anything that gets between them and the sun. If your home is near trees, make sure you visually inspect the modules as needed to ensure that leaves, needles, and other debris aren't robbing you of electric power. As needed, spray off the modules with a garden hose.

Keeping Track of Maintenance

As I've said, one of the great things about PV modules is that they have no moving parts. They sit there all day long soaking up the sun and converting it into electricity. It's an electro-chemical process and nothing is depleted or needs replacement.

Bright Idea _____

Your Solar Home Book is a good place to keep all information about your system—what's in it, when it was purchased and installed, its setpoints and normal operating range, its alarm-points, what maintenance is needed and when it is performed, and any problems you encounter.

In fact, they are *so* maintenance-free that some folks forget to perform basic maintenance that can keep their solar power system efficient longer, such as making sure that the surface is kept relatively clean so it can do its job. The PV module's surface may be plastic film or glass. In either case, follow the manufacturer's recommendation on cleaning the surface. That may mean simply squirting water on the units through a garden hose. (Don't worry about water; PV modules get wet every rainy season anyway.) Or you may need to clean them periodically with a special cleaner and squeegee. That's when you'll be glad you mounted the modules on a ground mount—or wish you had.

Other components will have maintenance issues, especially batteries. Batteries require more maintenance than just about any other component in a solar power system. The best way to manage these needs is to write them down in your Solar Home Book and make a plan. That plan may include cleaning modules yearly, performing battery and connection maintenance at least twice a year, watering battery cells four times a year, and inspecting the entire system four times a year. If you've invested in the highest-quality batteries, there may be little or no maintenance required. Even so, battery connections will need to be checked for corrosion and cleaned.

Troubleshooting Solar Power

Looking for trouble? You should be! Though well-designed and well-installed solar power systems are virtually trouble-free, we all know that stuff happens. A windstorm damages a module. Vermin nest in an inverter. A battery doesn't operate as long as it should. What to do?

Of course, you can *worry*—but that doesn't really fix anything. The best way to keep conditions from becoming problems is to be aware. First, be aware of how the system should be and is functioning. Maintaining and monitoring your solar power system will take care of that point. Second, know what problems mean; know how to troubleshoot your solar power system.

Let's say you discover that DC appliances in your home aren't functioning well. Your knowledge of the system suggests that the battery bank output is lower than normal, so you check it. Sure enough, there is a problem. So you use a VOM to check the output of each battery in the bank and find that two of the batteries are undercharged. You see that the connection cable between the two and the battery controller is corroded. Knowing how your system works has saved the day!

What about the bigger components? Fortunately, the solar components that manage your system typically have an owner's manual that includes troubleshooting tips. For example, a controller or inverter may have a troubleshooting chart that offers both symptoms and remedies. In most cases, the problem is something simple such as "no electricity" and a solution such as "check the main circuit breaker." More expensive controllers even have built-in diagnostic tests that you can run to make sure the system is running efficiently. Even less-expensive systems may have manual diagnostics that require you to push certain buttons to get the results of tests.

> **Bright Idea**
>
> If you used a solar power contractor to install your system, ask about a maintenance contract. Some contractors will perform annual and semi-annual maintenance at low cost on systems they have installed. Why? Because they want to keep you as a customer!

Need some troubleshooting tips? Here they are:

- Refer to your Solar Home Book and maintenance logs to see whether there are any probable causes that have shown up lately.

- If there's no AC, first check circuit breakers and fuses.

- Check the inverter, turning it off and then back on.

- Look for lights on the inverter that indicate low voltage, overcurrent, or other problems.

- Read the owner's manual for troubleshooting instructions.

- If battery bank output is low, disconnect the bank and check and clean all connections.

- Check the voltage of each battery in the bank.

- Check the array terminal that delivers DC electricity to the inverter or other controller.

- If in doubt about your safety, don't do it!

The best tip is to know your solar power system inside and out through careful monitoring and regular maintenance. Knowledge is power! The next best tip is to be aware of what you *don't* know or can't handle by yourself—and call in an expert for help.

For additional solar resources, turn to Appendix D or visit SolarHomeGuides.com online.

Solar Eclipse

Work safely! Always disconnect the system before doing any work on it to avoid electric shock.

The future of power technology is bright indeed! Congratulations! Your life is now more energy-efficient. You've learned to harness the sun's energy to power the important things in your life. And you've probably decided that other things really aren't that important. You've also discovered new ways of making life better for us and those who follow.

May the Source of all things reward you!

The Least You Need to Know

- Though solar power systems are low maintenance, they are not *no* maintenance. Automatic, manual, and observation monitoring can keep your solar power system running efficiently.

- Make sure you know your solar power system's setpoints and alarm-points—and what to do if there's a problem.

- Keep track of maintenance issues by writing down a plan in your Solar Home Book.

- Increase efficiency and reduce costs by taking time to maintain your solar power system.

- Troubleshooting solar equipment is relatively easy, especially if you know the system well and it comes with a troubleshooting guide.

- *Never* work on an electrical circuit unless you know it is safe to do so.

Estimating Your Home's Energy Needs

Home energy sources include electricity (produced from oil, gas, coal, biomass, solar, wind, and others) as well as heating fuel. The average U.S. home pays about $1,200 a year in energy costs. That's about a hundred bucks a month. In some parts of the country, winter bills for heating alone can be many hundreds of dollars. In other areas, summer air-conditioning costs can match that. In colder climates, the monthly heating bill can be bigger than the mortgage payment. And some lucky folks live in moderate climates where heating and cooling demands are lower.

Where does all this money for energy go? Those experts at the Department of Energy say that about 44 percent is used for heating and cooling; 33 percent for lighting, cooking, and appliances; about 14 percent for water heating; and the final 9 percent for refrigeration.

What's Home Energy?

Just as with people, homes use energy in everyday tasks. People's energy is typically measured in calories consumed. A calorie is a measurement of heat energy. Homes count Btu (pronounced *bee-tee-you*), a *British thermal unit*, as a measurement of heat energy. A barrel of fuel oil (42 U.S. gallons) offers

140,000 Btus of energy. To produce 1 million Btus of heat energy, you'd need one of the following:

- ◆ 80 pounds of coal

- ◆ 250 pounds of hardwood

- ◆ 11 gallons of propane

- ◆ 7 gallons of #2 fuel oil

- ◆ 293 kWh of electricity

Those Btus can be used to develop heat for the house's air or to develop electricity to run appliances. And the appliances really don't care whether the power originally came from oil, gas, sunlight, wind, or Uncle Bob on a treadmill. Utility companies count Btus in *quads*.

def•i•ni•tion

A **British thermal unit** (Btu) equals 252 calories and will raise a pound of water 1°F. It's about equal to a match or burning candle. Because a Btu is a small unit of measure, larger quantities are measured in quads. A **quad** is a quadrillion (1,000,000,000,000,000) Btus. The world's energy consumption is about 400 quads per year—with the United States using about *one fourth* of it.

Let's talk about electricity for a moment. Electricity is the flow of electrons through a wire similar to how water flows through a pipe. (This isn't exactly how it happens, but it's close enough for illustration purposes.)

def•i•ni•tion

A **volt** (V) is a unit of measure of the force given the electrons in an electric circuit. An **ampere** or **amp** (A) is a unit of measure of the flow of electrons. An **ohm** (Ω) is a unit of measure of the resistance to the flow of an electric current. One volt produces 1 ampere of current against a resistance of 1 ohm.

To get water moving through a pipe, you open up a faucet, where the water is under pressure to push it down the pipe to where there is less pressure. Electricity flows in the same manner. The difference in pressure between one prong on the electric plug and the other makes the electricity flow down one wire and to the electrical appliance. That difference in pressure is measured in *volts*. The amount of electricity that actually flows is the current measured in *amperes* or *amps*. The resistance to flow that the wire offers is measured in *ohms*.

Homes in the United States and Canada are wired for appliances that need voltage of 110 or 220 volts. The actual voltage delivered can fluctuate by about 10 percent (100 to 120 volts or 200 to 240 volts) and still cause no problems. Most appliances in the home are designed to use 110 volts of electricity. Things such as electric clothes dryers, electric stoves and ovens, and some big shop tools need 220 votes to run.

Actually, the work is done by the electrical current (amps), which is the flow of electrons in a wire, similar to the flow of water in a pipe. (Power used by most home appliances is alternating current [AC]. Solar power is produced as direct current [DC]. Batteries, too, use DC.) Current needed to run an alarm clock is less than an amp, measured in milliamps (mA) or thousandths of an ampere. A refrigerator needs a few amps. A toaster, surprisingly, needs even more amps of current than a refrigerator. That's because the toaster runs current through high-resistance wire to develop heat that toasts your bagels.

Of course, the toaster may be in use for only a few minutes each day, the refrigerator compressor is on for a few hours, and the TV seemingly always. So what's a better way to measure an appliance's power needs than reading the amps?

Electric power is measured in watts. A kilowatt (kW) is 1,000 watts of electrical power. A watt-hour (Wh) is a unit measure of energy, 1 watt of power during one hour of time. Power used over time also is measured in kilowatt-hours (kWh), or 1,000 watts used for one hour. Your electric power company charges you by the kilowatt-hour, so it will be an important measurement as you consider solar power.

Here's the power formula: $V \times A = W$. That is, volts multiplied by amps equals wattage. Power is the force times the flow. The amount of power used over a given time is the power in watts or kilowatts multiplied by the time in hours.

One more term: *load*. A load is anything in an electrical circuit that, when the circuit is turned on, draws power from that circuit. A refrigerator is a load. A toaster, when toasting, is a load. A light, when switched on, is a load. So figuring out how much energy your home needs starts with totaling up all the loads as measured in watt-hours. That's called a *load evaluation* (an example form is shown in the following figure).

Appliance	Qty.	Volts	AC DC	P Y/N	Run Watts	Hours/Day	Days/Week	W-hours/Day	Percent of Total	Surge Watts	Ph-L Y/N
Espresso Maker (example)	1	117	AC	N	1350	0.20	7	270.0	6.8%	1350	N

Total Daily Average Watt-Hrs

Simple load evaluation or analysis form for figuring a total of all electrical loads in your home.

Use the manufacturer's specs if possible, but be careful of nameplate ratings that are the highest possible electrical draw for that appliance. Beware of appliances that have a "standby" mode and are really "on" 24 hours a day. If you can't find a rating, call us for advice (800-919-2400).

DESCRIPTION	WATTS
Refrigeration:	
4-yr.-old 22 cu. ft. auto defrost (approximate run time 7-9 hours per day)	500
New 22 cu. ft. auto defrost (approximate run time 7-8 hours per day)	200
12 cu. ft. Sun Frost refrigerator (approximate run time 6-9 hours per day)	58
4-yr.-old standard freezer (approximate run time 7-8 hours per day)	350
Dishwasher: cool dry	700
hot dry	1450
Trash compactor	1500
Can opener (electric)	100
Microwave (.5 cu. ft.)	900
Microwave (.8 to 1.5 cu. ft.)	1500
Exhaust hood	144
Coffeemaker	1200
Food processor	400
Toaster (2-slice)	1200
Coffee grinder	100
Blender	350
Food dehydrator	600
Mixer	120
Range, small burner	1250
Range, large burner	2100
Water Pumping:	
AC Jet Pump (1/3 hp), 300 gal per hour, 20' well depth, 30 psi	750

DESCRIPTION	WATTS
AC submersible pump (1/2 hp), 40' well depth, 30 psi	1000
DC pump for house pressure system (typical use is 1-2 hours per day)	60
DC submersible pump (typical use is 6 hours per day)	50
Shop:	
Worm drive 7 1/4" saw	1800
AC table saw, 10"	1800
AC grinder, 1/2 hp	1080
Hand drill, 3/8"	400
Hand drill, 1/2"	600
Entertainment/Telephones:	
TV (27-inch color)	170
TV (19-inch color)	80
TV (12-inch black & white)	16
Video games (not incl. TV)	20
Satellite system, 12-ft dish/VCR	30
DVD/CD player	30
AC powered stereo (avg. volume)	55
AC stereo, home theater	500
DC powered stereo (avg. volume)	15
CB (receiving)	10
Cellular telephone (on standby)	5
Cordless telephone (on standby)	5
Electric piano	30
Guitar amplifier (avg. volume)	40
(Jimi Hendrix volume)	8500
General Household:	
Typical fluorescent light (60W equivalent)	15
Incandescent lights (as indicated on bulb)	
Electric clock	4
Clock radio	5
Electric blanket	400
Iron (electric)	1200

DESCRIPTION	WATTS
Clothes washer (vertical axis)	900
Clothes washer (horizontal axis)	250
Dryer (gas)	500
Dryer (electric)	5750
Vacuum cleaner, average	900
Central vacuum	1500
Furnace fan:	
1/4 hp	600
1/3 hp	700
1/2 hp	875
Garage door opener: 1/4 hp	550
Alarm/security system	6
Air conditioner: 1 ton or 10,000 BTU/hr	1500
Office/Den:	
Computer	55
17" color monitor	100
17" LCD "flat screen" monitor	45
Laptop computer	25
Ink jet printer	35
Laser printer	900
Fax machine: (plain paper)	
standby	5
printing	50
Electric typewriter	200
Adding machine	8
Electric pencil sharpener	60
Hygiene:	
Hair dryer	1500
Waterpik	90
Whirlpool bath	750
Hair curler	750
Electric toothbrush: (charging stand)	6

List of typical loads for common household appliances.

How does electricity get to you? Somewhere there's an electrical power-generating plant. It converts fuel, probably coal or oil, into electricity using turbines. High-voltage power lines then distribute the power to stations, then substations, and then to transformers that deliver the electricity to your home as 220 volts.

> ### Solar Eclipse
>
> If you've never done so before, go find the main power panel for your home or apartment and carefully take a peek. You'll see where the main power line comes in and the circuit breakers or fuses with amp ratings printed on them (15, 20, 30, and so on). Just don't touch anything except circuit breaker switches or you may get electrocuted and not be able to finish reading this book!

So how do you get 110-volt electric service out of this? The power comes in on three wires: two have 110 volts each and the other is neutral. The main power panel in your house is wired to provide voltage between the neutral wire (ground) and one hot wire (for 110 volts) or both hot wires (for 220 volts). The power panel then distributes the power to specific circuits wired when your home was built. The circuits might be wired for loads of 15 amps, 20 amps, 30 amps, or some other value. To protect the appliance(s), the electricity first goes through a circuit breaker that stops electricity flow if it exceeds the rating.

Where Does the Energy Go?

A load evaluation adds up all the energy loads in your home to help you figure out what things cost—and where you can save money. In the preceding load evaluation form, there's a place to list each appliance in your home and calculate the average watt-hours it uses on an average day.

The table after that shows typical watt-hour loads for many household loads. Use it to complete your home's load evaluation form.

For example, a 19-inch cathode-ray tube (CRT) television may require 70 watts for three hours of viewing a day. That's 210 Wh (70 × 3). For an 800-watt coffeemaker that's on four hours daily, it has a load of 3.2 kWh. You get the picture.

What's average? It depends on how much you rely on electricity to heat your water, air, and food. Your daily average will probably be somewhere between 15 kWh and 20 kWh. Below 15 kWh is relatively efficient and above 20 kWh is wasteful. Your usage may vary.

Bright Idea _____

Want to let the pros perform your home energy audit? Your state energy office (see Appendix B) can refer you to a certified home-energy auditor who will go through your house with meters and infrared cameras, compiling an action list. Professional energy auditors typically charge $200 to $400 for their services. However, your electric utility or solar contractor may perform a simpler audit for you for *free*. Ask!

Add up all the loads and you should have a good idea of how much energy it takes to keep your home comfortable. Next comes reality. Pull out your latest electric bill. It will probably be shown in kilowatt-hours and will include the service dates (from, to), number of billing days, the prior and current meter readings, and the difference or total usage. The electric bill will then multiply usage by your rate to come up with a subtotal.

As you compile your load evaluation form, there will be many head scratchers—appliances that seem to use up more power than you think they should. That's because they're on even when they say "off." What gives? Actually, these are called *phantom loads*. Examples include instant-on televisions in which power is on to keep video components warmed up and ready to view. Electric clocks on appliances are also phantom loads, albeit low-amp loads. (Don't we already have enough clocks in the house!) Appliances such as computer speaker systems and telephone answering systems that use a transformer box or "wall wort" are also phantom loads. Sure, they don't take much juice, but each one adds up. A little 4-watt phantom load can cost $5 or $10 a year in electricity. An instant-on TV can cost lots more. It all adds up.

def•i•ni•tion _____

A **phantom load** is a device that draws a small electrical current when plugged in, typically to provide instant-on power to a larger device (such as a television) or to transform power from one voltage to another (such as 110 volts to 4 volts). If such a device, when plugged into the wall, becomes warm to the touch, it is drawing current.

What can you do about phantom loads? Unplug ones you really don't need. Or plug them into a power strip that has an on-off switch so you can turn off more than one.

Besides electricity, your home uses lots of other energy. Depending on where you live (or where you're planning to live), the primary heat source may be electricity, fuel oil, natural gas, coal, wood, or, near state capitals, gas-generating rhetoric. So pull out the utility bills for the last 12 months—or ask for a printout—and figure out how much you spent to heat water, air, and food.

To keep folks from using more energy than what's considered normal, many electric utilities have a lower baseline rate and a higher rate for any usage above the baseline. Your bill may also include energy surcharges. What's important for estimating electric costs is the final charge divided by the kilowatt-hours of power used to get a final kWh rate.

Want to know how much power you've bought from your local utility over the last year? Ask them! Most utilities can check their records (or let you do so online) to calculate your power usage. In fact, based on answers to usage questions, they can often tell you how much you spent on power for your refrigerator, oven, computer, television, dishwasher, and aquarium. To calculate home energy usage and discover savings opportunities, visit Pacific Gas & Electric's SmartEnergy Analyzer site at pge.com/energysurvey.

How Much Does Home Energy Cost?

Which heating fuel is the most economical and efficient? The answer depends on the following:

- ◆ Cost of raw materials (crude oil, natural gas, sunlight, wind, and so on)
- ◆ Cost to process the material into usable power
- ◆ Cost to deliver the power to you
- ◆ Energy content of the fuel, measured in Btus
- ◆ Efficiency of the furnace or appliance
- ◆ Cost of maintaining the appliance

In many situations, the fuel resource used to develop electricity is already determined by local availability and costs. In the Pacific Northwest, hydroelectric power is cheapest because water is abundant. In the eastern United States, the fuel is typically coal. In the Midwest, fuel oil and natural gas provide much of the heating fuel and most of the electricity. In California, it's a combination, but primarily natural gas.

Many home appliances use electricity. Heating appliances such as furnaces, stoves, and water heaters might use electricity or a less-expensive heat source such as fuel oil or natural gas. The key here is what's least expensive.

Solar Eclipse

Where does the power come from? In California, for example, Pacific Gas & Electric (PG&E) currently produces 47 percent of its power from natural gas, 20 percent from nuclear, 16 percent from hydroelectric, and just 2 percent from coal fuel. About 15 percent is produced from renewable sources: biomass/waste, geothermal, small hydroelectric, solar, and wind sources.

Heating fuel prices fluctuate. Recently, the Energy Information Administration figured out the national average residential fuel costs and divided it by the typical fuel appliance efficiency to come up with some interesting comparisons:

- Coal heat costs $9.06 per million Btus.

- Wood heat costs $9.09 per million Btus.

- Natural gas in a central heating system costs $12.61 per million Btus.

- Oil in a central heating system costs $18.53 per million Btus.

- Propane in a central heating system costs $24.66 per million Btus.

- Electric resistance heat costs $33.25 per million Btus.

That's right, electric heat costs more than three times as much as coal or wood heat!

So how much do electric appliances cost to run? Not that much—unless you add it all up. Consider the following examples (source: Pacific Gas & Electric):

- Electric baseboard or central air heater (2,000-square-foot home): $160 to $500 or more per month

- Natural or propane gas furnace heater (2,000-square-foot home): $75 to $300 or more per month

- Frost-free refrigerator (20 cubic feet): $20 to $35 per month

- Water heater: electric, $35 to $90 per month; gas, $12 to $30 per month

- Window air conditioner: $0.15 to $0.40 per hour

- Central air conditioner: $0.60 to $0.85 per hour

- Laundry water: $0.62 for electric water heater or $0.18 for gas water heater per load

- Clothes washer: $0.07 to $0.35 per load

- Clothes dryer: electric, $0.40 to $0.75 per load; gas, $0.15 to $0.28 per load

- Electric oven: $0.40 to $0.90 per hour

- Gas oven: $0.10 to $0.22 per hour

- Microwave oven: $0.03 to $0.05 for 10 minutes

- Dishwasher: $0.12 to $0.16 per load

- Hair dryer: $0.03 for five minutes

- Incandescent light bulb (100 W): $0.03 per hour

- Equivalent compact fluorescent light bulb (27 watts): $0.03 for four hours

- CRT television: $0.03 to $0.08 per hour

- Personal computer: $0.03 to $0.05 per hour

Here's another important fact: it takes the power company about 3.3 kWh of energy to deliver 1 kWh of electricity to your home! That means your solar electric system saves more than just the power you don't use.

Bright Idea

Let's talk money! Compact fluorescent bulbs that replace incandescent bulbs can save enough electricity in one year to pay for themselves—and light up your life for many more years for free. Putting all your phantom power loads on a power strip that you turn off when the attached devices are not needed can save you up to 5 percent on your electric bill. And here's a big money saver: buy ENERGY STAR replacement appliances because they reduce power needs over older models by at least 30 percent. That's money you can use to lay in the sun!

Considering a Solar Power System

You can save money by reducing the costs of heat and power your home needs. Every watt not used is at least a watt that doesn't have to be produced, distributed, stored, or purchased!

So how does the sun fit into all this? The sun is an efficient source of solar energy that can be used to heat and/or power your home. There are two ways you can utilize solar energy to power your home.

First, you can encourage your local utility and state utility board to use more renewable energy sources, especially solar. You can become involved in the political and economic battle being fought over energy. Check Appendix B for more information.

Second, you can enlist as a soldier in the battle against nonrenewable energy. You can install solar thermal and solar electric systems in your current home, next home, apartment, vacation cabin, recreation vehicle, business, or other energy-dependent residence.

Exactly how much will solar power systems cost you? Unfortunately, it's not easy to come up with an estimate. Solar power systems are becoming a commodity that you can quickly size and buy at your local super-hardware store. Even so, there are incentives and rebates (see Chapter 2), equipment life, depreciation, and many other factors that vary based on what you're doing and where you live. Be wary regarding government incentives and rebates, though, as no program is safe from cuts while the legislature is in session.

Sun Spots

How much will your new solar power system cost and what are the benefits? Find out with one of the free Clean Power Estimator programs available online. Search for "clean power estimator." California's version is at consumerenergycenter.org, but it works for locations outside of California, too. Enter your zip code and the type of system, verify the assumptions, and get the results, including estimated cost, net savings, production, and emissions eliminated with clean renewable energy power.

Fortunately, this book was written to take you through each step of the process, offering the information you need to make wise decisions.

Fifty Ways to Cut Your Home Energy Bills Right Now!

This appendix offers some practical solutions for making your home more energy efficient. Included are ideas on how to reduce your home's dependency on costly energy. After the fuel bill is cut and you're still living comfortably, you can begin investing in solar solutions. According to *Home Power Magazine* (homepower.com), every dollar you spend on making your home more efficient decreases the cost of your power system by approximately $3 to $5!

Understanding Heat Transfer

Here's how it works: Heat energy seeks equilibrium. That is, heat on the outside of a cooler house wants to get in. Heat on the inside wants to go outdoors and play. If only nice, dense walls stood in its way, heat transfer would be very slow. But most houses have doors and windows and lots of little air leaks to speed up the transfer.

Of course, that wouldn't be a problem if climate maintenance were free. Unfortunately, keeping a house cool in hot weather and warm in a cold climate costs lots of bucks. When purchased, that high-priced warm (or cool) air needs to stay where you put it. The trick is to minimize heat transfer through the house's walls, doors, and windows.

Auditing Your Energy

How efficiently is your home using the energy you buy for it? In human terms, what's its metabolic rate?

Good question. You can get a good answer with a *home energy audit*. You can do the audit yourself, hire a contractor to do some or all of it, or ask your energy provider(s) to do it for you. Let's take a closer look at your options.

Do It Yourself

You can easily conduct a home energy audit yourself. During a simple walk-through, you can spot the more obvious energy losses, the ones that cost the most. Drafts or air leaks can suck up 5 to 30 percent of your home's energy, so that's a good place to start. On a very cold or very hot day, walk around the inside of your home feeling for temperature differences around windows, doors, fireplace dampers, attic hatches, and window air conditioners. Also check under sinks for gaps around pipes and around electrical outlets, especially on exterior walls. The solution is insulation, weatherstripping, and caulking.

def•i•ni•tion

A **home energy audit** is an analysis of how things in your home use and lose energy. It checks not only appliances (users), but also doors and windows (losers). An audit helps you determine where costly energy is wasted.

Sun Spots

Home-energy audit tools and instructions are available online. One popular website, hes/lbl.gov, is provided by the Environmental Energy Technologies Division at Lawrence Berkeley National Laboratory. Based on your location and specific home, it can help you identify ways to save energy. And it's *free!*

Next, take a closer look at those windows and doors. Depending on how much energy you're losing through them, more energy-efficient windows may be a good investment. Before spending the money, though, consider hiring an expert who can give you exact costs and estimate how long it will take for energy savings to pay you back.

A better way to find drafts is to do a pressurization test. To perform the test, close all exterior doors, windows, and fireplace flues. For safety, turn off all gas-burning appliances with pilot lights. Then turn on all exhaust fans, typically in the bathrooms and kitchen, to pull air out of the house. Finally, walk around inside the house perimeter with a burning incense stick or candle and watch the smoke or flame point *away* from drafts. Check closely around windows, doors, electric outlets, and fireplaces. The flame or smoke indicates how much of a draft there is by making the results of the draft visible. Remember to restart any gas appliances you turned off for the test.

In addition to losing energy through drafts, many homes lose energy through walls and ceilings. Insulation is installed in walls, as they are built to keep expensive interior air inside the house. You can check your home's insulation in various ways. The easiest is to look at the building plans if you have them, as they will indicate the R value of the home when built. An R value is a laboratory standard that defines a material's resistance to heat transfer. The higher the number, the more it will resist the transfer of heat through it. Otherwise, you may need to crawl up into the attic and below the house to see what insulation is exposed and try to read or estimate its R value.

You can sometimes check a wall's insulation by carefully uncovering an exterior electrical wall plug. Visually inspect the insulation for type and depth and whether it has a plastic or paper vapor barrier intended to keep moisture away from the insulation.

After you've checked your home's insulation, call your energy company or an insulation contractor to determine whether it's adequate for the local climate.

The next part of your energy audit is to figure out how efficient your heating and/or cooling system is. If it is more than about 15 years old, chances are a new energy-efficient model is a good investment. Newer heating furnaces surpass 90 percent efficiency. Newer air conditioners and heat pumps, too, are designed to use less energy. Also make sure that the ducts and pipes leading to and from these units are insulated and sealed as needed.

Sun Spots

About one third of escaping air in a home moves through floors, walls, and ceilings. Another third climbs out through plumbing, ducts, electrical outlets, and vents. One sixth goes through the fireplace or furnace flue, if any. And the final sixth makes its escape through doors and windows.

At least 10 percent of your energy bills pay for lighting. You can cut energy costs now with just a few lighting tips.

- Buy bulbs by their lumens (light) and life expectancy rather than their wattage (60 watts, 75 watts, 100 watts, and so on).

- In bright rooms, remove some of the light bulbs.

- Replace incandescent bulbs with new compact fluorescent bulbs, as they can last 10 times longer and use a quarter of the electricity.

Professional Energy Audits

House doctors and energy-efficiency contractors have more tools and knowledge than you do. If you think your house is losing lots of energy, consider investing in a professional audit to determine where the problems are. You can find house doctors and energy-efficiency contractors in the telephone book's yellow pages under "Energy Conservation Services and Products" or a similar heading. Plan on spending up to $300 for a professional energy audit.

In addition, many public and private utility companies will do an energy audit on your home at little or no cost. To find one, drag out your utility bills and look for a customer service telephone number or Internet address. Utilities are listed in the phone book under "Electric Service and Utility Providers," "Gas Utility Companies," and similar headings.

What can these pros do that you can't? They have the knowledge and equipment to conduct a *blower door test* and a *thermographic scan* of your house. They also have the eyes and know-how to see things you may miss in your energy audit.

def•i•ni•tion

A **blower door test** uses a powerful fan installed in an exterior door frame to pull air out of the house and lowers the interior air pressure. It's similar to the pressurization test you can perform, except better. The auditor will probably use a smoke pencil or other equipment instead of incense or candles to find air leaks. Calibrated blower doors will actually tell the auditor how much air leakage the house has and indicate how effective air-sealing will be. A **thermographic scan** uses infrared light to detect places in your home where air and heat are leaking. In good weather, the auditor will do an exterior scan; in inclement weather, the scan will probably be done on the interior of the home. Thermographic scans are quite accurate. The test costs between $300 and $500.

Before the energy auditor arrives at your house, make a list of anything you recognize as an energy loss, such as an especially drafty room or door. In addition, make sure the auditor can easily access your furnace or other heat source, as well as the main power panel and main gas shutoffs as appropriate. Have your energy bills nearby or get a printout of the last 12 months from all your utilities.

Where can you find a qualified energy auditor? Again, check the telephone book and your utility companies. In addition, try the National Association of Energy Service Companies (NAESCO) on the Internet at naesco.org.

Also, if you'll be financing your solar power system with an energy-efficient mortgage (read: lower interest rates!), you'll probably need a certified inspection by an accredited Home Energy Rating System (HERS) inspector.

You've Been Audited—Now What?

After your home has been audited for energy use and waste, what can you do about it? Solar power is an excellent resource. However, it requires an investment. And the less energy your home wastes, the smaller that investment will be. So there are many things you can do to your existing home or the one you're building to keep solar energy investment costs down.

First, prioritize. Where does your audit tell you that you're losing the most energy? Also factor in that some energy sources are more expensive than others. The question you're trying to answer is: Where can I most efficiently spend my money to cut energy costs?

Next, consider how much of the work you can do yourself and how much others should do. For example, following the instructions on the box, you can probably install window weatherstripping products. However, you may decide not to tackle installing new energy-efficient windows. Or you may have to hire an insulation contractor to drill holes in your home's walls and blow in insulation, but you might be able to install insulation in an open attic yourself. You can probably also buy and change out all your light bulbs without any assistance.

Finally, work by priority. Make a plan that gets you working on or paying for those projects with the highest return on your investment of time and money.

Payback, what business folks call the payback period, is as important to you as it is to businesses. Simply put, payback is the time it takes for total savings to catch up with total costs. If a $1,000 investment in energy efficiency saves you $250 a year in energy costs, the payback is four years. After that, the savings continue, although the costs don't. You profit. If the equipment lasts 20 years, you'll get 16 years of virtually free service (other than required maintenance).

Here are some projects that can pay you back relatively quickly and for little or no money:

- Wear a sweater inside during the winter or a light shirt or blouse during the summer to reduce heating and cooling needs.
- Close doors, windows, and heater vents in unoccupied rooms.

- Only use bathroom and kitchen fans as necessary because they pull conditioned air from your home.

- Caulk around plumbing and ducting, especially near the house's crawlspace and exterior.

- Install gasket seals (available from hardware stores) under the cover plate on electrical outlets installed along outside walls.

- Caulk and weather strip doors and windows.

- Use solar awnings, shades, drapes, and other window coverings to keep excess heat from entering your home through south- or west-facing windows.

- If you have a fireplace, keep the flue damper or firebox doors tightly closed when not in use.

- Reset heat thermostats for greater efficiency.

- Replace old thermostats with new digital controllers (cost: less than $75).

- Repair or replace leaky faucets, especially hot water faucets.

- Move refrigerators away from stoves or other heat sources.

- Keep the dryer's lint trap clean.

- Change incandescent light bulbs for more efficient fluorescent ones.

- Install storm windows and doors.

- Install ceiling fans as needed to circulate conditioned air.

- Clean or replace dirty furnace filters every two to three months during use seasons.

- Insulate your hot water heater and related hot water pipes to minimize energy loss.

- Lower the hot water heater temperature to 115°F.

- Take more showers and fewer baths, as a five-minute shower takes half the water of a bath.

- Maintain appliances and plumbing systems so energy isn't wasted.

- At least four times a year, vacuum the areas behind and under your refrigerator to keep it from working too hard; older refrigerators need to be cleaned more often. Let as much air circulate around the refrigerator as possible by not jamming it into a tight space; let it breathe!

♦ Replace worn-out appliances with those that have higher energy-efficiency ratings. Talk with the salesperson; a high-cost but more efficient unit may pay for itself in short order.

The U.S. Department of Energy has an ENERGY STAR program (energystar.gov) that rates and labels major appliances and other products for energy efficiency. An EnergyGuide is posted on new major appliances to show what the typical energy costs for the appliances are (see the following figure).

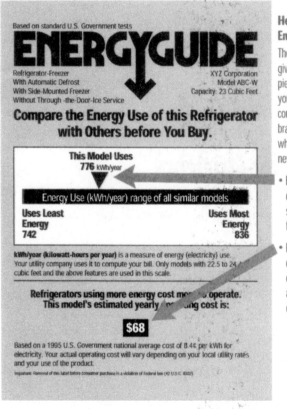

How to Read the EnergyGuide Label

The EnergyGuide label gives you two important pieces of information you can use for comparison of different brands and models when shopping for a new refrigerator:

• Estimated energy consumption on a scale showing a range for similar models

• Estimated yearly operating cost based on the national average cost of electricity.

An EnergyGuide on new appliances compares the typical energy used in a year based on averages.

In addition, here are some suggestions for projects with longer paybacks and the chapters of this book where you'll find more information:

♦ In moderate climates, consider an energy-efficient heat pump, because it can save 30 to 40 percent in energy costs compared to a furnace and air conditioner (see Chapter 5).

- Install a solar water heater (see Chapter 9) to reduce water heating costs.

- Install a solar space heater (see Chapter 10) to cut heating bills.

Bright Idea _____

At least twice a year, use the spigot near the bottom to drain a gallon of water from your water heater. This removes sediment that impedes heat transfer.

- Install a solar electric generating system (see Chapter 7) to reduce the need for outside electricity.

- Consider installing wind, water, and other power-producing systems for your home (see Chapter 8).

- Replace inefficient windows and doors (see Chapter 5).

- Take advantage of any tax credits and rebates available to you (see Chapter 2).

- If you're building a new home or refinancing your current one, consider an energy-efficient mortgage (see Chapter 3).

Building and Retrofitting for Efficiency

Fortunately, you can design your house to minimize heat transfer at little relative expense. Experts know lots more about how to do this than our parents knew when they shopped for housing.

What you're looking for as you consider which building materials to buy are those materials with the highest R value. If materials have an R value, more is better. That is, 4 inches of fiberglass has an R-13 value. Six inches is rated at R-23. That's why 2- × 6-inch insulated exterior walls are more energy efficient than 2- × 4-inch walls.

Local code and building practices will dictate the minimum R values you should have in your house. Obviously, you don't need the same value for a home in sunny San Diego as you do for one in chilly Minneapolis.

There's a point of diminishing returns, however. For example, the cost of increasing the R value to its upper limits may be greater than the amount of money you would save from the decreased energy use you would achieve. Smart planning is important.

So here are some ideas to consider as you plan your house to be more energy efficient:

- Build your house with 2- × 6-inch exterior walls if you need a higher R value and pack it with thicker insulation.

◆ Use the most efficient insulation you can afford.

◆ Install low-emissivity (low-e) glass coated to reduce heat conductivity without reducing light.

◆ Insulate ceilings well, even higher than the local recommended R value.

◆ Ventilate the attic above well-insulated ceilings to allow trapped heat to escape.

◆ Install radiant barriers under the rafters to limit significantly heat infiltration during warm weather.

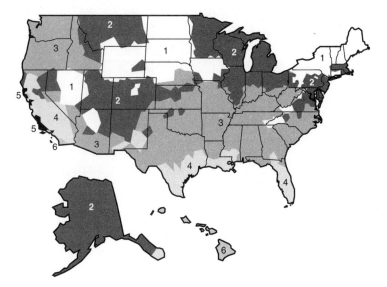

National insulation zones.

◆ Check walls as they are built to fill up any air leaks from the outside.

◆ Include a supplier-recommended moisture barrier in walls to keep them from sweating.

◆ Place heat registers near the floor and return vents near the ceiling, because heat rises.

◆ Buy the most efficient model fireplace you can afford if you must have one in your home. Fireplaces in general are inefficient heat sources.

◆ Buy a 92-plus percent efficient heating furnace rated in Btus to match or exceed your house's needs.

Insulation R values by zone.

Zone	Gas	Heat pump	Fuel oil	Electric furnace	Ceiling Attic	Ceiling Cathedral	Wall (A)	Floor	Crawl space (B)	Slab edge	Basement Interior	Basement Exterior
1	✓	✓	✓		R-49	R-38	R-18	R-25	R-19	R-8	R-11	R-10
1				✓	R-49	R-60	R-28	R-25	R-19	R-8	R-19	R-15
2	✓	✓	✓		R-49	R-38	R-18	R-25	R-19	R-8	R-11	R-10
2				✓	R-49	R-38	R-22	R-25	R-19	R-8	R-19	R-15
3	✓	✓	✓	✓	R-49	R-38	R-18	R-25	R-19	R-8	R-11	R-10
4	✓	✓	✓		R-38	R-38	R-13	R-13	R-19	R-4	R-11	R-4
4				✓	R-49	R-38	R-18	R-25	R-19	R-8	R-11	R-10
5	✓				R-38	R-30	R-13	R-11	R-13	R-4	R-11	R-4
5		✓	✓		R-38	R-38	R-13	R-13	R-19	R-4	R-11	R-4
5				✓	R-49	R-38	R-18	R-25	R-19	R-8	R-11	R-10
6	✓				R-22	R-22	R-11	R-11	R-11	(C)	R-11	R-4
6		✓	✓		R-38	R-30	R-13	R-11	R-13	R-4	R-11	R-4
6				✓	R-49	R-38	R-18	R-25	R-19	R-8	R-11	R-10

(A) R-18, R-22, and R-28 exterior wall systems can be achieved by either cavity insulation or cavity insulation with insulating sheathing. For 2 in x 4 in walls, use either 3-1/2-in thick R-15 or 3-1/2-in thick R-13 fiber glass insulation with insulating sheathing. For 2 in x 6 in walls, use either 5-1/2-in thick R-21 or 6-1/4-in thick R-19 fiber glass insulation.

(B) Insulate crawl space walls only if the crawl space is dry all year, the floor above is not insulated, and all ventilation to the crawl space is blocked. A vapor retarder (e.g., 4- or 6-mil polyethylene film) should be installed on the ground to reduce moisture migration into the crawl space.

(C) No slab edge insulation is recommended.

♦ Make sure your thermostat is computerized and can be set to make multiple temperature changes during the day. Every degree you turn down your heat setting can save you about 2 percent of your fuel bill.

Solar Eclipse

A standard exterior door without a threshold and weatherstripping allows as much air to pass through as a 5- × 5-inch hole.

♦ Include double-glazed or low-e windows in your budget for long-term energy savings.

♦ Insulate any heating ducts that run through unheated basements or crawl spaces.

♦ Remember to use weatherstripping and apply caulking around exterior doors and windows.

Expanding Awareness

The biggest step you can take toward making a better world is to become more aware of our limited resources. You've already started by learning about the limits of fossil fuels and where we're headed. You're now more aware of the *long-term* costs of energy—not just the monthly electric bill. Good for you!

You can carry that awareness over into other aspects of your life. You have daily choices: how to spend your money, what to drive, whether to recycle, what efforts to support, and which to discourage. Your decisions have long-term implications. You can make them with an eye on greater energy efficiency.

Want some examples?

◆ Take a closer look at miles per gallon (mpg) estimates when buying a new or used car or selecting a rental car for a trip. Or consider an electric or hybrid car.

◆ Think about long-term fuel costs as you plan your daily or weekly errands. Run as many of your errands as you can at one time to avoid making a lot of short trips.

◆ Find out what recycling opportunities your solid waste (trash) service offers. (In many places, recycling your trash is required; if it's still not required in your area, why not get in the habit anyway?)

◆ Reuse whatever you can around the house. For example, used computer paper makes great drawing paper for kids, and kitchen scraps can be composted for the garden.

Bright Idea

Numerous alternative, back-to-basics magazines are available at bookstores and larger newsstands. They include *Mother Earth News*, *Home Power*, *Backwoods Home*, *Popular Science*, and others.

◆ Read and consider the ENERGY STAR label when buying major appliances.

◆ Rinse out and reuse plastic food bags.

◆ When grocery shopping, ask for paper bags instead of plastic bags; paper bags are kinder to the environment. Or better yet, bring your own reusable grocery bags.

◆ Use natural light or less light whenever possible. Use lower-watt light bulbs and dimmer switches where possible. Install solar tubes in your home's ceiling. And don't forget to turn off the lights when you don't need them.

◆ Consider alternative transportation, such as the bus or train, for commuting. Carpool if possible. If there's no carpool available, organize one!

- Walk or ride your bike instead of taking the car on short trips; it saves on gas and it's good for you!

- Start planning your *next* solar home right now based on what you've learned with this one.

These suggestions are just a start. By being aware of what you're using up and how to reuse it or reduce your use of it, you're helping to cut costs and our dependency on borrowing from the future.

That's more than 50 ways you can not only cut home energy bills, but also reduce the initial costs of any renewable energy system that you install. Again, for every dollar you spend on making your home more efficient, you decrease the cost of your power system by approximately $3 to $5! It makes smart sense to consider low-cost efficiencies before planning solar power for your home.

Solar Glossary

absorbers   Dark-colored objects that soak up heat in solar collectors.

absorption coefficient   The factor by which photons are absorbed as they travel a unit distance through a material.

acceptor   A dopant material, such as boron, which has fewer outer shell electrons than required in an otherwise balanced crystal structure, providing a hole that can accept a free electron.

activated shelf life   The time it takes for the capacity of a charged battery to fall to an unusable level when stored at a specified temperature.

activation voltage   The voltage at which the controller will operate to protect the batteries.

active solar heater   A solar water or space-heating system that moves heated air or water using pumps or fans.

adjustable setpoint   A feature allowing the user to adjust the voltage levels at which a charge controller will become active.

alternating current (AC)   Electric current in which the direction of flow is reversed at frequent intervals, usually 100 or 120 times per second (50 or 60 cycles per second or 50/60 Hz).

alternator   A device for producing alternating current (AC) electricity. It is usually driven by a motor, but can also be driven by other means, including water and wind power.

ambient temperature   The temperature of the surroundings.

American Wire Gauge (AWG)   A standard system for designating the size of electrical wire. The higher the number, the smaller the wire. Most house wiring is AWG 12 or 14.

ammeter   A device used for measuring current flow at any point in an electrical circuit.

amorphous silicon   A thin-film solar PV cell material that has a glassy rather than crystalline structure. It is manufactured by depositing layers of doped silicon on a substrate.

amp-hour (Ah)   The quantity of electrical energy corresponding to the flow of current of one ampere for one hour. The term is used to quantify the energy stored in a battery. Most batteries are rated in Ah.

ampere or **amp (A)**   The unit for the electric current; the flow of electrons. One amp is 1 coulomb passing in one second. One amp is produced by an electric force of 1 volt acting across a resistance of 1 ohm.

anemometer   A device used to measure wind speed.

angle of incidence   The angle between horizontal and the angle of a solar panel.

annual solar savings   The energy savings of a solar building attributable to a solar feature relative to the energy requirements of a nonsolar building.

anode   The positive electrode in a battery. The positive terminal of a diode.

antireflection coating   A thin coating of a material that reduces the light reflection and increases light transmission, applied to a photovoltaic cell surface.

array   A group of solar electric modules connected together in a power system.

array current   The electrical current output of a PV array when exposed to sunlight.

array operating voltage   The voltage output of a PV array when exposed to sunlight and feeding a load.

autonomous system   A stand-alone PV system that has no backup generating source. It may or may not include storage batteries.

availability   The quality or condition of a PV system that is available to provide power to a load. It is usually measured in hours per year.

avoided cost   The minimum amount that an electric utility is required to pay an independent power producer under the Energy Policy Act of 2005. It is equal to the costs the utility calculates it avoids in not having to produce that power (usually substantially less than the retail price charged by the utility for power it sells to customers).

azimuth   The angle (in degrees) between north and a specific location. As applied to the PV array, 180° azimuth means the array faces due south.

balance of system   All components and costs other than the PV modules. It includes design costs, land, site preparation, system installation, support structures, power conditioning, operation and maintenance costs, indirect storage, and related costs.

ballast   A circuit used to stabilize an electric current, for example, in a fluorescent light.

base power   Power generated by a utility unit that operates at a very high capacity factor.

battery   A system in which stored chemical energy is converted directly into electrical energy. It can be either rechargeable or nonrechargeable.

battery bank   A group of batteries wired together to store power in a solar electric system. It allows you to use the stored power at night and on cloudy days or to run more power than the array can produce at one time.

battery capacity   The total number of ampere-hours (Ah) that a fully charged battery can output.

battery cell   An individual unit of a battery that can store electrical energy and is capable of furnishing a current to an external load. For lead-acid batteries, the voltage of a cell (fully charged) is about 2.2 volts DC. A battery may consist of a number of cells.

battery charger   A device used to charge a battery by converting AC voltage to a DC voltage suitable for the battery. Chargers often incorporate some form of regulator to prevent overcharging and damage to the battery.

battery cycle life   The number of times a battery can undergo a cycle of discharge and recharge before failing. Cycle life is normally specified as a function of discharge rate and temperature.

battery self-discharge   Energy loss by a battery that is not under load.

battery state of charge (SOC)   The extent of battery charge status as a percentage of full charge. Also 100 percent minus the depth of discharge.

blocking diode   A diode used to prevent current flow in an undesirable direction (for example, from the rest of the PV array to a failed module, or from the battery to the PV array when current generation is low).

boron (B)   A chemical element, atomic number 5, semimetallic in nature, used as a dopant to make p-semiconductor layers.

British thermal unit (Btu)   The amount of heat energy required to raise 1 pound of water from a temperature of 60°F to 61°F at one atmosphere pressure. One watt-hour equals 3,413 Btu.

building-integrated PV (BIPV)   A term for the design and integration of PV into the building envelope, typically replacing conventional building materials. This integration may be in vertical facades, replacing view glass, spandrel glass, or other facade material; in semitransparent skylight systems; in roofing systems, replacing traditional roofing materials; in shading "eyebrows" over windows; or other building envelope systems.

bypass diode   A diode connected across one or more solar cells in a photovoltaic module such that the diode will conduct if the cell(s) change polarity.

cadmium (Cd)   A chemical element, atomic number 48, used in making certain types of solar cells and batteries.

cadmium telluride (CdTe)   A polycrystalline thin-film photovoltaic material.

capacitor   An electronic component used for the temporary storage of electricity, as well for removing unwanted noise in circuits. A capacitor blocks direct current but passes alternating current.

captive electrolyte battery   A battery with an immobilized electrolyte (gelled or absorbed in a material).

cathode   The negative electrode in an electrochemical cell. Also, the negative terminal of a diode.

cell   The basic unit of a PV module or battery. The most basic unit that contains the necessary materials, such as electrodes and electrolyte in a battery, to produce electricity.

cell barrier   A very thin region of static electric charge along the interface of the positive and negative layers in a photovoltaic cell. The barrier inhibits the movement of electrons from one layer to the other, so that higher-energy electrons from one side diffuse preferentially through it in one direction, creating a current and thus a voltage across the cell. Also called depletion zone, cell junction, or space charge.

cell efficiency   The ratio of the electrical energy produced by a photovoltaic cell (under full sun conditions or 1 kW per square meter) to the energy from sunlight falling upon the photovoltaic cell.

charge   The process of adding electrical energy to a battery for storage.

charge controller   A component that controls the flow of current to and from the battery subsystem to protect the batteries from overcharge and overdischarge. It is essential for ensuring that batteries obtain the maximum state of charge and longest life. The charge controller may also monitor system performance and provide system protection. Charge controllers are also sometimes called regulators.

charge factor   The time in hours during which a battery can be charged at a constant current without damaging the battery.

charge rate   A measure of the current used to charge a battery as a proportion of its capacity.

chlorofluorocarbon   A family of chemicals composed primarily of carbon, hydrogen, chlorine, and fluorine whose principal applications are that of refrigerants and industrial cleansers and whose principal drawback is the tendency to destroy Earth's protective ozone layer.

circuit   A continuous system of conductors providing a path for electricity.

circuit breaker   A device that acts like an automatic switch that can shut the power off when it senses too much current.

cloud enhancement   The increase in solar intensity due to reflected light from nearby clouds.

coal   A black, solid fossil fuel found in the earth. Coal is often burned to make electricity.

cogeneration   The process in which fuel is used to produce heat for a boiler-steam turbine or gas for a turbine. The turbine drives a generator that produces electricity, while the excess heat is used to process steam.

combined collector   A photovoltaic device or module that provides useful heat energy in addition to electricity.

compact fluorescent lights   Lights that use a lot less energy than regular light bulbs. We can use compact fluorescent lights for reading lights and ceiling lights.

concentrator   A photovoltaic device that uses optical elements (such as mirrors or lenses) to increase the amount of light incident on a solar PV cell. Concentrator arrays track the sun and use only direct sunlight since the diffuse portion cannot be focused. Concentrators therefore work best in clear-sky locations. Efficiency is increased, but cell life may be reduced because operating temperatures are higher.

conductor   A material used to transfer, or conduct, electricity, often in the form of wires.

conduit   A pipe or elongated box used to house and protect electrical cables.

constant-speed wind turbines   Turbines that operate at a constant rotor revolutions per minute (RPM) and are optimized for energy capture at a given rotor diameter at a particular speed in plotting wind power.

contact resistance   The resistance between metallic contacts and the semiconductor.

controller   The device that regulates the current from solar charger to your battery bank.

conversion efficiency   The ratio of the electrical energy generated by a solar PV cell to the solar energy impacting the cell.

converter   Equipment that converts a direct current (DC) voltage into another DC voltage.

cross-flow turbine   A turbine where the flow of water is at right angles to the axis of rotation of the turbine.

crystalline silicon   A type of PV cell material made from a single crystal or poly-crystalline ingot of silicon.

current   The flow of electric charge in a conductor between two points having a difference in electrical potential (voltage); it is measured in amps.

current at maximum power (Imp)   The current at which maximum power is available from a module.

cutoff voltage   The voltage levels at which the charge controller (regulator) disconnects the PV array from the battery or the load from the battery.

cycle   One complete discharge and recharge cycle of a battery.

cycle life   The number of discharge-charge cycles that a battery can tolerate under specified conditions before it fails to meet specified criteria for performance (for example, capacity decreases to 80 percent of the nominal capacity).

days of storage   The number of days that a stand-alone system will power a specified load without solar energy input. It is a measure of system autonomy.

DC daily power budget   The number of watts that DC appliances use daily.

DC to DC converter   An electronic circuit that converts DC voltages (such as a PV module voltage) into other levels (such as load voltage). The converter can be part of a maximum power point tracker.

deep discharge   The discharging of a battery to 20 percent or less of its full charge.

deep-cycle battery   A battery designed to regularly discharge 80 percent of its capacity before recharging.

depth of discharge (DOD)   The amount of energy withdrawn from a battery or cell expressed as a percentage of its rated capacity.

diffuse insolation   Incident sunlight received indirectly because of scattering due to clouds, fog, particulates, or other obstructions in the atmosphere. The other component of sunlight is direct.

diode   An electronic device that allows current to flow only in one direction.

direct current (DC)   Electrical current that flows only in one direction, although it may vary in magnitude. It contrasts with alternating current (AC).

direct insolation   Sunlight falling directly upon a collector. It is the opposite of diffuse insolation.

direct radiation   Light that has traveled in a straight path from the sun (also referred to as beam radiation). An object in the path of direct radiation casts a shadow on a clear day.

direct-gain building   A building in which sunlight directly enters the structure through the windows and is absorbed and stored in massive floors or walls. These buildings are elongated in the east-west direction, and most of their windows are on the south side. The area devoted to south windows varies throughout the country. It could be as much as 20 percent of the floor area in sunny cold climates, where advanced glazings or movable insulation are recommended to prevent heat loss at night. These buildings have high insulation levels and added thermal mass for heat storage.

discharge factor   A number equivalent to the time in hours during which a battery is discharged at constant current usually expressed as a percentage of the total battery capacity; for example, C/5 indicates a discharge factor of five hours.

discharge rate   A measure of the current withdrawn from a battery over time, expressed as a percentage of battery capacity. A C/5 discharge rate indicates a current of one fifth of the rated capacity of the battery.

disconnect   A switch used to connect or disconnect individual components in a PV system.

distributed power   The generic term for any power supply located near the point where the power is used.

distributed systems   Systems that are installed at or near the location where the electricity is used, as opposed to central systems that supply electricity to grids. A residential photovoltaic system is a distributed system.

dopant   A chemical element (impurity) added in small amounts to an otherwise pure semiconductor material to modify the electrical properties of the material. An n-dopant introduces more electrons. A p-dopant creates electron vacancies (holes).

doping   Adding an impurity (dopant) to a material to modify its properties to achieve an enhanced effect.

downtime   Time during which the PV system cannot provide power to the load, expressed either in hours per year or as a percentage.

dry cell battery   A battery that uses a solid paste for an electrolyte.

duty cycle   The ratio of active to total time, used to describe the operating regime of loads in PV systems.

duty rating   The amount of time an inverter can operate at full rated power. Some inverters can operate at their rated power for only a short time without overheating.

earth   Refers to connecting a part of an electrical system physically to the ground. Earthing is done as a safety measure, by means of a conductor embedded in suitable soil.

efficiency   The ratio of output power or energy to input power or energy, expressed as a percentage.

electric circuit   The path followed by electrons from a power source (generator or battery) through an external line (including devices that use the electricity) and returning through another line to the source.

electric current   The flow of electrons measured in amps.

electrical grid   A network for electricity distribution across a large area.

electricity   The movement of electrons (subatomic particles), produced by a voltage power, through a conductor.

electrode   An electrically conductive material, forming part of an electrical device, often used to lead current into or out of a liquid or gas. In a battery, the electrodes are also known as plates.

electrolyte   A liquid conductor of electricity.

electron volt   An energy unit equal to the energy that an electron acquires when it passes through a potential difference of 1 volt.

energy   The ability to do work. Stored energy becomes working energy when we use it.

energy audit   A survey that shows how much energy you use in your house or apartment to help find ways to use less energy.

energy payback time   The time required for any energy-producing system or device to produce as much energy as was required in its manufacture.

environment   All the natural and living things around us. The Earth, air, weather, plants, and animals all make up our environment.

ethylene vinyl acetate (EVA)   An encapsulant used between the glass cover and the solar cells in PV modules. It is durable, transparent, resistant to corrosion, and flame retardant.

extrinsic semiconductor   The product of doping a pure semiconductor.

fall   The vertical descent of water, usually measured in vertical feet. Also called *head*.

fill factor   The ratio of a photovoltaic cell's actual power to its power if both current and voltage were at their maximums. It is a key characteristic in evaluating cell performance.

fixed tilt array   A solar PV array set at a fixed angle to the horizontal.

flat-plate PV   A solar PV array or module that does not contain concentrating devices and so responds to both direct and diffuse sunlight.

flooded-cell battery   A form of rechargeable battery with plates completely immersed in a liquid electrolyte. Most cars use flooded-cell batteries. They are the most commonly used type of battery for independent and remote-area power supplies.

flow rate   The speed at which water moves.

fluorescent light   A form of lighting that uses long, thin tubes of glass that contain mercury vapor and various phosphor powders (chemicals based on phosphorus) to produce white light. It is generally considered to be the most efficient form of home lighting.

fossil fuels   Fuels formed in the ground from the remains of dead plants and animals. It takes millions of years to form fossil fuels. Oil, natural gas, and coal are fossil fuels.

frequency   The number of cycles or repetitions per unit time of a complete waveform; in electrical applications, it is usually expressed in cycles per second or hertz (Hz). Electrical equipment in the United States requires 60 Hz, whereas in Europe it requires 50 Hz.

fresnel lens   A concentrating lens, positioned above and concave to a PV material to concentrate light on the material.

fuel   Any material that can be burned to make energy.

fuel cell   An electrochemical device that converts the energy of a fuel directly into electricity and heat and is therefore very energy efficient.

fuse   A device used to protect electrical equipment from short circuits. Fuses are made with metals that are designed to melt when the current passing through them is high enough. When the fuse melts, the electrical connection is broken, interrupting power to the circuit or device.

gallium arsenide (GaAs)   A crystalline, high-efficiency semiconductor/photovoltaic material.

gel-type battery   A lead-acid battery in which the electrolyte is immobilized in a gel. Gel-type batteries are usually used for mobile installations and when batteries will be subject to high levels of shock or vibration.

generator   A mechanical device used to produce DC electricity. Power is produced by coils of wire passing through magnetic fields inside the generator. Most alternating current generating sets are also referred to as generators.

gigawatt (GW)   One billion watts, 1 million kilowatts, or 1,000 megawatts.

gigawatt-hour (GWh)   A measurement of energy. One gigawatt-hour is equal to one gigawatt being used for a period of one hour or one megawatt being used for 1,000 hours.

glazings   Clear materials (such as glass or plastic) that allow sunlight to pass into solar collectors and solar buildings, trapping heat inside.

GPM   Gallons per minute. GPM is used in measuring water flow in hydroelectric power systems.

greenhouse effect   The effect of Earth's atmosphere, due to certain gases, in trapping heat from the sun; the atmosphere acts like a greenhouse.

greenhouse gases   Gases that trap the heat of the sun in Earth's atmosphere, producing the greenhouse effect. The two major greenhouse gases are water vapor and carbon dioxide; lesser greenhouse gases include methane, ozone, chlorofluorocarbons, and nitrogen oxides.

grid   An electrical utility distribution network.

grid-connected PV system   A PV system in which the PV array acts like a central generating plant, supplying power to the grid. Also known as an intertied system.

ground loop   An undesirable feedback condition caused by two or more circuits sharing a common electrical line, usually a grounded conductor.

ground mount   A piece of equipment upon which solar modules are mounted.

halogen lamp   A special type of incandescent globe made of quartz glass and a tungsten filament, enabling it to run at a much higher temperature than a conventional incandescent globe. It is more efficient than a normal incandescent, but not as efficient as a fluorescent light.

heat pump   A device, like an air conditioner or refrigerator, that moves heat from one location to another. In the cooling mode, heat pumps reduce indoor temperatures in the summer by transferring heat to the ground. Unlike an air-conditioning unit, however, a heat pump's cycle is reversible. In winter, a heat pump can extract heat from the ground and transfer it inside. The energy value of the heat thus moved can be more than three times the cost of the electricity required to perform the transfer process.

hertz (HZ)   The frequency of electrical current described in cycles per second. Appliances in the United States use 60 Hz. Appliances in other countries generally use 50 Hz. Sometimes also referred to as cycles.

high-voltage disconnect   Voltage at which the charge controller will disconnect the array to prevent overcharging the batteries.

hot spot   A phenomenon in which one or more cells within a PV module or array act as a resistive load, resulting in local overheating or melting of the cells.

hybrid system   A PV system that includes other sources of electricity generation, such as wind or diesel generators.

hydroelectricity   Electricity created by water power.

hydrometer   An instrument used to measure state of charge (voltage) of a battery.

i-type semiconductor   Semiconductor material that is left intrinsic, or undoped, so that the concentration of charge carriers is characteristic of the material itself rather than of added impurities.

I-V curve   A graph that plots the current versus the voltage from a PV cell as the electrical load (or resistance) is increased from short circuit (no load) to open circuit (maximum voltage). The shape of the curve characterizes cell performance. Three important points on the I-V curve are the open-circuit voltage, short-circuit current, and peak or maximum power (operating) point.

incandescent light   An electric lamp that is evacuated or filled with an inert gas and contains a filament (commonly tungsten). The filament emits visible light when heated to extreme temperatures by passage of electric current through it.

incident light   Light that shines onto the face of a solar cell or module.

independent power system   A power generation system that is independent of the electric grid.

infrared radiation   Electromagnetic radiation whose wavelengths lie in the range from 0.75 micrometer to 1,000 micrometers.

insolation   The amount of sunlight reaching an area, usually expressed in watt-hours per square meter per day.

insulation   Materials that prevent or slow down the movement of heat.

interconnect   A conductor within a module or other means of connection that provides an electrical interconnection between the solar cells.

inverter   A device that converts DC power from the PV array/battery to AC power. It is used either for stand-alone systems or grid-connected systems.

irradiance   The solar power incident on a surface, usually expressed in kilowatts per square meter. Irradiance multiplied by time gives insolation.

joule (J)   The energy conveyed by 1 watt of power for one second; a unit of energy equal to ⅓,₆₀₀ kilowatt-hours.

junction   A region of transition between semiconductor layers, such as a p/n junction, which goes from a region that has a high concentration of acceptors (p-type) to one that has a high concentration of donors (n-type).

junction box   For a PV generator, an enclosure on the module where PV strings are electrically connected and where protection devices can be located, if necessary.

junction diode   A semiconductor device with a junction and a built-in potential that passes current better in one direction than the other. All solar cells are junction diodes.

kilowatt (kW)   A unit of electrical power, 1,000 watts.

kilowatt-hour (kWh)   One thousand watts acting over a period of one hour. The kilowatt-hour is a unit of energy. 1 kWh = 3,600 kJ (kilo-joules).

lead-acid battery   A type of battery that consists of plates made of lead, lead-antimony, or lead-calcium and lead-oxide, surrounded by a sulfuric acid electrolyte. The most common type of battery used in remote area power supply (RAPS) systems.

life-cycle cost   The estimated cost of owning, operating, and disposing of a system over its useful life.

line loss   Voltage drop over the length of electric line wire. Line loss robs your system of power when wire is too small for the load being run through the line or when voltage is too low for the distance the power must travel.

linear current booster   An electronic circuit that matches PV output directly to a motor. It is used in array direct water pumping.

liquid electrolyte battery   A battery containing a liquid solution of an electrolyte in a solvent (such as sulfuric acid in water). It is also called a flooded battery because the plates are covered with the electrolyte solution.

load   Anything in an electrical circuit that, when the circuit is turned on, draws power from that circuit.

load circuit   The wiring, including switches and fuses, which connects the load to the power source.

load current   The current required to power the electrical device.

load resistance   The electrical resistance of the load.

low voltage disconnect (LVD)   The voltage at which the charge controller will disconnect the load from the batteries to prevent overdischarging.

maintenance-free battery   A sealed battery to which water cannot be added to maintain the level of the electrolyte solution.

maximum power point (MPP)   The point on the current-voltage (I-V) curve of a module under illumination, where the product of current and voltage is maximum. For a typical silicon cell, this is at about 0.45 volts.

megawatt (MW)   One million watts, or 1,000 kilowatts.

megawatt-hour (MWh)   A measurement of power with respect to time. One MWh is equal to 1 MW being used for a period of one hour, or 1 kW being used for 1,000 hours.

micrometer   One millionth of a meter.

milliamps (mA)   One thousandth of an ampere.

modified sine wave   A waveform with at least three states (positive, off, and negative) used to simulate a sine wave. It has less harmonic content than a square wave. This type of waveform is better than a square wave but not as suitable for some appliances as a sine wave.

modularity   The use of complete subassemblies to produce a larger system. Also the use of multiple inverters connected in parallel to service different loads.

module   A modular solar electric charger; used interchangeably with a solar electric panel.

monocrystalline solar cell   A form of solar cell made from a thin slice of a single large crystal of silicon.

monolithic   PV modules fabricated as a single structure.

multicrystalline   Material that is solidified at such as rate that many small crystals (crystallites) form. The atoms within a single crystallite are symmetrically arranged, whereas crystallites are jumbled together. These numerous grain boundaries reduce the device efficiency. Also, a material composed of variously oriented, small, individual crystals (sometimes referred to as polycrystalline or semicrystalline).

multijunction device   A photovoltaic device containing two or more cell junctions, each of which is optimized for a particular part of the solar spectrum to achieve greater overall efficiency.

multistage controller   A charge controller that allows different charging currents as the battery approaches full state of charge.

n-type silicon   Silicon doped with an element that has more electrons in its atomic structure than does silicon (phosphorus, for example).

National Electrical Code (NEC)   The U.S. code specifying guidelines for all types of electrical installations. It should be followed when installing a PV system.

National Electrical Manufacturers Association (NEMA)   The U.S. trade association that sets standards for some nonelectronic products such as junction boxes.

net metering   The practice of exporting surplus solar power during the day to the electricity grid, which either causes the homeowner's electric meter to run backward or simply creates a financial credit on the homeowner's electricity bill.

nickel-cadmium battery (NiCad)   A rechargeable battery with higher storage densities than that of lead-acid batteries; it uses a mixture of nickel hydroxide and nickel oxide for the anode and cadmium metal for the cathode. The electrolyte is potassium hydroxide.

nominal voltage   A rounded voltage value used to describe batteries, modules, or systems based on their specification (for example, a 12-volt, 24-volt, or 48-volt battery, module, or system).

nonrenewable fuels   Fuels that cannot be easily made or renewed, meaning that it is possible for mankind to use them up. Oil, natural gas, and coal are nonrenewable fuels.

nuclear energy   Energy that comes from splitting atoms of radioactive materials, such as uranium.

ohm   The resistance between two points of a conductor when a constant potential difference of 1 volt applied between these points produces in the conductor a current of 1 amp.

Ohm's Law   A mathematical formula that allows either voltage, current, or resistance to be calculated when the other two values are known. The formula is: $V = I \times R$, where V is the voltage, I is the current, and R is the resistance.

oil   A black liquid fossil fuel found deep in Earth. Gasoline, diesel, and most plastics are refined from oil.

one-axis tracking   A PV system structure that is capable of rotating on a single axis to track the movement of the sun.

open-circuit voltage (VOC)   The maximum possible voltage across a photovoltaic cell or module. Also, the voltage across the cell in sunlight when no current is flowing.

operating point   The current and voltage that a module or array produces when connected to a load. It is dependent on the load or the batteries connected to the output terminals.

orientation   Position with respect to the cardinal directions, north, south, east, and west.

overcharge   To apply current to a fully charged battery. This can damage the battery.

p-i-n   A semiconductor device structure that layers an intrinsic semiconductor between a p-type semiconductor and an n-type semiconductor. This structure is most often used with amorphous silicon devices.

p-type semiconductor   A semiconductor in which holes carry the current. It is produced by doping an intrinsic semiconductor with an electron acceptor impurity (such as adding boron to silicon).

p/n   A semiconductor device structure in which the junction is formed between a p-type layer and an n-type layer.

panel   In reference to photovoltaics, a modular solar electric charger; used interchangeably with *module*.

parallel connection   A way of joining two or more electricity-producing devices (PV cells or modules) by connecting positive leads together and negative leads together. Such a configuration increases the current.

passive solar home   A house that utilizes part of the building as a solar collector.

peak load   The maximum usage of electrical power occurring in a given period of time, typically a day. The electrical supply must be able to meet the peak load if it is to be reliable.

peak power   Power generated by a utility unit that operates at a very low capacity factor. It is generally used to meet short-lived and variable high-demand periods.

peak sun hours   The equivalent number of hours per day when solar irradiance averages 1,000 watts per square meter.

photocurrent   An electric current induced by radiant energy.

photoelectrochemical cell   A special type of photovoltaic cell in which the electricity produced is used immediately within the cell to produce a useful chemical product, such as hydrogen. The product material is continuously withdrawn from the cell for direct use as a fuel or as an ingredient in making other chemicals, or it may be stored and used subsequently.

photon   A particle of light that acts as an individual unit of energy.

photovoltaic (PV)   Of or having to do with the conversion of light into electricity. *Photo* means "light," and *voltaic* means "electric." Also referred to as *solar electric*.

photovoltaic array   An interconnected system of PV modules that function as a single electricity-producing unit. The modules are assembled as a discrete structure, with a common support or mounting.

photovoltaic cell   The smallest semiconductor element within a PV module to perform the immediate conversion of light into electrical energy (DC voltage and current).

photovoltaic conversion efficiency   The ratio of the electrical power generated by a PV device to the power of the light incident on it. This is typically in the range of 5 percent to 15 percent for commercially available modules.

photovoltaic effect   The effect that causes a voltage to be developed across the junction of two different materials when they are exposed to light.

photovoltaic generator   The total of all PV strings of a PV power supply system, which are electrically interconnected.

photovoltaic module   A single assembly of solar cells and ancillary parts, such as interconnections, terminals, and protective devices such as diodes, intended to generate DC power under unconcentrated sunlight. The structural (load carrying) member of a module can be either the top layer (superstrate) or the back layer (substrate).

photovoltaic panel   A connected collection of modules (a laminate string of modules used to achieve a required voltage and current). The term is often used interchangeably with *PV module* (especially in one-module systems).

photovoltaic peak watt   The maximum rated output of a cell, module, or system. Typical rating conditions are 0.645 watts per square inch (1,000 watts per square meter) of sunlight.

photovoltaic system   A complete set of components for the photovoltaic process to convert sunlight into electricity. The system includes the array and balance of system components.

photovoltaic-thermal (PV/T) system   A photovoltaic system that, in addition to converting sunlight into electricity, collects the residual heat energy and delivers both heat and electricity in a usable form. Also called a *total energy system*.

plates   The electrodes in a battery, usually taking the form of metal plates.

polycrystalline silicon   A material used to make solar PV cells; it consists of many crystals, compared to single-crystal silicon.

polyvinyl chloride (PVC)   A plastic used as an insulator on electrical cables. This toxic material is being replaced with alternatives made from more benign chemicals such as polyethylene and polypropylene.

power   The rate of doing work. It is expressed as watts (W). For example, a generator rated at 800 watts can provide that amount of power continuously.

power conditioning equipment   Electrical equipment, or power electronics, used to convert power from a photovoltaic array into a form suitable for subsequent use. It is also a collective term for the inverter, converter, battery charge regulator, and blocking diode.

power conversion efficiency   The ratio of output power to input power (of an inverter, for example).

primary battery   A battery that cannot be recharged.

pulse-width-modulated (PWM) wave inverter   The most expensive inverter, which produces a high-quality output signal at minimum current harmonics.

PV   Photovoltaic.

PV array   Two or more photovoltaic panels wired in series or parallel.

PV system   All the parts in combination required to generate solar electricity.

quad   A measure of energy equal to 1 trillion Btus; an energy equivalent to approximately 172 million barrels of oil.

quasi sine wave   The type of waveform produced by some inverters.

rated battery capacity (Ah)   A rating used by battery manufacturers to indicate the maximum amount of energy that can be withdrawn from a battery at a specified discharge rate and temperature.

rated module current (A)   The current output of a PV module measured under standard test conditions of 1,000 watts per square meter and 25°C cell temperature.

rated power   Nominal power output of an inverter; some units cannot produce rated power continuously.

rechargeable battery   A type of battery that uses a reversible chemical reaction to produce electricity, allowing it to be reused many times. The chemical reaction is reversed by forcing electricity through the battery in the direction opposite to normal discharge.

rectifier   A device that converts AC to DC, as in a battery charger or converter.

regulator   A device used to limit the current and voltage in a circuit, normally to allow the correct charging of batteries from power sources such as solar panels and wind generators.

remote area power supply (RAPS)   A power generation system used to provide electricity to remote and rural homes, usually incorporating power generated from renewable sources such as solar panels and wind generators, as well as nonrenewable sources such as gas- or diesel-powered generators.

remote systems   Systems off of the utility grid.

renewable fuels   Fuels that can be easily made or renewed and never used up. Types of renewable fuels are solar, wind, and hydropower energy.

reserve capacity   The amount of generating capacity that a central power system must maintain to meet peak loads.

resistance (R)   The property of a material that resists the flow of electric current when a potential difference is applied across it, measured in ohms.

resistive voltage drop   The voltage developed across a cell by the current flow through the resistance of the cell.

resistor   An electronic component used to restrict the flow of current in a circuit. It is sometimes used specifically to produce heat, such as in a water heater element.

reverse current protection   Any means of preventing current flow from the battery to the solar PV array (usually at night) that would discharge the battery.

sealed lead-acid battery   A form of lead-acid battery where the electrolyte is immobilized, either by being contained in an absorbent fiber separator or gel between the battery plates.

secondary battery   A battery that can be recharged; a rechargeable battery.

self discharge rate   The rate at which a battery will lose its charge when at open circuit (with no load connected).

semiconductor   A material that has an electrical conductivity in between that of a metal and an insulator. Transistors and other electronic devices are made from semiconducting materials and are often called semiconductors. Typical semiconductors for PV cells include silicon, gallium arsenide, copper indium diselenide, and cadmium telluride.

series connection   A way of joining photovoltaic cells by connecting positive leads to negative leads; such a configuration increases the voltage.

series regulator   Type of battery charge regulator where the charging current is controlled by a switch connected in series with the PV module or array.

series resistance   Resistance to current flow within a cell due to factors such as the bulk resistance of the cell materials and contact resistances.

series wiring   A system of wiring, for solar electric modules or batteries, that increases voltage. Series wiring is + to – (positive to negative).

shallow-cycle battery   A battery with small plates that cannot withstand many deep discharges (to a low state of charge).

shelf life   The amount of time a device, such as a battery, can be stored and still retain its specified performance.

shunt regulator   A type of battery charge regulator that controls the charging current by a switch connected in parallel with the PV generator. Overcharging of the battery is prevented by shorting the PV generator.

silicon (Si)   A chemical element with atomic number 14, a dark gray semimetal. Silicon occurs in a wide range of silicate minerals and makes up approximately 28 percent of Earth's crust (by weight). Silicon has a face-centered cubic lattice structure like a diamond. It is the most common semiconductor material used in making PV cells either traditionally in its crystalline form or more recently as an amorphous thin film.

sine wave   A waveform in which one variable is proportional to the sine of the other. The sine wave is the ideal form of electricity for running more sensitive appliances, such as radios, TVs, and computers.

sine wave inverter   An inverter that produces utility-quality, sine wave power forms.

single-crystal silicon   Silicon material with a single crystal structure. It is a common material used for the construction of solar PV cells.

solar cell   The smallest basic solar electric device that generates electricity when exposed to light.

solar constant   The strength of sunlight: 1,353 watts per square meter in space and about 1,000 watts per square meter at sea level at the equator at solar noon.

solar electric   Of or having to do with the conversion of sunlight into electricity. This is the common term, although *photovoltaic* is the more technical term.

solar energy   Energy from the sun.

solar module   A device used to convert light from the sun directly into DC electricity by using the photovoltaic effect. It is usually made of multiple solar cells bonded between glass and a backing material. A typical solar module would produce approximately 100 watts of power output (but module powers can range from 1 watt to 300 watts) and typically has dimensions of 2 feet by 4 feet.

solar noon   The midpoint between sunrise and sunset, the time when the sun reaches its highest point in its daily arc across the sky.

solar power   Electricity generated by conversion of sunlight, either directly through the use of photovoltaic panels or indirectly through solar-thermal processes.

solar resource   The amount of solar insolation received at a site, normally measured in units of kilowatt-hours per square meter per day, which equates to the number of peak sun hours.

solar thermal   A form of power generation using concentrated sunlight to heat water or other fluid that may then be used to drive a motor or turbine.

solar-grade silicon   Intermediate-grade silicon used in the manufacture of solar cells. It is less expensive than electronic-grade silicon.

specific gravity   The ratio of the weight of a solution to the weight of an equal volume of water at a specified temperature. It is used with reference to the sulfuric acid electrolyte solution in a lead-acid battery as an indicator of battery state of charge.

split-spectrum cell   A compound photovoltaic device in which sunlight is first divided into spectral regions by optical means. Each region is then directed to a different photovoltaic cell optimized for converting that portion of the spectrum into electricity. Such a device achieves significantly greater overall conversion of incident sunlight into electricity.

square wave   A train of rectangular voltage pulses that alternate between two fixed values for equal lengths of time.

square wave inverter The simplest and the least-expensive type of inverter, which produces the lowest quality of power. The inverter uses switches that can carry a large current and withstand a high voltage; these switches are turned on and off in the correct sequence and at a certain frequency.

stand-alone system A solar PV system that operates without connection to a grid or another supply of electricity.

stand-off mounting The technique for mounting a PV array on a sloped roof. The technique involves mounting the modules a short distance above the pitched roof and tilting them to the optimum angle.

standby current The current used by the inverter when no load is active, corresponding to lost power.

state of charge (SOC) The available capacity remaining in the battery, expressed as a percentage of the rated capacity.

static head The height of the water level above the point of free discharge of the water, normally measured when the pump is off.

storage density The capacity of a battery, in amp-hours compared to its weight. It is measured in watt-hours per kilogram (Wh/kg).

substrate The physical material upon which a photovoltaic cell is made.

sunspace A room that faces south, or a small structure attached to the south side of a house.

superstrate The covering on the sun side of a PV module, providing protection for the PV materials from impact and environmental degradation while allowing maximum transmission of the appropriate wavelengths of the solar spectrum.

surge An excessive amount of power drawn by an appliance when it is first switched on. An unexpected flow of excessive current, usually caused by excessive voltage, can damage appliances and other electrical equipment.

surge capacity The ability of an inverter or generator to deliver instantaneous high currents when starting motors, for example.

system operating voltage The output voltage of a solar PV array under load, dependent on the electrical load and size of the battery stack connected to the output terminals.

thermal electric Electric energy derived from heat energy, usually by heating a working fluid, which drives a turbogenerator.

thermal mass Materials that store heat within a sunspace or solar collector.

thermal storage walls A south-facing wall that is glazed on the outside. Solar heat strikes the glazing and is absorbed into the wall, which conducts the heat into the room over time. The walls are at least 8 inches thick. Generally, the thicker the wall, the less the indoor temperature fluctuates.

thick cells Conventional solar cells in most types of PV modules, such as crystalline silicon cells, which are typically from 200 to 400 micrometers thick. In contrast, thin-film cells are several microns thick.

thin film A solar PV module constructed with sequential layers of thin-film semiconductor materials usually only micrometers thick. Currently, thin-film technologies account for around 12 percent of all solar modules sold worldwide. This share is expected to increase, since thin-film technologies represent a potential route to lower costs.

tilt angle The angle of inclination of a solar collector or solar module measured from the horizontal.

total daily power budget (TDPB) In a DC system, the daily amount of watts your DC appliances use, plus the battery power allowance. In a DC and AC system, the daily amount of watts that DC and AC appliances use, plus battery and inverter power allowances.

tracking array A PV array that is moved to follow the path of the sun to maintain the maximum incident solar radiation on its surface. The two most common methods are *single-axis tracking*, in which the array tracks the sun from east to west, and *two-axis tracking*, in which the array points directly at the sun all the time. Two-axis tracking arrays capture the maximum possible daily energy. Typically, a single-axis tracker will give 15 to 25 percent more power per day and dual-axis tracking will add a further 5 percent.

transformer A device that converts the generator's low-voltage electricity to higher voltage levels for transmission to the load center, such as a city or factory.

transistor A semiconductor device used to switch or otherwise control the flow of electricity.

transmission lines Power lines that transmit high-voltage electricity from the transformer to the electric distribution system.

trickle charge A charge at a low rate, balancing through self-discharge losses, to maintain a cell or battery in a fully charged condition.

two-axis tracking   A PV module mount system capable of rotating independently about two axes (vertical and horizontal).

uninterruptible power supply (UPS)   A power supply capable of providing continuous uninterruptible service. Normally batteries provide energy storage.

utility-interactive inverter   An inverter that can operate only when connected to the utility grid supply and an output voltage frequency fully synchronized with the utility power.

VAC   Volts alternating current.

VDC   Volts direct current.

VMP   The voltage at which a PV device is operating at maximum power.

VOC   Open-circuit voltage.

volt (V)   A unit of measure of the force, or pressure, given the electrons in an electric circuit. One volt (V) produces 1 ampere of current (A) when acting on a resistance of 1 ohm (R or Ω).

volt-ohmmeter (VOM)   An electrical or electronic device used to measure voltage, resistance, and current.

voltage drop   The voltage lost along a length of wire or conductor due to the resistance of that conductor. This also applies to resistors. The voltage drop is calculated by using Ohm's Law.

voltage regulator   A device that controls the operating voltage of a photovoltaic array.

wafer   A thin sheet of crystalline semiconductor material made either by mechanically sawing it from a single-crystal boule or multicrystalline ingot or block, or by casting. The wafer is "raw material" for a solar cell.

watt (W)   The unit of electric power, or amount of work (J), done in a unit of time. One ampere of current flowing at a potential of 1 volt produces 1 watt of power.

watt-hour (Wh)   A unit of energy equal to 1 watt of power being used for one hour.

waveform   The shape of a wave or pattern representing a vibration. The shape characterizing an AC current or voltage output.

zenith angle   The angle between directly overhead and a line through the sun. The elevation angle of the sun above the horizon is 90° minus the zenith angle.

Additional solar power definitions are available online at www1.eere.energy.gov/solar/solar_glossary.html.

Appendix D

Solar Resources

The following solar resources are current as of fall 2009. Updated Solar Resources with links are available online at SolarHomeGuides.com.

First-Stop Solar Information

American Planning Association
1776 Massachusetts Avenue, NW
Washington, DC 20036-1904
Phone: 202-872-0611
Fax: 202-872-0643
Website: planning.org

American Solar Energy Society (ASES)
2400 Central Avenue, Suite G-1
Boulder, CO 80301
Phone: 303-443-3130
Fax: 303-443-3212
Website: ases.org

Ask an Energy Expert
Energy Efficiency and Renewable Energy Clearinghouse (EREC)
P.O. Box 3048
Merrifield, VA 22116
Phone: 1-800-DOE-EREC (363-3732)
Fax: 703-893-0400
Website: www1.eere.energy.gov/informationcenter

Center for Excellence in Sustainable Development (CESD)
U.S. Department of Energy, Denver Regional Office
1617 Cole Boulevard
Golden, CO 80401
Fax: 303-275-4830
Website: smartcommunities.ncat.org

Federal Energy Regulatory Commission (FERC)
Public Reference Room
888 First Street, NE, Room 2-A
Washington, D.C. 20426
Phone: 1-866-208-3372
Website: ferc.gov

National Association of Energy Service Companies (NAESCO)
1615 M Street, NW, Suite 800
Washington, D.C. 20036
Phone: 202-822-0950
Fax: 202-822-0955
Website: naesco.org

National Center for Appropriate Technology (NCAT)
3040 Continental Drive
Butte, MT 59701
Phone: 406-494-4572
Fax: 406-494-2905
Website: ncat.org

National Center for Photovoltaics
National Renewable Energy Laboratory (NREL)
1617 Cole Boulevard
Golden, CO 80401
Website: nrel.gov/ncpv

National Climatic Data Center
Federal Building
151 Patton Avenue
Asheville, NC 28801-5001
Phone: 828-271-4800
Fax: 828-271-4876
Website: ncdc.noaa.gov

National Technical Information Service (NTIS)
5285 Port Royal Road
Springfield, VA 22161
Phone: 1-800-553-6847 or 703-605-6000
Fax: 703-605-6900
Website: ntis.gov

Solar Energy Industries Association (SEIA)
1616 H Street, NW, 8th Floor
Washington, D.C. 20006
Phone: 202-628-7745
Fax: 202-628-7779
Website: seia.org

Solar Energy International (SEI)
P.O. Box 715
Carbondale, CO 81623
Phone: 970-963-8855
Fax: 970-963-8866
Website: solarenergy.org

Sustainable Buildings Industry Council (SBIC)
1331 H Street, NW, Suite 1000
Washington, D.C. 20005-4706
Phone: 202-628-7400
Fax: 202-393-5043
Website: sbicouncil.org

U.S. Government Printing Office (GPO)
New Orders, Superintendent of Documents
P.O. Box 371954
Pittsburgh, PA 15250-7954
Phone: 202-512-1800 (orders)
Fax: 202-512-2250
Website: gpo.gov

Energy Efficiency Resources

Air Conditioning and Refrigeration Institute (ARI)
4301 North Fairfax Drive, Suite 425
Arlington, VA 22203
Phone: 703-524-8800
Fax: 703-528-3816
Website: ari.org

American Council for an Energy-Efficient Economy (ACEEE)
1001 Connecticut Avenue, NW, Suite 801
Washington, D.C. 20036
Research and Conferences: 202-429-8873
Publications: 202-429-0063
Website: aceee.org

American Institute of Architects (AIA)
1735 New York Avenue, NW
Washington, D.C. 20006
Phone: 202-626-7300 or contact Ed Jackson 202-626-7446
Website: aia.org

American National Standards Institute (ANSI)
25 West 43rd Street
New York, NY 10036
Phone: 212-642-4900
Fax: 212-398-0023
Website: ansi.org

American Nursery and Landscape Association (ANLA)
1250 I Street, NW, Suite 500
Washington, D.C. 20005
Phone: 202-789-2900
Fax: 202-789-1893
Website: asla.org

American Society for Testing and Materials (ASTM)
100 Barr Harbor Drive
West Conshohocken, PA 19428
Phone: 610-832-9585
Fax: 610-832-9555
Website: astm.org

American Society of Heating, Refrigerating, and Air Conditioning Engineers (ASHRAE)
1791 Tullie Circle, NE
Atlanta, GA 30329-2305
Phone: 404-636-8400
Fax: 404-321-5478
Website: ashrae.org

American Society of Landscape Architects (ASLA)
636 Eye Street, NW
Washington, D.C. 20001-3736
Phone: 202-898-2444
Fax: 202-898-1185

American Society of Mechanical Engineers (ASME)
Headquarters:
3 Park Avenue
New York, NY 10016-5900
Service Center:
22 Law Drive
P.O. Box 2300
Fairfield, NJ 07007
Phone: 1-800-843-2763
Website: asme.org

Center for Energy Efficiency and Renewable Technologies (CEERT)
1100 Eleventh Street, Suite 311
Sacramento, CA 95814
Phone: 916-442-7785
Fax: 916-447-2940
Website: cleanpower.org

E SEAL Program
Edison Electric Institute
701 Pennsylvania Avenue, NW
Washington, D.C. 20004-2696
Phone: 202-508-5557
Website: eei.org

Efficient Windows Collaborative
Alliance to Save Energy
1200 18th Street, NW, Suite 900
Washington, D.C. 20036
Phone: 202-857-0666
Website: ase.org

Energy Efficiency and Renewable Energy Clearinghouse (EREC)
P.O. Box 3048
Merrifield, VA 22116
Phone: 877-337-3463
Website: eere.energy.gov/consumer

ENERGY STAR Homes
U.S. EPA
Climate Protection Partnerships Division
ENERGY STAR Programs Hotline and Distribution (MS-6202J)
1200 Pennsylvania Avenue, NW
Washington, D.C. 20460
Phone: 1-888-STAR-YES (782-7937)
Website: energystar.gov

Gas Appliance Manufacturers Association, Inc. (GAMA)
2107 Wilson Boulevard, Suite 600
Arlington, VA 22201
Phone: 703-525-7060
Fax: 703-525-6790
Website: gamanet.org

Institute of Electrical and Electronics Engineers (IEEE)
445 Hoes Lane
P.O. Box 1331
Piscataway, NJ 08855-1331
Phone: 732-981-0060 for inquiries; 1-800-678-IEEE (4333) for publications
Website: ieee.org

Lawrence Berkeley National Laboratory
Building Technologies Department
MS 90-3111
Berkeley, CA 94720
Phone: 510-486-6845
Fax: 510-486-4089
Website: lbl.gov

National Arbor Day Foundation (NADF)
100 Arbor Avenue
Nebraska City, NE 68410
Phone: 402-474-5655
Website: arborday.org

National Association of Home Builders (NAHB)
1201 15th Street, NW
Washington, D.C. 20005
Phone: 1-800-368-5242
Website: nahb.com

National Fire Protection Association (NFPA)
1 Batterymarch Park
Quincy, MA 02269-9101
Phone: 1-800-344-3555 or 617-770-3000
Fax: 1-800-593-6372 or 508-895-8301
Website: nfpa.org

National Hydropower Association (NHA)
1 Massachusetts Avenue, NW, Suite 850
Washington, D.C. 20001
Phone: 202-682-1700
Fax: 202-682-9478
Website: hydro.org

National Institute of Standards and Technology (NIST)
100 Bureau Drive, Stop 1070
Gaithersburg, MD 20899
Phone: 301-975-5864
Website: nist.gov

National Spa and Pool Institute (NSPI)
2111 Eisenhower Avenue, Suite 500
Alexandria, VA 22314
Phone: 1-800-323-3996 or 703-838-0083
Fax: 703-549-0493
Website: nspi.org

Oak Ridge National Laboratory (ORNL)
Buildings Technology Center
P.O. Box 2008, MS-6070
Oak Ridge, TN 37831-6070
Phone: 865-574-4160
Website: ornl.gov

Sheet Metal and Air Conditioning Contractors National Association, Inc. (SMACNA)
4201 Lafayette Center Drive
Chantilly, VA 20151-1209
Phone: 703-803-2980
Fax: 703-803-3732
Website: smacna.org

Solar Rating and Certification Corporation (SRCC)
c/o Florida State Energy Center
1679 Clearlake Road
Cocoa, FL 32922
Phone: 321-638-1537
Fax: 321-638-1010
Website: solar-rating.org

Sustainable Buildings Industry Council (SBIC)
1331 H Street, NW, Suite 1000
Washington, D.C. 20005-4706
Phone: 202-628-7400
Fax: 202-393-5043
Website: sbicouncil.org

Underwriters Laboratories, Inc. (UL)
Corporate Headquarters
333 Pfingsten Road
Northbrook, IL 60062-2096
Phone: 847-272-8800
Fax: 847-272-8129
Website: ul.com

Publications

2009 Code of Federal Regulations. Chapter 29 Part 1926–Safety and Health Regulations for Construction. U.S. Department of Labor/OSHA, OSHA Publications, P.O. Box 37535, Washington, D.C. 20013-7535; osha.gov. Also available online at gpoaccess. gov/CFR/.

2010 National Electrical Code. NFPA 70, National Fire Protection Association, 1 Batterymarch Park, Quincy, MA 02269 (*2005 National Electrical Code Handbook* is an acceptable substitute; nfpa.org/nec).

A Guide to Photovoltaic System Design and Installation. California Energy Commission Consultant Report 500-01-020, June 2001; energy.ca.gov (FREE).

Battery Service Manual, 12th Edition. Battery Council International, 401 North Michigan Avenue, Chicago, IL 60611; batterycouncil.org.

Hybrid Power Systems: Issues and Answers. Sandia National Laboratories, Photovoltaic Systems Assistance Center, Albuquerque, NM 87185-0753; sandia.gov (FREE).

Installing Photovoltaic Systems (Course Manual). Florida Solar Energy Center, 1679 Clearlake Road, Cocoa, FL 32922-5703, 2002. Contact Joann Stirling at 321-638-1014; fsec.ucf.edu.

Maintenance and Operation of Stand-Alone Photovoltaic Systems. Sandia National Laboratories, Photovoltaic Systems Assistance Center, Albuquerque, NM 87185-0753, December 1991; sandia.gov/pv (FREE).

One and Two Family Dwelling Electrical Systems, 6th Edition. J. Philip Simmons, International Association of Electrical Inspectors, Richardson, TX. 2002; iaei.org.

Photovoltaic Power Systems and the National Electrical Code: Suggested Practices. SAND2001-0674, Sandia National Laboratories, Photovoltaic Systems Assistance Center, Albuquerque, NM 87185-0753, March 2001; sandia.gov/pv. Also available from Southwest Technology Development Institute; nmsu.edu (FREE).

Photovoltaic Systems Engineering, 2nd Edition. Roger A. Messenger and Gerard G. Ventre, CRC Press, 2004; crcpress.com.

Solar Hot Water Systems Lessons Learned 1977 to Today. Tom Lane, Energy Conservation Services, 6120 SW 13th Street, Gainesville, FL 32608, 2004; ecs-solar.com.

Stand-Alone Photovoltaic Systems: A Handbook of Recommended Design Practices. Sandia National Laboratories, Photovoltaic Systems Assistance Center, Albuquerque, NM 87185-0753; sandia.gov/pv (FREE).

Working Safely with Photovoltaic Systems. Sandia National Laboratories, Photovoltaic Systems Assistance Center, Albuquerque, NM 87185-0753; sandia.gov/pv (FREE).

Financial Resources

Electric and Gas Industries Association (EGIA)
Nationwide Solar Financing
Phone: 1-866-367-3442
Website: egia.com

Fannie Mae
3900 Wisconsin Avenue, NW
Washington, D.C. 20016-2892
Phone: 1-800-7FANNIE (732-6643)
Website: fanniemae.com; homepath.com (consumer)

Federal Housing Authority (FHA)
U.S. Department of Housing and Urban Development (HUD)
451 7th Street, SW
Washington, D.C. 20410
Website: hud.gov

Freddie Mac
8200 Jones Branch Drive
McLean, VA 22102-3107
Phone: 1-800-FREDDIE (373-3343)
Website: freddiemac.com

Internal Revenue Service (IRS)
P.O. Box 25866
Richmond, VA 23260
Phone: 1-800-829-3676
Website: irs.gov

Renewable Energy Policy Project (REPP)
1612 K Street, NW, Suite 202
Washington, D.C. 20006
Phone: 202-293-2898
Fax: 202-293-5857
Website: repp.org

Residential Energy Services Network (RESNET)
P.O. Box 4561
Oceanside, CA 92052-4561
Phone: 760-806-3448
Fax: 760-806-9449
Website: natresnet.org

U.S. Department of Energy (DOE)
Office of Energy Efficiency and Renewable Energy
Website: eere.energy.gov

U.S. Department of Veterans Affairs (VA)
Phone: 1-800-848-4904
Website: homeloans.va.gov

Solar Equipment Catalogs

Affordable Solar
E-mail: sales@affordable-solar.com
Website: affordable-solar.com
(online catalog only)

Backwoods Solar Electric Systems
1395 Rolling Thunder Ridge
Sandpoint, ID 83864
Phone: 208-263-4290
Fax: 208-265-4788
E-mail: info@backwoodssolar.com
Website: backwoodssolar.com

Gaiam/Real Goods
360 Interlocken Boulevard
Broomfield, CO 80021
Phone: 303-222-3600
Website: gaiam.com; realgoods.com

Kansas Wind Power
13569 214th Road
Holton, KS 66436
Phone: 785-364-4407
Fax: 785-364-5123
Website: kansaswindpower.net

New England Solar Electric, Inc.
401 Huntington Road
P.O. Box 435
Worthington, MA 01098
Phone: 413-238-5974
Fax: 413-238-0203
Website: newenglandsolar.com

Off Line Independent Energy Systems
P.O. Box 231
North Fork, CA 93643
Phone: 559-877-7080
Fax: 559-877-2980
Website: psnw.com/~ofln

Positive Energy Conservation Products
P.O. Box 7568
Boulder, CO 80306
Phone: 1-800-488-4340 or 303-444-4340
Website: positive-energy.com

Sierra Solar Systems
563 C Idaho Maryland Road
Grass Valley, CA 95945
Phone: 1-888-667-6527
Fax: 530-273-1760
Website: sierrasolar.com

Solar Components Corporation
121 Valley Street
Manchester, NH 03103
Phone: 603-668-8186
Fax: 603-668-1783
E-mail: solarcomponents@yahoo.com
Website: solar-components.com

Solar Depot
1240 Holm Road
Petaluma, CA 94954
Phone: 415-499-1333; 1-800-822-4041 (orders)
Fax: 415-499-0316
Website: solardepot.com

Sunelco, Inc.
2068 U.S. Highway 93N
Victor, MT 59875
Phone: 1-800-338-6844
Fax: 406-363-6046
Website: sunelco.com

Regional and State Energy Resources

The following information is provided by the American Solar Energy Society (ases.org).

Alabama

Alabama Solar Association
2117 Rothmore Drive, SW
Huntsville, AL 35803-1431
Phone: (256) 658-5189
E-mail: morton@al-solar.org
Website: al-solar.org
Contact: A. Morton Archibald, Jr.

Arizona

Arizona Solar Energy Association
P.O. Box 5583
Scottsdale, AZ 85261
Phone: (520) 883-8880
E-mail: j2envarch@aol.com
Website: azsolarcenter.com
Contact: Daniel Aiello

California

Los Angeles Solar Energy Society
Phone: 310-734-6613
E-mail: zoecstarr@gmail.com
Contact: Zoe Starr

Northern California Solar Energy Association (NorCal Solar)
P.O. Box 3008
Berkeley, CA 94703
Phone: 510-647-3774
E-mail: solarinfo@norcalsolar.org
Contact: Rachel Huang

Redwood Empire Solar Living Association
13771 S. Highway 101
Hopland, CA 95449
Phone: 707-744-2017 XT 2102
E-mail: coral.mills@solarliving.org
Website: solarliving.org
Contact: Coral Mills

San Diego Renewable Energy Society (SDRES)
1857 Altozano Drive
El Cajon, CA 92020
Phone: 858-677-1230
E-mail: info@sdres.org
Website: sdres.org
Contact: Ted Stern

Colorado

Colorado Renewable Energy Society
P.O. Box 933
Golden, CO 80402
Phone: 303-806-5317
E-mail: info@cres-energy.org
Website: cres-energy.org
Contact: Sheila Townsend

Connecticut

Northeast Sustainable Energy Association
50 Miles Street
Greenfield, MA 01301
Phone: 413-774-6051
Fax: 413-774-6053
E-mail: nesea@nesea.org
Website: nesea.org
Executive Director: David Barclay

Delaware

Northeast Sustainable Energy Association
50 Miles Street
Greenfield, MA 01301
Phone: 413-774-6051
Fax: 413-774-6053
E-mail: nesea@nesea.org
Website: nesea.org
Executive Director: David Barclay

Florida

Florida Renewable Energy Association
430 North Street
Clermont, FL 34711
Phone: 352-241-4733
E-mail: info@cleanenergyflorida.org
Website: cleanenergyflorida.org
Contact: Craig Williams

Student Chapter
University of Florida–Gainesville
Mechanical Engineering Department MAE-B 228
Gainesville, FL 32612
Phone: 561-827-3608
E-mail: ases.uf@gmail.com
Website: ufases.org
Contact: Alex Palomino

Georgia

Georgia Solar Energy Association
100 Colony Square, Suite 400
Atlanta, GA 30361-3500
Phone: 404-879-2229
E-mail: info@gasolar.org
Website: gasolar.org
Contact: Walter Brown

Idaho

Idaho Renewable Energy Association
6444 N. Portsmouth
Boise, ID 83714
Phone: 208-639-0656
E-mail: dustin@idahosolar.org
Website: idahosolar.org
Contact: Dustin W. Baker

Illinois

Illinois Solar Energy Association
800 West Evergreen Avenue
Chicago, IL 60642
Phone: 312-376-8245
E-mail: contactisea@illinoissolar.org
Website: illinoissolar.org
Contact: Mike Johnson 312-401-4859,
Mark Burger 708-267-7965

Midwest Renewable Energy Association
7558 Deer Road
Custer, WI 54423
Phone: 715-592-6595
Fax: 715-592-6596
E-mail: info@the-mrea.org
Website: the-mrea.org
Contact: Amy Heart

Indiana

Indiana Renewable Energy Association
1013 Elroy Drive
Middlebury, IN 46540
Phone: 574-536-9483
E-mail: indianarenew@homeandmobileenergy.com
Website: indianarenew.org
Contact: Leon Bontrager

Iowa

Midwest Renewable Energy Association
7558 Deer Road
Custer, WI 54423
Phone: 715-592-6595
Fax: 715-592-6596
E-mail: info@the-mrea.org
Website: the-mrea.org
Contact: Amy Heart

Kansas

Heartland Renewable Energy Society
P.O. Box 1157
Blue Springs, MO 64013-1157
Phone: 816-224-5550
E-mail: sharla@hathmore.com
Website: heartland-res.org
Contact: Sharla Riead

Kentucky

Kentucky Solar Energy Society
2235 Gregory Woods Road
Frankfort, KY 40601
E-mail: solar@kysolar.org
Website: kysolar.org
Contact: Andy McDonald

Louisiana

Louisiana Solar Energy Society
5261 Highland Road #217
Baton Rouge, LA 70808
Phone: 225-933-3216
E-mail: info@lses.org
Website: lses.org
Contact: Jeff Shaw

Maine

Northeast Sustainable Energy Association
50 Miles Street
Greenfield, MA 01301
Phone: 413-774-6051
Fax: 413-774-6053
E-mail: nesea@nesea.org
Website: nesea.org
Executive Director: David Barclay

Maryland

Potomac Region Solar Energy Association
4619 Oakview Court
Ellicott City, MD 21042
E-mail: info@prsea.org
Website: prsea.org
Contact: Nelson Buck

Massachusetts

Northeast Sustainable Energy Association
50 Miles Street
Greenfield, MA 01301
Phone: 413-774-6051
Fax: 413-774-6053
E-mail: nesea@nesea.org
Website: nesea.org
Executive Director: David Barclay

Michigan

Great Lakes Renewable Energy Association
257 South Bridge Street
P.O. Box 346
Dimondale, MI 48821
Phone: 517-646-6269 or 1-800-434-9788
E-mail: info@glrea.org
Website: glrea.org
Contact: Samantha Keeney

Midwest Renewable Energy Association
7558 Deer Road
Custer, WI 54423
Phone: 715-592-6595
Fax: 715-592-6596
E-mail: info@the-mrea.org
Website: the-mrea.org
Contact: Amy Heart

Minnesota

Minnesota Renewable Energy Society
2928 5th Avenue S.
Minneapolis, MN 55408
Phone: 612-308-4757
E-mail: info@mnrenewables.org
Website: mnRenewables.org
Contact: David Boyce

Mississippi

Mississippi Solar Energy Society
P.O. Box 141
Columbia, MS 39429
E-mail: sdlewis@megagate.com
Contact: Steve Lewis

Missouri

Heartland Renewable Energy Society
P.O. Box 1157
Blue Springs, MO 64013-1157
Phone: 816-224-5550
Fax: 816-224-5150
E-mail: sharla@hathmore.com
Website: Heartland-RES.org
Contact: Sharla Riead

Nevada

Solar NV
P.O. Box 31665
Las Vegas, NV, 89173
Phone: 702-507-0093
E-mail: contact@solarnv.org
Website: solarnv.org
Contact: Deidre Radford

Sunrise Sustainable Resources Group
P.O. Box 19074
Reno, NV 89511
Phone: 775-224-1877
E-mail: Philip_Moore@charter.net
Website: sunrisenevada.org
Contact: Philip Moore

New Hampshire

Northeast Sustainable Energy Association
50 Miles Street
Greenfield, MA 01301
Phone: 413-774-6051
Fax: 413-774-6053
E-mail: nesea@nesea.org
Website: nesea.org
Executive Director: David Barclay

New Jersey

Northeast Sustainable Energy Association
50 Miles Street
Greenfield, MA 01301
Phone: 413-774-6051
Fax: 413-774-6053
E-mail: nesea@nesea.org
Website: nesea.org
Executive Director: David Barclay

New Mexico

New Mexico Solar Energy Association
1009 Bradbury, SE #35
Albuquerque, NM 87106
Phone: 505-246-0400
Fax: 505-246-2251
E-mail: info@nmsea.org
Website: nmsea.org
Contact: Mary McArthur and Ron Herman

New York

New York Solar Energy Society, Inc.
5270 Sycamore Avenue
Bronx, NY 10471-2838
Phone: 917-974-4606 (cell)
E-mail: wyldon1@gmail.com
Website: nyses.org
Contact: Wyldon Fishman

Northeast Sustainable Energy Association
50 Miles Street
Greenfield, MA 01301
Phone: 413-774-6051
Fax: 413-774-6053
E-mail: nesea@nesea.org
Website: nesea.org
Executive Director: David Barclay

North Carolina

North Carolina Sustainable Energy Association
P.O. Box 6465
Raleigh, NC 27628
Phone: 919-832-7601
E-mail: officemanager@energync.org
Website: energync.org
Executive Director: Ivan Urlaub

NCSU Renewable Energy Society
c/o North Carolina Solar Center
P.O. Box 7401
North Carolina State University
Raleigh, NC 27695-7401
Phone: 919-515-9782
Fax: 919-515-5778
E-mail: ccmaurer@unity.ncsu.edu
Contact: C. C. Maurer

Student Chapters
Appalachian State University
Department of Technology
P.O. Box 9096
Boone, NC 28608
Phone: 252-717-9730
E-mail: ASUSES@gmail.com
Website: asuses.net
Contact: David Quint

Ohio

Green Energy Ohio
7870 Olentangy River Road, #209
Columbus, OH 43235
Phone: 614-985-6131
Fax: 614-888-9716
E-mail: geo@greenenergyohio.org
Website: greenenergyohio.org
Executive Director: William A. Spratley

Oregon

Solar Oregon
205 SE Grand, Suite 205
Portland, OR 97214
Phone: 503-231-5662
E-mail: Hadley@solaroregon.org
Website: solaroregon.org
Contact: Hadley Price

Pennsylvania

Northeast Sustainable Energy Association
50 Miles Street
Greenfield, MA 01301
Phone: 413-774-6051
Fax: 413-774-6053
E-mail: nesea@nesea.org
Website: nesea.org
Executive Director: David Barclay

Rhode Island

Northeast Sustainable Energy Association
50 Miles Street
Greenfield, MA 01301
Phone: 413-774-6051
Fax: 413-774-6053
E-mail: nesea@nesea.org
Website: nesea.org
Executive Director: David Barclay

South Carolina

South Carolina Solar Council
1200 Senate Street
408 Wade Hampton Building
Columbia, SC 29201
Phone: 803-737-8030
E-mail: emyers@energy.sc.gov
Website: scsolarcouncil.org
Contact: Erika Myers

Texas

Texas Solar Energy Society
P.O. Box 1447
Austin, TX 78767-1447
Phone: 512-326-3391 or 800-465-5049
Fax: 512-444-0333
E-mail: info@txses.org
Website: txses.org
Executive Director: Natalie Marquis

Utah

Utah Solar Energy Association
P.O. Box 25263
Salt Lake City, UT 84125-0263
Phone: 801-501-9353
E-mail: ofarnsworth@aeesolar.com
Website: utsolar.org
Contact: Orrin Farnsworth

Vermont

Northeast Sustainable Energy Association
50 Miles Street
Greenfield, MA 01301
Phone: 413-774-6051
Fax: 413-774-6053
E-mail: nesea@nesea.org
Website: nesea.org
Executive Director: David Barclay

Virginia

Potomac Region Solar Energy Association
4619 Oakview Court
Ellicott City, MD 21042
E-mail: info@prsea.org
Website: prsea.org
Contact: Nelson Buck

Washington State

Solar Washington
16415 29th Place SW
Burien, WA 98166
Phone: 206-246-1200
E-mail: info@solarwashington.org
Website: solarwashington.org
Contact: Peter Barton

Washington, D.C.

Potomac Region Solar Energy Association
4619 Oakview Court
Ellicott City, MD 21042
E-mail: info@prsea.org
Website: prsea.org
Contact: Nelson Buck

Wisconsin

Midwest Renewable Energy Association
7558 Deer Road
Custer, WI 54423
Phone: 715-592-6595
Fax: 715-592-6596
E-mail: info@the-mrea.org
Website: the-mrea.org
Contact: Amy Heart

Photovoltaic Periodicals and Websites

Connections Newsletter
Interstate Renewable Energy Council (IREC)
P.O. Box 1156
Latham, NY 12110-1156
Phone: 518-458-6059
Website: irecusa.org
Offers consumer information on photovoltaic systems for consumers and small businesses.

Database of State Incentives for Renewable Energy (DSIRE)
North Carolina Solar Center
P.O. Box 7401
North Carolina State University
Raleigh, NC 27695-7401
Phone: 919-515-5666
Fax: 919-515-5778
Website: dsireusa.org
The one-stop-shop for the latest rebate and incentive programs for your state.

Home Power Magazine (periodical)
P.O. Box 520
Ashland, OR 97520
Phone: 1-800-707-6585
Fax: 541-512-0343
Website: homepower.com
Excellent magazine for do-it-yourselfers.

Photon International (periodical)
Publishing and Editorial Office
Solar Verlag GmbH
Wilhelmstrasse 34
52070 Aachen
Germany
Phone: 49-241-4003-0
Fax: 49-241-4003-300
Website: photon-magazine.com
A terrific magazine for professionals and serious enthusiasts. Great articles on world market conditions and end-user and manufacturing equipment.

PV News, PV Energy Systems (subscription report)
4539 Old Auburn Road
Warrenton, VA 20187
Phone: 540-349-4497
Website: pvenergy.com
PV News reports developments in PV technologies and applications from around the world, and includes information on markets, new technologies, policies, and projects.

Renewable Energy World (periodical)
James and James Science Publishers Ltd.
35-37 William Road
London, NW1 3ER, England
Website: renewableenergyworld.com
This journal reports on applications of renewable energy technologies around the world.

Solar Buzz (online resource only)
Website: solarbuzz.com
A hot site for the latest in international solar industry updates, technologies, and prices.

Sun-E News (online resource only)
Website: sun-enews.com
Another great online informational site.

Solar Software

Awnshade
Florida Solar Energy Center (FSEC)
1679 Clearlake Road
Cocoa, FL 32922-5703
Phone: 321-638-1000
Fax: 321-638-1010
Website: fsec.ucf.edu
Calculates the unshaded fraction of diffuse sky irradiance or illuminance incident on a
rectangular window for any given solar position coordinates relative to the window.

Energy-10
Sustainable Buildings Industry Council
1331 H Street, NW, Suite 1000
Washington, DC 20005
Phone: 202-628-7400
Fax: 202-393-5043
Website: sbicouncil.org
Enables building designers to optimize energy-efficient building strategies including
daylighting, passive solar heating, insulation, improved windows, shading, high-
efficiency mechanical systems, and other building components.

Home Energy Efficient Design (HEED)
Department of Architecture and Urban Design
University of California at Los Angeles
Los Angeles, CA 90095-1467
Website: aud.ucla.edu/energy-design-tools
Plots sunlight penetrating through a window with any combination of rectangular fins
and overhangs, and can provide a printout of annual tables of percent of window in
full sun, radiation on glass, and so on. SOLAR-5 is a DOS-based tool that can simulate the performance of up to 40 different solar energy components in a building. It
plots thermal mass, heat transfer, temperatures, daylighting, HVAC parameters, and
fuel and electricity costs, and it estimates air pollution emissions.

PV-Designpro
Maui Solar Energy Software Corporation
810 Haiku Road 113
P.O. Box 1101
Haiku, HI 96708
Phone: 808-573-6712
Fax: 808-879-5060
Website: mauisolarsoftware.com
Simulates photovoltaic system operation on an hourly basis for one year, based on a user-selected climate and system design.

PV F-Chart
F-Chart Software
4406 Fox Bluff Road
Middleton, WI 53562
Phone: 608-836-8531
Fax: 608-836-8536
Website: fchart.com
Estimates monthly performance for photovoltaic systems with and without storage and utility feedback.

PVform
Photovoltaic Systems Assistance Center
Sandia National Laboratories
P.O. Box 5800
Albuquerque, NM 87185-0753
Phone: 505-844-3698
Fax: 505-844-6541
Website: sandia.gov
A free photovoltaic system simulation program for stand-alone and grid-interactive applications. It simulates hourly performance for a one-year period.

PVWatts
Website: pvwatts.org
An Internet-accessible tool developed by the National Renewable Energy Laboratory that calculates electrical energy produced by a grid-connected PV system for locations within the United States and its territories.

Retscreen
CANMET Energy Diversification Research Laboratory/Natural Resources Canada
Website: retscreen.gc.ca
Available for free, Retscreen can be used to evaluate the energy production, life-cycle costs, and greenhouse gas emissions reduction for various solar and other renewable energy technologies.

Solar Environmental Benefits Calculator
U.S. Environmental Protection Agency
Website: epa.gov or srpnet.com
Estimates the pollution reduction benefits of using solar photovoltaic, water heaters, and pool-heating systems.

Solar Pathfinder
3953 Marsh Creek Road
Linden, TN 37096
Phone: 317-501-2529
Website: solarpathfinder.com
Calculates the position of the center of the sun in the sky at locations, dates, and times specified by the user. Numerous calculation options are available.

Solar-Pro
Maui Solar Energy Software Corporation
810 Haiku Road 113
P.O. Box 1101
Haiku, HI 96708
Phone: 808-573-6712
Fax: 808-879-5060
Website: mauisolarsoftware.com
For active solar water heating system design, simulation, and prediction.

Sun or Moon Altitude/Azimuth Table for One Day
U.S. Naval Observatory's Astronomical Applications Department
Website: usno.navy.mil/USNO/astronomical-applications
Provides altitudes and azimuths for the sun for locations in the United States. This provides a simple way to determine whether a landscape feature will shade a potential solar collector site.

Sunspec
Florida Solar Energy Center (FSEC)
1679 Clearlake Road
Cocoa, FL 32922-5703
Phone: 321-638-1000
Fax: 321-638-1010
Website: fsec.ucf.edu
A DOS-based program that calculates the spectral distribution of solar irradiance and the integrated irradiances and illuminances for clear-sky direct beam, diffuse sky, and ground-reflected radiation incident upon an arbitrarily oriented flat surface.

Educational Opportunities

Workshops and courses on solar system design and installation can be found at many universities and community colleges. In addition, Solar Energy International (SEI) offers courses on solar and radiant heating systems, grid-tied PV systems, advanced PV installation, and renewable energy for rural villages. Classes are held in the U.S. and foreign countries as well as online. For more information, visit solarenergy.org.

Index

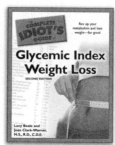
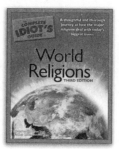

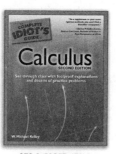

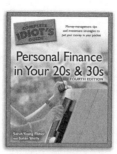

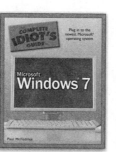

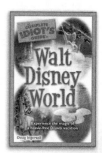